THE EMPLOYMENT RELATIONS ACT 1999

A PRACTICAL GUIDE

THE EMPLOYMENT RELATIONS ACT 1999

A PRACTICAL GUIDE

Deborah J Lockton LLB, MPhil
De Montfort University

JORDANS
1999

Published by
Jordan Publishing Limited
21 St Thomas Street
Bristol BS1 6JS

British Library Cataloguing-in-Publication Data
A catalogue record for this book is available from the British Library.

ISBN 0 85308 574 9

Typeset by Mendip Communications Limited, Frome, Somerset
Printed by MPG Books Ltd, Bodmin, Cornwall

PREFACE

The Employment Relations Act 1999 received Royal Assent on 27 July 1999. It enacts many of the proposals put forward in the White Paper, *Fairness at Work*, and represents a shift in the law in that many of the rights protect workers and not only those workers who are employees. The substance of some of the new rights will be enacted by statutory instrument and in these areas this book has attempted to give guidance as to what the provisions may be. While introducing many new rights, it will take some time before the extent and content of all of these rights are known and, where the law is set out in the Act, in many cases we will need a body of case-law to determine the limits of such rights.

The Act was the result of major amendments throughout its parliamentary passage which was not without controversy and, accordingly, some of the original proposals in *Fairness at Work* have been toned down. However, the Act has also introduced provisions which were not proposed in the White Paper, in particular in the areas of part-time work and employment agencies.

A book such as this takes a great deal of patience on the part of the publisher. I must express my thanks to Jordans, particularly when frequent amendments and my son's chicken pox held up the final submission of the manuscript. I must also express my thanks to my colleagues who have borne my frustrations with their usual support. Finally, I must thank my husband, Keith, and my son, James, who gave me the time to complete this book with no complaint as to the loss of my company. Despite all of this help, any mistakes are my own.

Deborah Lockton
October 1999

CONTENTS

		Page
PREFACE		v
TABLE OF CASES		xi
TABLE OF STATUTES		xiii
TABLE OF STATUTORY INSTRUMENTS		xxiii
TABLE OF EUROPEAN LEGISLATION		xxv
TABLE OF ABBREVIATIONS		xxvii
Chapter 1	**INTRODUCTION**	1
	1.1 BACKGROUND	1
	Fairness at work	1
	The proposals	2
	Rights for individuals	2
	Collective rights	3
	Family friendly policies	5
	1.2 THE EMPLOYMENT RELATIONS BILL 1999	6
	Rights for individuals	7
	Collective rights	7
	Family friendly policies	8
	Other provisions	8
Chapter 2	**TRADE UNIONS**	11
	2.1 COLLECTIVE BARGAINING: RECOGNITION	11
	Introduction	11
	2.2 STATUTORY RECOGNITION	12
	Introduction	12
	Request for recognition	13
	Parties agree	15
	Employer rejects request	15
	Negotiations fail	15
	Withdrawal of application/notice to cease consideration of application	18
	Appropriate bargaining unit	19
	Union recognition	19
	Competing applications	21
	Secret ballot	22
	Consequences of recognition	24
	Method not carried out	25
	2.3 VOLUNTARY RECOGNITION	25
	Introduction	25
	Agreement for recognition	25
	Determination of type of agreement	26

Termination of the agreement 27
Application to the CAC to specify method 27
2.4 CHANGES AFFECTING THE BARGAINING UNIT 28
Introduction 28
Either party believes unit no longer appropriate 28
Employer believes unit has ceased to exist 30
CAC decides new bargaining unit 32
Residual workers 34
2.5 DERECOGNITION 35
Introduction 35
Employer employs fewer than 21 employees 35
Employer's request to end arrangements 37
Workers' request to end arrangements 39
Ballot on derecognition 39
2.6 DERECOGNITION WHERE RECOGNITION
AUTOMATIC 40
Introduction 40
Employer's request to end arrangements 41
2.7 DERECOGNITION WHERE UNION NOT
INDEPENDENT 42
Introduction 42
Workers' application to end arrangements 42
Derecognition in other cases 44
2.8 LOSS OF INDEPENDENCE 44
Introduction 44
2.9 PROTECTION FOR WORKERS 45
Detriment 45
Dismissal 47
Power to amend procedures and issue guidance 47
2.10 DETRIMENT RELATED TO TRADE UNION
MEMBERSHIP 48
Introduction 48
Detriment 49
Time-limit for proceedings 49
2.11 BLACKLISTS 50
Introduction 50
2.12 NOTICE RELATING TO INDUSTRIAL ACTION 51
Introduction 51
Informing employers of the ballot result 51
Notice to the employers of ballots and the taking of
industrial action 51
Requirement to send sample voting papers to
employers 53
Inducing members to take industrial action 53
Separate workplace ballots 54
Overtime and call-out bans 55

Conduct of ballot – merchant seaman   55
Disregard of certain minor breaches and accidental
failures   55
Ballots for industrial action: periods of effectiveness   56
Suspension of industrial action   56
2.13 TRAINING   57
Introduction   57
2.14 UNFAIR DISMISSAL CONNECTED WITH
RECOGNITION: INTERIM RELIEF   59
Introduction   59

Chapter 3   **LEAVE FOR FAMILY AND DOMESTIC REASONS**   61
3.1   MATERNITY LEAVE   61
Introduction   61
Ordinary maternity leave   61
Compulsory maternity leave   62
Additional maternity leave   63
Redundancy and dismissal   63
Supplemental   64
3.2   PARENTAL LEAVE   65
Introduction   65
Entitlement   65
Rights during and after parental leave   66
Supplemental   67
Complaint to an employment tribunal   68
3.3   TIME OFF FOR DEPENDANTS   68
Introduction   68
Dependants   69
Right not to suffer a detriment   71
Dismissal   71

Chapter 4   **OTHER RIGHTS OF INDIVIDUALS**   73
4.1   RIGHT TO BE ACCOMPANIED IN DISCIPLINARY
AND GRIEVANCE HEARINGS   73
Introduction   73
Detriment and dismissal   76
National security   78
4.2   UNFAIR DISMISSAL OF STRIKING WORKERS   78
Introduction   78
4.3   COLLECTIVE AGREEMENTS: DETRIMENT AND
DISMISSAL   81
4.4   AGREEMENT TO EXCLUDE DISMISSAL RIGHTS   82
Introduction   82
4.5   PART-TIME WORK   83
Introduction   83
4.6   EXEMPTION FROM THE NATIONAL MINIMUM
WAGE   85
4.7   POWER TO CONFER RIGHTS ON INDIVIDUALS   86

              Introduction   86

**Chapter 5 CAC, ACAS, COMMISSIONERS AND THE
             CERTIFICATION OFFICER**   87
      5.1   CENTRAL ARBITRATION COMMITTEE   87
             Introduction   87
             CAC members   87
             CAC proceedings   88
      5.2   ACAS   88
             Introduction   88
             General duty   89
      5.3   ABOLITION OF COMMISSIONERS   89
             Introduction   89
      5.4   THE CERTIFICATION OFFICER   90
             Introduction   90
             Register of members   91
             Accounting records   92
             Offenders   93
             Elections   94
             Application of funds for political objects   95
             Political ballot rules   95
             Political fund   96
             Amalgamations or transfer of engagements   96
      5.5   BREACH OF UNION RULES   97
             Introduction   97
             Employers' associations   98
             Procedure before the Certification Officer   99

Chapter 6 MISCELLANEOUS PROVISIONS   101
      6.1   PARTNERSHIPS AT WORK   101
      6.2   EMPLOYMENT AGENCIES   102
             Regulations   102
             Charges   104
             Inspection   105
             Self-incrimination   106
             Offences   106
      6.3   COMPENSATION   107
             Unfair dismissal: special and additional awards   107
             Indexation of amounts   108
             Compensatory award   109
             Guarantee payments   110
      6.4   NATIONAL SECURITY   110
      6.5   EMPLOYMENT OUTSIDE GREAT BRITAIN   112
      6.6   TRANSFERS OF UNDERTAKINGS   113
      6.7   MINIMUM WAGE INFORMATION   113
      6.8   DISMISSAL OF SCHOOL STAFF   114

Appendix EMPLOYMENT RELATIONS ACT 1999   115

INDEX   249

TABLE OF CASES

References in the right-hand column are to paragraph numbers.

Associated British Ports v Palmer [1995] 2 AC 454; [1995] 2 All ER 100; [1995]
  2 WLR 354   1.1.7, 2.9.1, 2.10.1, 4.3.1
Associated Newspapers v Wilson [1995] 2 AC 454; [1995] 2 All ER 100; [1995]
  2 WLR 354   1.1.7, 2.9.1, 2.10.1, 4.3.1

BBC v Kelly-Phillips [1998] 2 All ER 845; [1998] ICR 587; [1998] IRLR 294   4.4.1
Blackpool and Fylde College v NAFTHE [1994] ICR 982; [1994] IRLR 227;
  (1994) *The Times*, 23 March   1.1.7, 2.12.3, 2.12.4
BP Chemicals v Gillick [1995] IRLR 128   6.2.1

Campey & Sons Ltd v Bellwood [1987] ICR 311   4.2.1
Carver v Saudi Arabian Airlines [1999] 3 All ER 61; [1999] IRLR 370; (1999)
  149 NLJ 521   6.5.1
Coates v Modern Methods and Materials Ltd [1983] QB 192; [1982] 3 WLR
  764; [1982] ICR 763   4.2.1

Dekker v Stichting Vormingscentrum Voor Jonge Volwassenen (VJ Centram)
  Plus [1992] ICR 325; [1991] IRLR 27; (1990) *The Times*, 12 December   3.3.6
Dixon v BBC [1979] QB 546; [1979] 2 WLR 647; [1979] ICR 281   4.4.1

H Campey & Sons Ltd v Bellwood [1987] ICR 311   4.2.1

Lavery v Plessey Communications [1983] ICR 534; [1983] IRLR 202   3.1.1

McMeechan v Secretary of State for Employment [1995] ICR 365; [1995] IRLR
  461   4.7.1, 6.2.1
Mulrine v University of Ulster [1993] IRLR 545   4.4.1

Nethermere (St Neots) Ltd v Taverna and Another [1984] IRLR 240   4.7.1
Norton Tool Co Ltd v Tewson [1972] ICR 501; [1973] 1 All ER 183; [1973] 1
  WLR 45   6.3.3

O'Kelly v Trust House Forte plc [1984] QB 90; [1983] 3 All ER 456; [1983]
  IRLR 369   4.7.1

P&O Ferries (Dover) Ltd v Byrne [1989] ICR 779; [1989] IRLR 254; (1989)
  The Times, 12 April   4.2.1

R v Secretary of State for Employment ex p Seymour-Smith and Perez [1999]
    All ER (EC) 97; [1999] 3 WLR 460; [1999] 2 CMLR 273   1.1.6
Rank Xerox (UK) Ltd v Goodchild & Ors [1979] IRLR 185   4.1.1

Saunders v United Kingdom [1997] 23 EHRR 313; [1998] 1 BCLC 362; [1997]
    BCC 872   6.2.5
South West Launderettes Ltd v Laidler [1986] ICR 455; [1986] IRLR 305   2.2.2

Tidman v Aveling Marshall Ltd [1977] ICR 506; [1977] IRLR 218; (1977) 12
    ITR 290   6.3.3

WA Goold (Pearmak) Ltd v McConnell [1995] IRLR 516   4.1.1
Webb v EMO Air Cargo (UK) Ltd (No 2) [1995] 4 All ER 577; [1995] 1 WLR
    1454; [1995] IRLR 645   3.3.6
Wickens v Champion Employment Agency Ltd [1984] ICR 365; (1984) 134
    NLJ 544   6.2.1

TABLE OF STATUTES

References are to paragraph numbers. The entry in bold is where the text is set out in full.

Broadcasting Act 1990	6.4.2	s 11B	6.2.6
		s 12(5)	6.2.7
		(6)	6.2.7
Criminal Procedure (Scotland)		s 13(2)	6.2.1
Act 1995		(3)	6.2.2
s 136	6.2.6	(7)(i)	6.2.7
		Employment Protection Act	
		1975	5.1.1, 5.2.1, 5.4.1
Disability Discrimination Act		**Employment Relations Act 1999**	4.7.2,
1995	6.4.1		**App**
		s 1	2.2.1, 2.13.1, 5.1.1
		s 2	1.2.4, 2.10.2
Employment Act 1988	5.3.1	s 3	1.2.4, 2.11.2
Employment Agencies Act 1973	1.2.6,	(1)	2.11.2
	6.2.1	(2)	2.11.2
s 5	6.2.7	(3)	2.11.2
s 5(1)	6.2.1	(4)	2.11.2
(1A)	6.2.2	(5)	2.11.2
s 6	6.2.7	s 4	1.2.4, 2.12.1, 3.3.6
(1)	6.2.3	s 5	1.2.6
(b)	6.2.3	s 7	3.1.1
(c)	6.2.3	s 8	1.2.5, 3.3.3
s 9	6.2.4, 6.2.5	s 10	1.2.4
(1)(a)	6.2.4	s 12(3)	4.1.7
(b)	6.2.3, 6.2.4	(4)	4.1.7
(d)	6.2.4, 6.2.5	(5)	4.1.7
(c)	6.2.5	(6)	4.1.7
(1A)	6.2.4, 6.2.5	s 15	1.2.6, 4.1.8, 6.4.1
(1B)	6.2.4	s 16	4.1.6
(a)	6.2.4	s 17(1)	4.3.1
(b)	6.2.4	(2)	4.3.1
(c)	6.2.4	(3)	4.3.1
(1C)	6.2.4	(4)	4.3.1
(2)	6.2.5	s 18	1.2.3
(2A)	6.2.5	(1)	4.4.2
(2B)	6.2.5	(2)	4.4.2
(3)	6.2.5, 6.2.6	(3)	4.4.2
(4)(a)(iv)	6.2.5	(4)	4.4.2
s 11	6.2.6	(5)	4.4.2
s 11A(2)	6.2.6	s 19	1.2.6, 4.5.1
(3)	6.2.6	(2)(a)	4.5.2
(4)	6.2.6	(b)	4.5.2

Employment Relations Act 1999

  – *cont*

(c)	4.5.2
(d)	4.5.2
(3)(a)	4.5.2
(b)	4.5.2
(c)	4.5.2
(d)(i)	4.5.2
(e)	4.5.2
(g)	4.5.2
(4)	4.5.2
(5)	4.5.2
s 20	1.2.6, 4.5.3
(1)	4.5.3
(3)	4.5.3
(4)	4.5.3
s 21	1.2.6
(1)	4.5.3
(2)	4.5.3
(3)	4.5.3
s 22	1.2.6, 4.6.1
s 23	6.2.1
s 24	5.1.2
s 25	5.1.3
s 26	5.2.2
s 28	1.2.4
(1)	5.3.2
(2)	5.3.2
s 29	5.4.2
s 30	1.2.4
(1)	6.1.2
(2)	6.1.2
s 31	1.2.6, 6.2.1
s 32	1.2.6, 6.5.1
s 33	1.2.3, 6.3.1
(2)	6.3.1
s 34	1.2.3
(4)	6.3.3
s 35	6.3.4
s 37	1.2.3
s 38	6.6.1
s 39	6.7.1
s 40	6.8.1
s 41	6.4.1
s 42	2.11.2, 4.7.2
Sch 1	1.2.4, 2.1.1, 2.11.2
Sch 2	1.2.4, 2.10.2
Sch 3	1.2.4, 2.12.1, 2.12.2, 2.12.4, 2.12.5, 2.12.8, 2.12.10, 2.12.12
Sch 4	1.2.5, 3.1.1, 3.3.3, 3.3.6
Sch 5	1.2.4, 4.1.6, 4.2.2
Sch 6	5.4.3, 5.4.6, 5.4.8, 5.4.10, 5.5.4
Sch 7	1.2.6, 5.4.7, 6.2.1–6.2.7
Sch 8	1.2.6, 4.1.8, 6.4.1–6.4.2

Employment Relations Bill 1999   1.2

Employment Rights Act 1996   4.7.2

s 3(1)(a)	4.1.1
(b)(ii)	4.1.1
(3)(a)	4.1.1
s 10	4.1.2
(2)	4.1.2, 4.1.5
(3)	4.1.2, 4.1.3
(a)	4.1.3
(4)	4.1.2, 4.1.5
(5)	4.1.2
(6)	4.1.2
(7)	4.1.2
s 11(1)	4.1.5
(2)	4.1.5
(3)	4.1.5
(4)	4.1.5
(5)	4.1.5
(6)	4.1.5
s 12(1)	4.1.6
(2)	4.1.6
s 13(3)	4.1.4
(4)	4.1.2
(5)	4.1.2
s 18	2.9.3
s 20	4.2.1
(2)	4.2.1
s 21	4.2.1
(1)	4.2.1
(2)	4.2.1
ss 28–35	6.3.4
s 31(1)	6.3.2
(2)	6.3.4
(3)	6.3.4
(4)	6.3.4
s 34	6.3.2
(2)	6.3.2
(3)	6.3.2
s 36(2)	6.3.2
ss 44–47	4.1.5
s 44	2.9.1, 4.4.2
(4)	4.4.2
s 45A	4.4.2
s 46	4.4.2
(2)	4.4.2
s 47	4.4.2
(2)	4.4.2

Employment Rights Act 1996 –		s 76(3)(b)	3.2.2	
cont		(4)(a)	3.2.2	
s 47A	4.4.2	(b)	3.2.2	
(2)	4.4.2	s 76(5)	3.2.2	
s 47C	3.3.6	s 77(1)(a)	3.2.3	
(1)	3.3.6	(b)	3.2.3	
(2)	3.3.6	(c)	3.2.3	
(3)	3.3.6	(2)(b)	3.2.3	
s 49(1)	4.1.6	(4)	3.2.3	
(2)	4.1.6	s 78(1)	3.2.3	
(5)	4.1.6	(2)	3.2.3	
s 50	3.3.3	(3)	3.2.3	
s 55	3.3.3	(4)	3.2.3	
s 56	3.3.3	(5)	3.2.3	
s 57A	1.2.5, 3.3.3	(7)	3.2.3	
(1)	1.2.5, 3.3.3	s 79	3.2.4	
(2)	3.3.4	(1)	3.2.4	
(3)	1.2.5, 3.3.3	(2)	3.2.4	
(4)	3.3.3	(3)	3.2.4	
(5)	1.2.5, 3.3.3	s 80(1)	3.2.5	
(6)	3.3.3	(2)	3.2.5	
s 57B(1)	3.3.5	(3)	3.2.5	
(2)	3.3.5	(4)	3.2.5	
(3)	3.3.5	s 94	2.9.3	
(4)	3.3.5	s 99	3.3.7	
s 71	3.1.2	(1)	3.3.7, 4.2.1	
(2)	3.1.2	(2)	3.3.7, 4.2.1	
(3)(a)	3.1.3	(3)	3.3.7, 4.2.1	
(3)(b)	3.1.3	(4)	3.3.7	
(4)(a)	3.1.2	s 100	4.2.1, 6.3.3	
(b)	3.1.2	(1)(a)	2.14.1	
(c)	3.1.2	(b)	2.14.1	
(5)	3.1.2	s 102(1)	2.14.1	
(6)	3.1.3	s 103	2.14.1, 4.2.1	
(7)	3.1.2	s 103A	6.3.3	
s 72	3.1.4	s 105(6A)	6.3.3	
(1)	3.1.4	s 108	2.9.3, 3.3.7, 4.1.6	
(3)(a)	3.1.4	s 109	2.9.3, 3.3.7, 4.1.6	
(b)	3.1.4	s 111	6.4.1	
s 74(1)	3.1.6	s 117(4)(b)	6.3.1	
(2)	3.1.6	(5)(a)	6.3.1	
(3)	3.1.6	(b)	6.3.1	
(4)	3.1.6	(6)	6.3.1	
s 75	3.1.7	s 118(2)	6.3.1	
(1)	3.1.7	(3)	6.3.1	
(2)	3.1.2	s 120(1)	6.3.2	
s 76	3.2.2	s 123(1)	6.3.3	
(1)	3.2.2	s 124(1)	6.3.2, 6.3.3	
(2)	3.2.2	s 125	6.3.1	
(3)	3.2.2	(1)	6.3.1	
(a)	3.2.2	(2)	6.3.1	

Employment Rights Act 1996 –
   cont
s 127A(2)   4.1.5
ss 128–132   2.14.1
s 128(1)(b)   2.14.2, 4.1.7
s 129(1)   2.14.2
s 130(5)   2.14.1
s 146   2.9.1
s 148   4.1.6
s 186(1)(a)   6.3.2
    (b)   6.3.2
s 193   6.4.1
s 196   1.2.6, 6.5.1
s 197(1)   4.4.1, 4.4.2
   (2)   4.4.1, 4.4.2
   (3)   4.4.1
s 203   4.1.7
   (2)(f)   6.3.3
s 208   6.3.2, 6.3.4
s 227   2.13.3, 6.3.2
   (1)   4.1.5
s 231   2.2.2
s 238   4.2.1
s 238A   4.1.6
Part VIII   3.1.1, 3.2.1
Part X   2.9.3, 4.1.7
Part XIV   4.1.5
Employment Tribunals Act 1996   5.5.5
s 10   6.4.1
   (1)   6.4.1
   (5)   6.4.1, 6.4.2
   (6)   6.4.1, 6.4.2
   (7)   6.4.1
s 10A(1)   6.4.2
   (2)   6.4.2
s 10B(2)   6.4.2
   (3)   6.4.2
   (4)   6.4.2
   (5)   6.4.2
   (6)   6.4.2
European Communities Act 1972
               4.5.1
s 2(2)   4.7.2, 6.6.1

Health and Safety at Work Act
   1974   6.2.1
s 3(1)   6.2.1

Income and Corporation Taxes
   Act 1988
s 134   6.2.1

Judicature (Northern Ireland)
   Act 1978
s 32   5.5.5

Late Payment of Commercial
   Debts (Interest) Act 1998   2.2.3

Magistrates' Courts Act 1980
s 127(1)   6.2.6
Minimum Wage Act 1998   1.2.6, 2.9.2,
               4.7.1
s 23(4)(a)   4.4.2
s 44A   4.6.1
   (2)   4.6.1
   (3)   4.6.1

Perjury Act 1911
s 5   6.2.5
Public Interest Disclosure Act
   1998   6.4.1
s 5   6.3.3
s 6   6.3.3
s 47B   4.4.2

Race Relations Act 1976   6.4.1
s 7   6.2.1

School Standards and
   Framework Act 1998
Sch 16   6.8.1
Sch 17   6.8.1
Sex Discrimination Act 1975   6.4.1
s 1(1)(a)   3.3.6
    (b)   3.3.6
s 9   6.2.1
Supreme Court Act 1981
s 42(1)   5.5.5

Tax Credits Act 1999
Sch 3   4.4.2
Trade Union and Labour
   Relations (Consolidation)
   Act 1992   2.13.1, 4.7.2, 5.5.1
s 1   4.1.2
s 5   2.2.2
s 7   2.8.1
s 8   5.4.2

Trade Union and Labour		s 70B(7)	2.13.2
Relations (Consolidation)		s 70C	2.13.2
Act 1992 – *cont*		(2)	2.13.3
s 9	2.8.1	(3)	2.13.3
s 24	5.4.3	(4)	2.13.3
(6)	5.4.3	(5)	2.13.3
s 24A(4)	5.4.3	(6)	2.13.3
(6)	5.4.3	s 71	5.4.9
s 25	5.4.1, 5.4.3, 5.4.4, 5.4.7	s 72A	5.4.9
(5)	5.4.4	(2)	5.4.9
(9)	5.4.4	(3)	5.4.9
(10)	5.4.4	(4)	5.4.9
s 26	5.4.1, 5.4.3, 5.4.5	(5)	5.4.9
(8)	5.4.5	(6)	5.4.9
s 30	5.4.6	(7)	5.4.9
(1)	5.4.6	(8)	5.4.9
s 31	5.4.6, 5.4.7	(9)	5.4.9
(1)	5.4.6	(10)	5.4.9
(4)	5.4.6	(11)	5.4.9
(5)	5.4.6	s 74	5.4.10
(6)	5.4.6	(2)	5.4.10
(7)	5.4.6	s 75	2.2.17
s 45(1)	5.4.7	s 79	5.4.10, 5.4.11
s 45A	5.4.7	s 80	5.4.10
s 45C	5.4.2, 5.4.7	(2)(b)	5.4.11
(2)	5.4.7	(5A)	5.4.11
(5A)	5.4.7	(5B)	5.4.11
(5B)	5.4.7	(5C)	5.4.11
(b)	5.4.7	(8)	5.4.11
(5C)(b)	5.4.7	(9)	5.4.11
(8)	5.4.7	(10)	5.4.11
(9)	5.4.7	s 81(8)	5.4.11
s 45D	5.4.7	s 82	5.4.11
s 49	2.2.17	(2A)	5.4.11
s 54	5.4.8	(3A)	5.4.11
s 55	5.4.2	s 103(2A)	5.4.13
(2)(b)	5.4.8	(6)	5.4.13
(5A)	5.4.8	(7)	5.4.13
(5B)	5.4.8	(8)	5.4.13
(5C)	5.4.8	(9)	5.4.13
(10)(b)	5.4.8	ss 99–103	5.4.13
s 56A	5.4.8	s 108A	5.5.2
s 56(8)(b)	5.4.8	(1)	5.5.1
s 70A	2.13.1	(2)	5.5.2
s 70B	1.2.6, 2.13.2, 2.13.3	(3)	5.5.2
(1)(a)	2.13.2	(4)	5.5.2
(b)	2.13.2	(5)	5.5.2
(2)	2.13.2	(6)	5.5.2
(3)	2.13.2	(7)	5.5.2
(4)	2.13.2	(8)	5.5.2
(6)	2.13.2	(9)	5.5.2

Trade Union and Labour		s 209	5.2.2
Relations (Consolidation)		s 210	5.2.1
Act 1992 – *cont*		s 211	5.2.1
s 108A(10)	5.5.2	s 212	5.2.1
(11)	5.5.2	(1)	5.1.1
(12)	5.5.2	s 213	5.2.1
(14)	5.5.2	s 214	5.2.1
(15)	5.5.2	ss 226–235	2.12.1
s 108B(1)	5.5.3	s 226	2.12.6
(2)	5.5.3	s 226A	1.1.7, 2.12.3
(3)	5.5.3	(1)	2.12.5
(4)	5.5.3	(2)(c)	2.12.3, 2.12.4
(5)	5.5.3	(3)(a)	2.12.3, 2.12.4
(6)	5.5.3	(3A)	2.12.4
(7)	5.5.3	(3B)	2.12.5
(8)	5.5.3	s 227(1)	2.12.6, 2.12.10
(9)	5.5.3	(2)	2.12.6
s 108C	5.5.3	s 228A(2)	2.12.7
s 109	5.3.1	(3)	2.12.7
s 119	4.1.2	(4)	2.12.7
s 132	5.5.4	(5)(a)	2.12.7
s 133	5.5.4	(b)	2.12.7
s 137	2.11.1	(c)	2.12.7
s 138	2.11.1	(d)	2.12.7
s 146	2.10.1, 4.3.1, 6.4.1	s 229(2)	2.12.8
(1)	2.10.2	(2A)	2.12.9
(2)	2.10.2	(2B)	2.12.9
(3)	2.10.2	(4)	2.12.8
(4)	2.10.2	s 230(2)	2.12.10
(5)	2.10.2	(2A)	2.12.9
s 147	2.10.3	s 231A	2.12.2
s 148	2.10.4	s 232A	2.12.6
s 149	2.10.4	s 232B(1)	2.12.10
s 150	2.10.4	(2)	2.12.10
s 156(1)	6.3.2	s 233	2.12.11
s 157	6.3.1	(3)	2.12.11
s 158	6.3.1	s 234	2.12.11
s 168(3)	4.1.2	(1)	2.12.3, 2.12.11
(4)	4.1.2	s 234A	2.12.3, 2.12.12
s 169	4.1.2	(3)	2.12.12
s 171	4.1.2	(a)	2.12.4
s 172	4.1.2	(5A)	2.12.4
s176(6)	6.3.2	s 234(4)	2.12.12
s 178(1)	2.7.1, 4.3.1	(7)	2.12.12
ss 181–185	5.1.1	(7A)	2.12.12
s 181	2.13.2	(7B)	2.12.12
s 182(1)	2.13.2	s 235A	5.3.2
s 199	2.2.17, 5.2.1	s 235B	5.3.1, 5.3.2
s 203	2.2.17	s 235C	5.3.2
s 207(1)	4.1.1	s 237	4.2.1
(2)	4.1.1	s 238	2.12.7

Trade Union and Labour
  Relations (Consolidation)
  Act 1992 – *cont*

s 238(2)	4.2.1
(3)	4.2.1
s 238A	2.12.7, 4.2.2
(8)	4.2.2
s 239(1)	4.2.2
(4)	4.2.2
s 244(1)(a)	2.12.7
(b)	2.12.7
(c)	2.12.7
(d)	2.12.7
(e)	2.12.7
(f)	2.12.7
s 246	2.12.11
s 254	5.4.1
s 256	5.5.5
s 256A	5.5.5
(4)	5.5.5
s 259	5.1.1
s 260	5.1.2
(1)	5.1.2
(2)	5.1.2
(3)	5.1.2
(3A)	5.1.2
s 263	5.1.3
(7)	5.1.3
s 263A	5.1.3
(1)	5.1.3
(2)	5.1.3
(4)	5.1.3
(5)	5.1.3
(6)	5.1.3
(7)	5.1.3
ss 266–271	5.3.2
s 285(1)	6.5.1
s 297	2.2.2
Sch A1	
para 2(2)–(6)	2.2.1
para 3(3)–(6)	2.2.1
para 4(1)	2.2.2
para 5	2.2.2
para 6	2.2.2
para 7(1), (3)–(6), (8)	2.2.2
para 8	2.2.2
para 9	2.2.2
para 10(1)–(7)	2.2.4
para 11	2.2.5
para 12(1)–(5)	2.2.6
para 13	2.2.6

para 14(1)–(8)	2.2.6
para 15(2)(a), (b)	2.2.7
(3)	2.2.7
(4)	2.2.2
(6)(a), (b)	2.2.7
para 16(1), (2)	2.2.11
para 17(1)–(3)	2.2.11
para 18	2.2.1
(1), (2)	2.2.12
para 19	2.2.1
(1)–(4)	2.2.12
para 20(1)–(4)	2.2.13
(5)	2.2.16
(6)	2.2.13
para 21(1), (2)	2.2.16
para 22(2)–(5)	2.2.16
para 23	2.2.16
para 24(2), (4), (5)	2.2.16
para 25(2)–(9)	2.2.17
para 26 (2)–(4), (6)–(8)	2.2.17
para 27(1)–(3)	2.2.17
para 28(2)–(7)	2.2.17
para 29(2)–(7)	2.2.17
para 30(2)–(4)	2.2.18
para 31(3), (4)	2.2.18
(5)	2.2.1, 2.2.18
(6), (7), (8)(a), (b)	2.2.18
para 32(1)–(3)	2.2.19
para 33	2.2.6
para 34(2)	2.2.6, 2.2.9
para 35(1)	2.2.1, 2.2.9
(2)	2.2.1
(4), (5)	2.2.9
para 36	2.2.10
para 37(1), (2)	2.2.10
para 38	2.2.10
para 39	2.2.10
para 40	2.2.10
para 41	2.2.10
para 42	2.2.10
para 44(1), (2), (4)	2.2.15
para 45	2.2.14
para 46	2.2.14
para 47	2.2.14
para 48	2.2.14
para 49	2.2.14
para 50	2.2.14
para 51	2.2.15
para 52(2)–(5)	2.3.2
para 54(2)–(4)	2.3.2
para 55(2), (4), (6)	2.3.3

Trade Union and Labour
  Relations (Consolidation)
  Act 1992 – *cont*
  Sch A1 – *cont*
    para 56(1)–(5)   2.3.4
    para 57(1)   2.3.4
    para 58(1)–(5)   2.3.5
    para 59   2.3.5
    para 60(2)–(4), (6)–(8)   2.3.5
    para 61   2.3.5
    para 62(1)–(5)   2.3.5
    para 63(1)–(5), (7), (8)   2.3.5
    para 66(2)   2.4.2
    para 67   2.4.2
    para 68(1), (2), (6)   2.4.2
    para 69(1)–(3), (4)(a),(b),
      (5)   2.4.3
    para 70(1)–(7)   2.4.4
    para 71   2.4.4
    para 73   2.4.4
    para 74(1)–(4), (6), (7)   2.4.5
    para 75   2.4.5
    para 76(1), (4)–(6)   2.4.6
    para 77(1), (5)   2.4.6
        (2)–(4), (6)   2.4.7
    para 78(1)–(5)   2.4.7
    para 79(1)–(6)   2.4.7
    para 82(1), (3)   2.4.8
    para 83(1)–(6)   2.4.8
    para 84(1), (2), (5)   2.4.8
    para 85(1), (2)   2.4.8
    para 86(1)–(3)   2.4.9
    para 87(1)–(5)   2.4.9
    para 88(1), (2)   2.4.9
    para 89(1)–(7)   2.4.9
    para 90   2.4.10
    para 91(1)–(5)   2.4.10
    para 92   2.4.2, 2.4.6
    para 96(1), (3)   2.5.1
    para 97   2.5.1, 2.5.2
    para 99(1), (2), (3)(f)   2.5.2
    para 100(1), (2), (4), (5)   2.5.3
    para 101   2.5.3
        (1)–(5)   2.5.3
    para 102(1)–(4), (6)   2.5.3
    para 103(1)(a), (2)–(4)   2.5.3
    para 104(2)   2.5.5
    para 105(1), (3), (5), (6),
      (7)   2.5.5
    para 106   2.5.6
    para 107(1)–(3)   2.5.6
    para 108(1), (2)   2.5.6

    para 109(1), (2)   2.5.6
    para 110(1), (2)   2.5.6
    para 111(2), (4)–(6)   2.5.6
    para 112(1)–(3)   2.5.7
    para 113(1), (2)   2.5.7
    para 114   2.5.7
    para 115(1), (3)–(6)   2.5.7
    para 116(1), (2)   2.5.7
    para 117(1)   2.5.8
        (2)   2.5.7, 2.5.8
        (3)   2.5.7, 2.5.8
    para 118   2.5.8
    para 119   2.5.8
    para 120   2.5.8
    para 121(1)–(4), (6)–(8)   2.5.8
    para 122   2.6.1
    para 123   2.6.1
    para 124   2.6.1
    para 127(1)–(3)   2.6.2
    para 128(1), (2)   2.6.2
    para 129(1), (2)   2.6.2
    para 130   2.6.2
    para 131   2.6.2
    para 132(1)–(6)   2.6.2
    para 133   2.6.2
    para 134   2.7.1
    para 135   2.7.1
    para 137(1)–(3)   2.7.2
    para 138   2.7.2
    para 139   2.7.2
    para 140   2.7.2
    para 141(2)–(4)   2.7.2
        (5)   2.7.3
    paras 142–148   2.7.3
    paras 149–150   2.8.1
    para 152   2.8.1
    para 153   2.8.1
    para 156(1)–(4)   2.9.1
        (5)   2.9.2
    para 157(1)(a), (b) (2), (3)   2.9.2
    para 158   2.9.2
    para 159(1)–(5)   2.9.2
    para 160   2.9.2
    para 161(1)–(3)   2.9.3
    para 162   2.9.3
    para 163   2.9.3
    para 164   2.9.3
    para 166   2.2.16
        (2)–(4)   2.9.4
    para 167   2.2.16
        (1), (3), (4)   2.9.4

Trade Union and Labour
    Relations (Consolidation)
    Act 1992 – *cont*
    Sch A1 – *cont*
    para 168   2.2.18, 2.3.5
        (1)–(3)   2.9.4
    para 169(1)–(3)   2.9.4

para 170   2.9.4
para 171   2.1.2

Vexatious Actions (Scotland) Act
    1898   5.5.5

TABLE OF STATUTORY INSTRUMENTS

References in the right-hand column are to paragraph numbers.

Conduct of Employment Agencies and Employment Businesses Regulations
1976, SI 1976/715   6.2.1

Employment Rights (Increase of Limits) Order 1998, SI 1998/924   6.3.3

Maternity (Compulsory Leave) Regulations 1994, SI 1994/2479   3.1.4

Social Security (Categorisation of Earners) Regulations 1978, SI 1978/1689   6.2.1

Transfer of Undertakings (Protection of Employment) Regulations 1981,
SI 1981/1794   6.6.1

Working Time Regulations 1998, SI 1998/1833   2.9.2, 4.1.6

TABLE OF EUROPEAN LEGISLATION

References in the right-hand column are to paragraph numbers.

Council Directive 77/187 relating to the safeguarding of employees' rights in
the event of transfers of undertakings   6.6.1

Council Directive 92/85 on the safety and health at work of pregnant workers
and workers who have recently given birth   3.1.2

Council Directive 93/104 on the organisation of working time   1.1.8

Council Directive 96/34 on the framework agreement on parental leave   1.1.8, 3.2.1,
3.3.1, 3.3.6

Council Directive 96/71 concerning the posting of workers in the framework
of the provision of services   6.5.1

Council Directive 97/81 concerning the framework agreement on part-time
work concluded by UNICE, CEEP and the ETUC   1.2.6, 4.5.1, 4.5.2

Council Directive 98/50 amending Directive 77/187 relating to the
safeguarding of employees' rights in the event of transfers of
undertakings   6.6.1

TABLE OF ABBREVIATIONS

Statutes

DDA 1995	Disability Discrimination Act 1995
EAA 1973	Employment Agencies Act 1973
EPA 1975	Employment Protection Act 1975
ERA 1996	Employment Rights Act 1996
ERA 1999	Employment Relations Act 1999
ETA 1996	Employment Tribunals Act 1996
NMWA 1998	National Minimum Wage Act 1998
PIDA 1998	Public Interest Disclosure Act 1998
RRA 1976	Race Relations Act 1976
SDA 1975	Sex Discrimination Act 1975
TULR(C)A 1992	Trade Union and Labour Relations (Consolidation) Act 1992
TURERA 1993	Trade Union Reform and Employment Rights Act 1993

Other

ACAS	Advisory, Conciliation and Arbitration Service
CAC	Central Arbitration Committee
CO	Certification Officer
CPAUIA	Commissioner for Protection Against Unlawful Industrial Action
CRTUM	Commissioner for the Rights of Trade Union Members

Chapter 1

INTRODUCTION

1.1 BACKGROUND

Fairness at work

1.1.1 On 21 May 1998, the Government published its White Paper on employment legislation entitled *Fairness at Work*.[1] The proposals contained therein heralded the biggest change in employment and union rights since the legislation of the Thatcher Government in the early 1980s. In the Foreword, the Prime Minister, Tony Blair, stated that the White Paper was part of the Government's programme 'to replace the notion of conflict between employers and employees with the promotion of partnership'. He continued:

> 'It goes along with our emphasis on education and skills – not over-burdensome regulation – in the labour market [and] steers a way between the absence of minimum standards of protection at the workplace, and a return to the laws of the past. It is based on the rights of the individual, whether exercised on their own or with others, as a matter of choice . . . It seeks to draw a line under the issue of industrial relations law.'

---

1   Cm 3968.

1.1.2 The White Paper described its proposals as creating a framework for the future, the three main elements of the framework being:

– provisions for the basic fair treatment of employees;
– new procedures for collective representation at work;
– policies that enhance family life.[1]

---

1   White Paper, para 1.9.

1.1.3 The White Paper also stated that the Government recognised that the proposals will take time to implement and bed in and that the Government did not intend to pass further legislation.[1] This indicates that the Government recognises the mammoth changes the proposals bring.

---

1   White Paper, para 1.11.

1.1.4 There were two other points noted by the Government in introducing the White Paper. First, the Government stated that the term 'employees' used within its proposals:

'is generally used to cover those who work for someone else rather than on their own account, regardless of whether or not they are strictly employed under a contract of employment.'[1]

Further, the Government stated that it was:

'committed to maintaining the key elements of the employment legislation of the 1980s. Laws on picketing, on ballots before industrial action and for increasing democratic accountability in trade unions have all helped to improve employment relations. They will stay.'[2]

---

1 White Paper, para 1.14.
2 Ibid, para 2.15.

The proposals

1.1.5 In the Summary to the White Paper, the Government identified 29 proposals or issues for consultation. Some of the proposals did not find their way into the Employment Relations Bill. In particular, the controversial issue of zero hours contracts was not addressed. Neither was the reduction in the continuity period for unfair dismissal, although the continuity period was reduced to one year from the beginning of June 1999, by statutory instrument.

Rights for individuals

1.1.6 The Government listed three major proposals in respect of individual rights. First, the reduction of the qualifying period for unfair dismissal to one year.[1] The aim behind this proposal was a better balance between competitiveness and fairness. The Government felt that the two-year period was too long and a reduction would mean that employees would be less inhibited about changing jobs and losing protection, thus encouraging a more flexible labour market, and also it would encourage employers to introduce good employment practices and thereby encourage a more committed and productive workforce.[2] Secondly, the abolition of the limit on awards for unfair dismissal.[3] The Government acknowledged that very few employment tribunals issue reinstatement or re-engagement orders and therefore the amount of compensation is very important. The Government also acknowledged that the limits meant that some employees were not fully compensated for the loss of their job and that the likelihood of proper compensation being awarded should encourage employers to put proper voluntary systems in place. The Government also stated that the abolition of the limit in sex discrimination cases has not led to a significant rise in the number of claims and, although the number of claims of race discrimination have increased since the removal of the limit on compensation, the number is still low.[4] The final proposal in *Fairness at Work* in respect of individual rights was the introduction of index-linking limits on statutory awards and payments subject to a maximum rate.[5] The reason behind this proposal was that annual reviews are time-consuming and costly and produce results which could generally be predicted.[6] In addition to specific proposals put forward, the Government also invited views on:

- whether the limits on additional and special awards should be retained or tribunals should be able to award aggravated damages;[7]
- options for changing the law allowing employees to waive their rights to unfair dismissal and redundancy payments in fixed-term contracts;[8]
- whether further action should be taken to address the potential abuse of zero hours contracts;[9] and
- whether legislation should be introduced to extend the coverage of some or all existing employment rights to all of those who work for another person.[10]

Some of these have found their way into the Employment Relations Act 1999.

---

1   White Paper, para 3.10. This appeared to pre-empt what many thought would be the decision of the ECJ in *R v Secretary of State for Employment ex p Seymour-Smith and Perez* [1999] IRLR 253 (ECJ). In fact, that Court held that the two-year qualifying period in respect of unfair dismissal claims, when it was introduced in 1985, did not have a disparate impact on women and therefore under the normal test was not indirectly discriminatory. The Court did, however, suggest a second test whereby it would be up to the national courts to determine whether a small difference in the number of men and women who could comply with the rule showed 'a persistent and relatively constant disparity over a long period' suggesting that there may be discrimination.
2   White Paper, para 3.9.
3   Ibid, para 3.5.
4   Ibid.
5   Ibid, para 3.8.
6   Ibid.
7   Ibid, para 3.7.
8   Ibid, para 3.13.
9   Ibid, para 3.16.
10   Ibid, para 3.18.

Collective rights

1.1.7   The Government made eight proposals in respect of collective rights:

(1) a statutory procedure for both recognition and derecognition of trade unions where the majority of the workforce wishes it.[1] The Government stated that out of the 50 largest UK companies, 44 recognise trade unions.[2] The Government also accepted, however, the importance of voluntary choices and acknowledged that 'mutually agreed arrangements for representation, whether involving trade unions or not, are the best ways for employers and employees to move forward'.[3] The White Paper states, however, that there will be occasions when the employees want the benefit of representation at work but are unable to get an agreement with their employer and, in these circumstances, there should be a statutory procedure in place to be used when voluntary agreement has not worked and the majority of the workforce want representation;[4]

(2) the second proposal was the introduction of the right to claim unfair dismissal for those dismissed for taking part in lawfully organised official industrial action.[5] The Government stated that the position at the time of

the White Paper, that is that employees dismissed for taking lawfully organised industrial action could claim unfair dismissal only if there were selective dismissals or selective re-engagements, was illogical and unsatisfactory;[6]

(3) the third proposal was to make it unlawful to discriminate by omission on the grounds of trade union membership, non membership or activities.[7] The Government saw this proposal as part of its commitment to ensuring that individuals should be free to choose whether to be a union member or not and felt that to leave the law as it stood would act as a deterrent to some employees who wanted to become union members;[8]

(4) in support of the third proposal was the fourth proposal which was to prohibit the blacklisting of trade unionists;[9]

(5) the White Paper also proposed to amend the law on industrial action ballots and notice so that the union does not have to name the employees being balloted.[10] The balloting rules were complex and some trade union members do not want their employers to know of their union membership;

(6) the White Paper also proposed the creation of a legal right to be accompanied during disciplinary and grievance hearings putting on a statutory footing the recommendations in the ACAS Code of Practice on Disciplinary Powers and Procedures;[11]

(7) the abolition of the posts of the Commissioner for the Rights of Trade Union Members and the Commissioner for Protection Against Unlawful Industrial Action and giving new powers to the Certification Officer to hear complaints currently heard by the former;[12] and

(8) making funds available to contribute to the training of managers and employee representatives in order to assist and develop partnerships at work.[13]

In addition, the Government invited views on:

– whether training should be among the matters automatically covered by an award of trade union recognition;[14]
– how the procedure for recognition should work;[15]
– how protection for those taking part in lawful industrial action should be implemented;[16] and
– how to simplify the law and Code of Practice on industrial action ballots and notice.[17]

---

1   White Paper, para 4.11.
2   Ibid, para 4.7.
3   Ibid, para 4.10.
4   Ibid, para 4.11.
5   Ibid, para 4.22.
6   Ibid.
7   Ibid, para 4.25. This proposal sought to reverse the House of Lords' decisions in *Associated Newspapers v Wilson* and *Associated British Ports v Palmer* [1995] 2 AC 454.
8   White Paper, para 4.25.

9   White Paper, para 4.25.
10   Ibid, para 4.27. The interpretation that s 226A of the Trade Union and Labour Relations
     (Consolidation) Act 1992 created an obligation on the union to give the names of the
     balloted members to the employer comes from the House, of Lords' decision in *Blackpool
     and Fylde College v NAFTHE* [1994] ICR 982.
11   White Paper, para 4.29.
12   Ibid, para 4.31.
13   Ibid, para 2.7.
14   Ibid, para 4.18.
15   Ibid.
16   Ibid, para 4.23.
17   Ibid, para 4.26.

Family friendly policies

1.1.8 The Government, in the final part of its framework, listed proposals in relation to family friendly policies. To some extent, these proposals built on existing initiatives which had been introduced to implement EU Directives such as the Working Time Directive[1] and the need to implement the Parental Leave Directive.[2] In addition, there had been criticism of the complex provisions in respect of maternity leave[3] and uncertainty as to whether the contract continued after the 14-week maternity leave period, if the woman took extended maternity leave.[4] The Government therefore proposed:

–   to extend maternity leave to 18 weeks to align it with maternity pay;[5]
–   to give employees rights to extended maternity absence and to parental leave after one year's service;[6]
–   to provide for the contract of employment to continue during the whole of the maternity or parental leave period, unless expressly terminated by either party;[7]
–   to provide similar rights for employees returning to their jobs after parental leave as apply to those employees on maternity leave;[8]
–   to provide three months parental leave for adoptive parents;[9]
–   to provide a right to reasonable time off for family emergencies for all employees regardless of length of service;[10] and
–   protection for employees from dismissal or detriment if they exercise the new rights.[11]

The majority of these proposals merely implement the Parental Leave Directive. The Government also invited views on:

–   simplifying notice of maternity leave;[12]
–   options for framing legislation to comply with the Parental Leave Directive;[13] and
–   the difficulties small firms might face in complying with the Parental Leave Directive.[14]

1   Council Directive 93/104/EC.
2   Council Directive 96/34/EC.
3   For example, House of Commons, Session 1994–5, Employment Committee First Report
     Mothers in Employment Vol 1: Report and Proceedings of the Committee, 15 February 1995.

4   White Paper, paras 5.20 and 5.21.
5   Ibid, para 5.14.
6   Ibid, para 5.19.
7   Ibid, para 5.21.
8   Ibid, para 5.22.
9   Ibid, para 5.23.
10   Ibid, para 5.28.
11   Ibid, para 5.29.
12   Ibid, para 5.17.
13   Ibid, para 5.16.
14   Ibid, para 5.26.

1.2   THE EMPLOYMENT RELATIONS BILL 1999

1.2.1   The Employment Relations Bill, as it was originally introduced into the House of Commons, bears little relation to the Employment Relations Act 1999 (ERA 1999) discussed in this book. Originally, it was an enabling piece of legislation giving powers to the Secretary of State to issue regulations to implement many of the proposals in *Fairness at Work*, causing one member of the House of Lords, at its second reading, to state: 'It is an enabling Bill, a mere skeleton, with the details to be filled in by statutory instrument, rather like the ministerial decrees that pass for law-making in Russia'[1] and another to comment: 'It is regrettable that this legislation has been drafted in that way'.[2]

1   HL Deb, vol 600, col 974, 10 May 1999 (Baroness Miller).
2   HL Deb, vol 600, col 980, 10 May 1999 (Lord Razzall).

1.2.2   Perhaps because of comments above, the Government undertook to place more of the law on the face of the Act, while retaining the power of the Secretary of State to issue regulations in other areas (for example, maternity rights). This meant that the Bill was extensively amended throughout its parliamentary passage. At report stage, in the House of Lords, one member of the House said:

> 'This Bill began in the other place, but it was completely recast by the government amendments, so that the Bill that left there was totally different in form from the one that had started. The Bill which your lordships have been asked to deal with was therefore the Employment Relations Bill Mark II. The Government extensively amended the Bill in Committee so that we now have Mark III. However, some 48 hours before this present stage, the Government tabled some 16 pages of amendments to Schedule 1 alone, plus about another dozen spread around the Bill. So what we are really being asked to consider is the Employment Relations Bill Mark IV.'[1]

In reality, there is much truth in this comment because the Employment Relations Bill Mark IV is the Employment Relations Act 1999 which contains much more detail than the original Bill and also introduces provisions which were not put forward in *Fairness at Work.*

---

1 HL Deb, vol 603, cols 1039–1040, 8 July 1999 (Baroness Miller).

Rights for individuals

1.2.3 The proposals put forward in *Fairness at Work* have been discussed above. In respect of individual rights, many of the proposals have been adopted. The qualifying period for unfair dismissal has been reduced to one year, albeit not by the Employment Relations Act 1999. While the Act does not remove the limit on compensatory awards in unfair dismissal, it increases the limit to £50,000[1], meaning that in very few cases will an employee not be adequately compensated for the loss of his job. The Act has introduced index-linking on statutory awards and payments[2] and has abolished special awards although increasing additional awards in all cases to between 26 and 52 weeks' pay.[3] The Act also prevents the use of waiver provisions in fixed-term contracts.[4] Nothing has been done, however, in respect of zero hours contracts and the Government is still out to consultation in respect of employment protection rights covering all workers and not just those under a contract of employment. This creates anomalies in that many of the new rights in the Act apply to workers, whereas existing employment protection rights apply to employees only.

---

1 ERA 1999, s 37.
2 Ibid, s 34.
3 Ibid, s 33.
4 Ibid, s 18.

Collective rights

1.2.4 In respect of the proposals on collective rights, all have been implemented. Schedule 1 introduces a statutory recognition and derecognition procedure, while encouraging voluntary agreement in respect of representation. Schedule 5 gives protection, in some circumstances, against unfair dismissal for employees engaged in lawfully organised industrial action. Detriment now includes:

- an omission to act;[1]
- blacklists of trade union members are now prohibited;[2]
- a union no longer has to name the members it will be balloting on industrial action;[3]
- there is now a right to be accompanied at disciplinary and grievance hearings;[4]
- the posts of the Commissioner for the Rights of Trade Union Members and the Commissioner for Protection Against Unlawful Industrial Action have been abolished;[5] and

–   the Secretary of State can make funds available to develop partnerships at work.[6]

---

1   ERA 1999, s 2 and Sch 2.
2   Ibid, s 3.
3   Ibid, s 4 and Sch 3.
4   Ibid, s 10.
5   Ibid, s 28.
6   Ibid, s 30.

Family friendly policies

1.2.5   While the Government is required to implement the Parental Leave Directive, it is arguable that, in its original iteration, the Employment Relations Bill went much further. The original Bill allowed reasonable time off for domestic incidents, giving a power to the Secretary of State to issue regulations defining what was meant by domestic incident and the limits of the right. Whilst the provisions on maternity leave and parental leave did not cause much debate, those on time off for domestic incidents did, and, as a result, major revisions were made at a late stage. The result is Part II of Sch 4 to the Employment Relations Act 1999[1] which inserts s 57A into the Employment Rights Act 1996 (ERA 1996). This creates a right to reasonable time off for dependants and, unlike the original proposals, the Act defines in what circumstances an employee is entitled to time off and what is meant by a dependant for the purposes of the section.[2] There is no residual power in the Secretary of State to issue regulations. Whilst this satisfied the opposition, the regulations would have listed factors to be taken into account when looking to see what would be reasonable time off and therefore would have taken into account the needs of the small employer. It will now be up to the Employment Appeal Tribunal and the courts to establish a body of case-law to determine what factors tribunals should take into account.

---

1   Implemented by s 8 of the Employment Relations Act 1999.
2   ERA 1996, s 57A(1), (3) and (4).

Other provisions

1.2.6   In addition to noting what proposals did not find their way into the Employment Relations Act 1999, it is interesting to note other provisions which were not proposed in *Fairness at Work* but which have now become law. In respect of individual rights, *Fairness at Work* did not mention part-time workers, although the Government must implement the Part Time Work Directive[1] by the year 2000. The Government, however, has taken advantage of the fact that the Employment Relations Act 1999 is creating so many new rights by inserting provisions relating to part-time work and giving power to the Secretary of State to issue regulations and Codes of Practice.[2] The Employment Relations Act 1999 also extends employment protection rights to persons who are based in the UK or who work for a majority of their time in the UK even though their base is elsewhere by repealing s 196 of ERA 1996.[3] In relation to collective rights, the Act gives rights to recognised trade unions, where the method of collective bargaining has been specified by the Central Arbitration Committee (CAC), to send representatives of those unions for regular meetings with the employer in order to consult about training for the workers in the bargaining unit.[4] In addition, although it is not mentioned in *Fairness at Work*, the Employment Relations Act 1999 amends the Employment Agencies Act 1973 and places many more restrictions on the operation of employment agencies and business.[5] In two areas, however, the Act has appeared to take away rights. It amends the National Minimum Wage Act 1998 by excluding from its provisions residential members of a religious or similar community who work for that community.[6] Whilst this may appear to be taking away rights, in reality those workers are really acting voluntarily and the provision was inserted on the recommendation of the Low Pay Commission. Finally, the 1997–98 report of the Intelligence and Security Committee recommended that employment protection rights should be extended to employees employed by organisations where national security could be an issue. Whereas to some extent the Act adopts this recommendation, the right to be accompanied at disciplinary and grievance hearings does not apply to employment for the purposes of the Security Services, the Secret Intelligence Service or the Government Communications Headquarters[7] and the enforcement of other rights by such employees can be prevented or restricted as described in Chapter 6.[8] Only when these provisions have been interpreted will it be clear whether the Act gives with one hand and takes away with the other.

---

1   Council Directive 97/81/EC.
2   ERA 1999, ss 19, 20 and 21.
3   Ibid, s 32.
4   Ibid, s 5 inserting s 70B into the Trade Union and Labour Relations (Consolidation) Act 1992.
5   Ibid, s 31 and Sch 7.
6   Ibid, s 22.
7   Ibid, s 15.
8   Ibid, Sch 8.

Chapter 2

TRADE UNIONS

2.1 COLLECTIVE BARGAINING: RECOGNITION

Introduction

2.1.1   Section 1 of and Sch 1 to ERA 1999 create a new statutory procedure for the recognition and derecognition of trade unions, in addition to rights for workers to participate or not to participate in the process and not to suffer dismissal or detriment as a consequence. It does so by the insertion of a new Chapter (Chapter VA) and the addition of Sch A1 into the Trade Union and Labour Relations (Consolidation) Act 1992 (TULR(C)A 1992). Part I of the Schedule deals with the statutory recognition process. Part II deals with voluntary recognition and the possibility that the employer could voluntarily recognise a union to avoid a declaration of recognition being made, and then fail to carry out the agreement reached. Part III deals with changes in the bargaining unit. Parts IV, V and VI deal with derecognition. Part VII deals with the situation when the union loses independence. Part VIII provides protection for workers who participate or choose not to participate in the processes and Part IX contains general provisions and powers for the Secretary of State to issue guidance on or amend certain procedures. In total, 172 paragraphs.

2.1.2   In *Fairness at Work* the Government stated that the starting point in the new procedures is voluntary agreement. Only if this does not work will the statutory procedure be invoked. The Government felt that, by setting out the procedure, employers, employees and trade unions will all understand the consequences of not reaching an agreement and thus lessen the likelihood of the procedure being invoked. However, should an agreement not be forthcoming, the statutory procedure described below offers a means of resolution of disputes without industrial action.[1] In dealing with cases under Sch A1, the CAC is to have regard to the object of encouraging and promoting fair and efficient practices and arrangements in the workplace, so far as having regard to that object is consistent with applying other provisions of the Schedule to the case concerned.[2]

---

1   *Fairness at Work*, paras 4.15 and 4.16.
2   TULR(C)A 1992, Sch A1, para 171.

2.2   STATUTORY RECOGNITION

Introduction

2.2.1   Part I of the new Sch A1 sets out the process for statutory recognition for a trade union or unions seeking recognition to be entitled to conduct collective bargaining on behalf of a group or groups of workers. Paragraph 2 contains definitions for the purposes of Part I of the Schedule. 'Bargaining unit' refers to the group of workers or groups of workers concerned.[1] The 'proposed bargaining unit' refers to the bargaining unit proposed in the request for recognition.[2] If the employer does not agree the bargaining unit, it may be changed by negotiation or, if there is a failure to agree, the CAC will rule on what constitutes the bargaining unit.[3] References to the 'employer' mean the employer of the workers constituting the bargaining unit.[4] References to the 'parties' mean the union or unions and the employer.[5] References to 'collective bargaining' in Part I of the Schedule are to negotiations relating to pay, hours and holidays,[6] although the parties can agree that other matters be included.[7] If, however, the CAC specifies the method of collective bargaining, that method shall apply only to pay, hours and holidays and not other matters agreed by the parties.[8] Even where the CAC does specify the method of collective bargaining, the parties can agree to vary it to include those matters agreed.[9] Furthermore, the restricted definition of collective bargaining does not apply in respect of an existing collective agreement which is in force.[10] This means that if a union already has an agreement with the employer which allows the union to negotiate in respect of other matters including pay, hours and holidays, there is a union recognised for the purposes of collective bargaining and this will prevent another union applying to be recognised unless certain conditions exist.[11] Conversely, if a union already has a long-standing arrangement with the employer to negotiate on matters other than pay, hours or holidays, that union can still apply for recognition on the 'core' issues without losing the limited recognition it enjoys.[12]

---

1   TULR(C)A 1992, Sch A1, para 2(2).
2   Ibid, para 2(3).
3   Ibid, para 18 and 19.
4   Ibid, para 2(4).
5   Ibid, para 2(5).
6   Ibid, para 3(3).
7   Ibid, para 3(4).
8   Ibid, para 3(5). The CAC specifies a method of collective bargaining under para 31(3) where the parties cannot reach an agreement as to the method.
9   Ibid, para 31(5).
10   Ibid, para 3(6).
11   Ibid, para 35(1).
12   Ibid, para 35(2).

Request for recognition

2.2.2 The process begins with the union or unions making a request for recognition to the employer.[1] Various conditions are laid down for a request to be valid and, if the conditions are not met, the CAC must reject the application.[2] First, the request must be received by the employer.[3] This provision may cause problems if the employer denies receipt of the request. The original proposals contained provisions whereby the CAC could resolve the dispute if the employer denied receipt, but these were removed in the amended Bill which went to the House of Lords. Secondly, each of the unions making the request must have a certificate of independence from the Certification Officer.[4] The procedure applies to employers who employ on the day the request is received at least 21 employees or employ an average of 21 employees in the 13 weeks ending with the day the request for recognition is received. These are either/or tests and therefore if the employer employs 21 workers for one day and on that day the union submits a request for recognition, the procedure will apply. Conversely, by also having the alternative test of the average number of employees in the preceding 13 weeks, it prevents an employer from sacking some employees for a short while to avoid the statutory recognition procedure. The number of employees includes those of an associated employer,[5] although the term 'associated employer' does not include companies incorporated outside Great Britain, but will include workers of associated employers incorporated outside Great Britain if the day the request was made fell within a period when they were ordinarily working in Great Britain.[6] In addition, where the employer employs an average of 21 workers in the preceding 13 weeks, any worker employed by an associated employer incorporated outside Great Britain will be included in relation to a week the worker worked the whole or part of the week in Great Britain.[7] For the purposes of the calculation of 21 workers, that calculation shall also apply to a worker employed on board a ship registered in Great Britain unless:

(a) the ship's entry in the register specifies a port outside Great Britain as the port to which the vessel is to be treated as belonging;
(b) the employment is wholly outside Great Britain; or
(c) the worker is not ordinarily resident in Great Britain.[8]

The original Bill placed a burden on the employer to show that the employer employed fewer than 21 employees but, again, this was removed by the House of Lords. The Secretary of State has the power to vary the number of employees and, in specified circumstances, exclude some of the conditions by statutory instrument, subject to affirmative resolution.[9] The final condition to be satisfied in order for a request to be valid is that it must comply with the minimum criteria laid down for the form and content of requests for recognition in that the request must be in writing; it must identify the union or unions and the bargaining unit, and state that it is made under Sch A1.[10] The Secretary of State has the power to issue a statutory instrument requiring more detail in requests and laying down a procedure for making them.[11] However, it is not intended at present to exercise this power unless the lack of a laid-down procedure causes problems.

---

1 TULR(C)A 1992, Sch A1, para 4(1).
2 Ibid, para 15(4).
3 Ibid, para 5.
4 Ibid, para 6. By s 5 of TULR(C)A 1992 an independent trade union:
  'is a trade union which –
    (a) is not under the domination or control of an employer or group of employers or of one or more employers associations, and
    (b) is not liable to interference by an employer or any such group or association (arising out of the provision of financial or material support or by any other means whatsoever) tending towards such control'.
5 TULR(C)A 1992, Sch A1, para 7(1). By s 297 of TULR(C)A 1992:
  'any two employers shall be treated as associated if –
    (a) one is a company of which the other (directly or indirectly) has control, or
    (b) both are companies of which a third person (directly or indirectly) has control.'
  Cases under an identical provision which is now s 231 of ERA 1996 have stated that control means legal control rather than share ownership (*South West Launderettes Ltd v Laidler* [1986] IRLR 305).
6 TULR(C)A 1992, Sch A1, para 7(3).
7 Ibid, para 7(4).
8 Ibid, para 7(5).
9 Ibid, para 7(6) and (8).
10 Ibid, para 8.
11 Ibid, para 9.

2.2.3 The figure of 21 workers was one of the most controversial parts of the Act as it completed the parliamentary process. The opposition quoted from the recommendation of the Commission of the European Union concerning the definition of a small enterprise which the Commission defined as an enterprise with fewer than 50 employees.[1] The opposition also quoted the Late Payment of Commercial Debts (Interest) Act 1998 in which a small company was defined as one with fewer than 50 employees[2] and argued that there should be a standard definition for the purposes of all legislation. In response, the Government stated that it did not feel that there should be a standard definition of a small business for the purpose of all legislation; the figure of 21 was reached after consultation; and that this will still exclude 8.1 million workers or 31 per cent of the total workforce from the statutory recognition procedure.[3]

---

1 HL Deb, vol 603, col 1042, 8 July 1999 (Baroness Miller).
2 Ibid.
3 HL Deb, vol 603, col 1045, 8 July 1999, (Lord McCarthy).

Parties agree

2.2.4 If, before the end of the first period, which is 10 working days starting with the day after the employer receives the request,[1] the parties agree the appropriate bargaining unit and that the union or unions are to be recognised as entitled to conduct collective bargaining on behalf of that unit, no further steps need be taken.[2] If the employer does not accept the request but informs the union before the end of the first 10-day period that he or she is prepared to negotiate, the parties may, in the second period, conduct negotiations with a view to agreeing the bargaining unit and that the union or unions are recognised to conduct collective bargaining on behalf of that unit. If an agreement is reached, no further steps are necessary.[3] The second period is 20 working days, starting the day after the first period expires, or any such longer period which the parties agree upon.[4] Either party may request the Advisory Conciliation and Arbitration Service (ACAS) to assist in the negotiations.[5]

1   TULR(C)A 1992, Sch A1, para 10(6).
2   Ibid, para 10(1).
3   Ibid, para 10(2), (3) and (4).
4   Ibid, para 10(7).
5   Ibid, para 10(5).

Employer rejects request

2.2.5 If the employer fails to respond to the request before the end of the first period, or before the end of the first period the employer rejects the request and does not indicate a willingness to negotiate, the union or unions may apply to the CAC to decide whether the proposed bargaining unit is appropriate, or some other bargaining unit is appropriate, and/or whether the union or unions have the support of the majority of the workers constituting the bargaining unit.[1]

1   TULR(C)A 1992, Sch A1, para 11.

Negotiations fail

2.2.6 If the employer has refused the request to recognise but has informed the union or unions that he or she is prepared to negotiate and no agreement has been reached in the second 20-day period, the union or unions may apply to the CAC to decide whether the proposed bargaining unit is appropriate, or some other unit is appropriate and whether the union or unions have the support of the majority of the workers constituting the appropriate bargaining unit.[1] Similarly, if, in the second period, the parties agree the bargaining unit but cannot agree that the union or unions be recognised, the union may apply to the CAC to decide whether the union or unions have the support of the majority of the workers constituting the unit.[2] No application may be made, however, if, within a period of 10 working days starting with the day that the employer informs the union that he or she is refusing the request but is willing to negotiate, the employer proposes that ACAS be asked to assist in the negotiations and the union rejects the proposal or fails to accept the proposal within 10 working days of it being made.[3] Any application made to the CAC must be in the form specified by the CAC and supported by any documents specified by the CAC.[4] The union or unions must give notice of the application to the employer complete with a copy of the application and any supporting documents.[5] The CAC must give the parties notice of receipt of an application.[6] If two or more applications are received by the CAC, and the bargaining units proposed overlap – that is at least one worker in one of the bargaining units also falls within another of the bargaining units which is the subject of an application – the CAC must apply the 10 per cent test.[7] The 10 per cent test means that at least 10 per cent of the workers in the relevant bargaining unit are members of the union making the application.[8] If more than one application satisfies the 10 per cent test or none of the applications satisfies it, then the CAC must not accept any application.[9] If only one application satisfies the test then the CAC must proceed with that application and not proceed with any others.[10] The CAC must inform the parties, within 10 working days starting with the day after the receipt of the last application, of its decision, unless the CAC extends that period by giving notice to the parties with reasons given for the extension.[11] The purpose of these provisions is to prevent a union which has no real support from jeopardising an application from a union which has support from the workers. If two unions have more than 10 per cent of union members, it would be practical for the unions to put in a joint application.

---

1   TULR(C)A 1992, Sch A1, para 12(1) and (2).
2   Ibid, para 12(3) and (4).
3   Ibid, para 12(5).
4   Ibid, para 33.
5   Ibid, para 34.
6   Ibid, para 13.
7   Ibid, para 14(1), (2), (3) and (4).
8   Ibid, para 14(5).
9   Ibid, para 14(7).
10   Ibid, para 14(8).
11   Ibid, para 14(6).

2.2.7   By para 15, when an application for recognition can proceed, it must be valid,[1] it must be made in accordance with either para 11 (employer rejects request) or para 12 (negotiations fail) and it must be admissible.[2] In deciding those questions the CAC must consider any evidence which it has been given by the union or unions and the employer.[3] The CAC has 10 working days starting with the day it receives the application in which to decide if the application is valid and admissible,[4] although this period can be extended by the CAC by giving notice to the parties stating reasons for the extension.[5]

1   TULR(C)A 1992, Sch A1, para 15(2)(a).
2   Ibid, para 15(2)(b).
3   Ibid, para 15(3).
4   Ibid, para 15(6)(a).
5   Ibid, para 15(6)(b).

2.2.8   In order to be valid and therefore proceed, the application must comply with paras 5–9. That is:

- it must be received by the employer (para 5);
- the union must have a certificate of independence (para 6);
- the employer employs at least 21 employees on the day of the request or an average of 21 employees in the 13 weeks preceding the request (para 7);
- the request is in writing, identifies the union and the bargaining unit and states that it is made under Sch A1 (para 8);
- complies with any requirements laid down by statutory instrument (para 9).

2.2.9   In addition to complying with the procedures in paras 11 or 12, for the application to proceed it must be admissible. To be admissible, paras 33–42 must be complied with. Paragraph 33 states that the application must be in the form prescribed by the CAC and supported by such documents specified by the CAC as stated above. The application must be copied to the employer, along with any supporting documents.[1] The application will be inadmissible if the CAC is satisfied that a union is already recognised in respect of any of the workers falling within the relevant bargaining unit (that is the proposed bargaining unit where the application is under paras 11(2) or 12(2) or the agreed bargaining unit where the application is under para 12(4)).[2] However, the application will be admissible if:

- the recognised union is the one making the application and the matters in respect of which the union is recognised do not include pay, hours or holiday;
- the recognised union does not have a certificate of independence;
- there has been an agreement between the employer and the union to recognise that union in respect of the same or substantially the same bargaining unit; and
- the agreement ceased to have effect in the period of three years ending with the date of the agreement.[3]

It is for the CAC to decide whether the bargaining unit is substantially the same but in deciding the matter the CAC may take into account the views of any person it believes has an interest in the matter.[4] These provisions ensure that where there are existing arrangements the procedure should not disrupt them.

1   TULR(C)A 1992, Sch A1, para 34.
2   Ibid, para 35(1).
3   Ibid, para 35(4).
4   Ibid, para 35(5).

2.2.10 Further, in order for the application to be admissible, the CAC must decide that members of the relevant union constitute 10 per cent of the relevant bargaining unit and the majority of the workers in the bargaining unit would be likely to support recognition.[1] In addition, if the application is made by more than one union, to be admissible the unions must show that they will co-operate with each other in a manner likely to secure and maintain stable collective bargaining arrangements and will enter into an arrangement under which the collective bargaining is conducted by the unions acting together on behalf of the bargaining unit, if the employer so wishes.[2] An application is inadmissible if:

–   it covers workers in respect of whom an application has already been accepted by the CAC;[3]
–   is substantially the same as an application made by the same union and accepted by the CAC in the previous three years;[4]
–   is made within three years of a declaration by the CAC that the union making the application is not entitled to recognition in respect of the same or substantially the same bargaining unit;[5]
–   is made within three years of a declaration by the CAC that the bargaining arrangements involving the union making the application are to cease to have effect.[6]

In respect of the above, it is for the CAC to decide if the bargaining units are the same or substantially the same and the CAC may take into account the views of any person it believes has an interest in the matter.[7] The aim of the last three provisions is to ensure stability in the bargaining arrangements in that, once a decision has been made on an application for recognition, it should not be re-opened for three years. The provisions do not appear to prevent another union applying for recognition in respect of the same bargaining unit where the first application has been rejected by the CAC.

---

1   TULR(C)A 1992, Sch A1, para 36.
2   Ibid, para 37(1) and (2).
3   Ibid, para 38.
4   Ibid, para 39.
5   Ibid, para 40.
6   Ibid, para 41.
7   Ibid, para 42.

Withdrawal of application/notice to cease consideration of application

2.2.11 If the CAC has accepted an application, the union may not withdraw the application after the CAC has issued a declaration that the union is recognised or given notice that a ballot on recognition will be held.[1] If an application is effectively withdrawn before those events take place, the CAC must give notice of the withdrawal to the employer and take no further steps in respect of the application.[2] If the CAC has received an application, the parties can give notice to the CAC that they want no further steps taken on the application before the final event occurs.[3] The final event is a declaration by the CAC that the union is recognised for collective bargaining purposes or the last day of the notification period, whichever occurs first.[4] The notification period is 10 working days after the union and the employer have received notice from the CAC that the CAC is proposing to hold a ballot on recognition.[5]

1   TULR(C)A 1992, Sch A1, para 16(1).
2   Ibid, para 16(2).
3   Ibid, para 17(1) and (2).
4   Ibid, para 17(3).

Appropriate bargaining unit

2.2.12   Where the parties have agreed a bargaining unit then the application under para 12(4) leads directly to a determination of support. If the parties have not decided the appropriate bargaining unit and the application is under paras 11(2) or 12(2), the CAC must try to help the parties to reach an agreement as to the appropriate bargaining unit within 20 days after it accepts the application, or a longer period which the CAC may specify.[1] If the parties cannot reach an agreement, the CAC must decide the appropriate bargaining unit within 10 working days, that period beginning with the end of the 20 days (or at the end of the longer period if the CAC extended it).[2] The 10-day period may also be extended. In deciding on the appropriate bargaining unit, the CAC must take into account:

–   the need for the unit to be compatible with effective management;
–   the views of the employer and the union or unions;
–   existing national and local bargaining arrangements;
–   the desirability of avoiding small, fragmented bargaining units within the undertaking;
–   the characteristics of workers falling within the unit and of other relevant employees of the employer;
–   the location of the workers.[3]

1   TULR(C)A 1992, Sch A1, para 18(1) and (2).
2   Ibid, para 19(1) and (2).
3   Ibid, para 19(3) and (4).

Union recognition

2.2.13   If the CAC accepts an application and either the parties or the CAC have decided the appropriate bargaining unit and it differs from the proposed bargaining unit, the CAC cannot proceed with the application until it is satisfied that the application is valid within the terms of paras 43–50.[1] In considering whether the application is valid, the CAC must consider any evidence given to it by the employer or union.[2] The CAC must make a decision on the validity of the application within a period of 10 working days starting with the day after the one on which the parties agreed the bargaining unit or the day the CAC decided the appropriate unit, although the CAC can extend this period.[3] If the CAC decides that the application is invalid, it must give notice of the decision to the parties and must not proceed with the application.[4]

---

1   TULR(C)A 1992, Sch A1, para 20(1) and (2).
2   Ibid, para 20(3).
3   Ibid, para 20(6).
4   Ibid, para 20(4).

2.2.14   An application will be invalid for a variety of reasons:

– there is already a collective agreement in force under which a union is recognised as entitled to conduct collective bargaining in respect of any workers falling within the relevant bargaining unit (that is the unit agreed by the parties or decided by the CAC).[1] This does not apply if the collective agreement is in respect of the union making the application and the matters for which the union is recognised do not include pay, hours or holidays.[2] This provision also does not apply: if the union is not independent; there is an old recognition agreement recognising the union for collective bargaining purposes for the same or substantially the same bargaining group; and the old agreement ceased to have effect in the period of three years ending with the date of the agreement;[3]

– the application is invalid unless the CAC decides that members of the union or unions constitute at least 10 per cent of the workers constituting the relevant bargaining unit and that a majority of the workers constituting the unit support recognition;[4]

– the CAC has accepted an application under paras 11 or 12 or is proceeding with an application under para 20 and at least one worker falls within the unit under that application and the unit which is the subject of the investigated application and, in addition, the application is being made by another union;[5]

– the CAC has accepted an application under paras 11 or 12 or is proceeding with an application under para 20 and an application is made within three years starting with the day the CAC gave notice of acceptance of the application, the relevant bargaining unit is the same or substantially the same and the application is made by the same union;[6]

– the CAC has made a declaration under para 29(4) that the union is not entitled to be recognised and the application is made within three years of the date of the declaration for the same or substantially the same bargaining unit and by the same union which was subject to the declaration;[7]

– the CAC has issued a declaration under para 121(3) that the bargaining arrangements are to cease to have effect, and the application is made within three years of the declaration, the bargaining unit is the same or substantially the same and the application is made by the union which was the party leading to the declaration.[8]

In all of the above, it is for the CAC to decide whether the bargaining unit is the same or substantially the same.[9] As before, the purpose of these provisions is to ensure stability in the collective bargaining arrangements for three years.

---

1   TULR(C)A 1992, Sch A1, para 44(1).
2   Ibid, para 44(2).
3   Ibid, para 44(4).
4   Ibid, para 45.
5   Ibid, para 46.
6   Ibid, para 47.
7   Ibid, para 48.
8   Ibid, para 49.
9   Ibid, para 50.

Competing applications

2.2.15   There are special provisions relating to two applications where the parties to the original application have not agreed, nor has the CAC decided, the appropriate bargaining unit. If there is an original application accepted by the CAC under paras 11(2) or 12(2) and there is a competing application, then the CAC has the power to dismiss the original application in certain circumstances. These are where the competing application is inadmissible by para 38 or invalid by para 46; at the time that decision is made, the parties to the original application, nor the CAC, have decided the appropriate bargaining unit, but the 10 per cent test is satisfied in relation to the competing application. In this situation, the CAC must cancel the original application and take no further steps.[1] This prevents a union which has a valid and admissible application but which clearly has less support than the union presenting the competing application from being recognised.

---

1   TULR(C)A 1992, Sch A1, para 51.

2.2.16   If the CAC decides that the application is not invalid, it must proceed with the application, giving notice to the parties that it is proceeding.[1] If the agreed bargaining unit or the CAC-decided unit is the same as the proposed unit, the CAC must proceed with the application[2] and the CAC must proceed if the parties have agreed a bargaining unit but have not agreed that the union is recognised and the union applies to the CAC, under para 12(4), for a decision that the union has the support of the majority of the workers constituting the bargaining unit.[3] If the CAC is satisfied that the union's or unions' members constitute the majority of the bargaining unit, the CAC must issue a declaration that the union or unions are recognised for the purposes of collective bargaining for that unit unless any of the qualifying conditions are fulfilled.[4] In that case the CAC must arrange for the holding of a secret ballot of the workers constituting the bargaining unit to determine whether those workers want the union to represent them.[5] The qualifying conditions are:

– the CAC is satisfied that a ballot should be held in the interests of good industrial relations;

– a significant number of the union members within the bargaining unit inform the CAC that they do not want the union or unions to conduct collective bargaining on their behalf;

– membership evidence is produced which leads the CAC to conclude that there are doubts whether a significant number of members within the bargaining unit want the union or unions recognised.[6]

Membership evidence is evidence about the circumstances in which the workers became union members and evidence about the length of time for which they have been members if the CAC is satisfied that such evidence should be taken into account.[7] The CAC must also call a secret ballot if it is not satisfied that a majority of workers within the bargaining unit are members of the union or unions.[8] Either the union or the union and the employer can give notice to the CAC, within the notification period, that they do not want a ballot to be held.[9] If the CAC does not receive such notification, it must arrange for the holding of a ballot.[10] The notification period is 10 working days starting with the day the party notifying the CAC receives the notice from the CAC that a ballot will be held.[11] These rather clumsy arrangements will be monitored in that the CAC may make representations to the Secretary of State that the procedure outlined above has an unsatisfactory effect and should be amended; the Secretary of State has the power to make amendments by statutory instrument subject to affirmative resolution.[12] Further, the Secretary of State can issue guidance to the CAC as to the exercise of its functions in relation to the procedure.[13]

---

1   TULR(C)A 1992, Sch A1, para 20(5).
2   Ibid, para 21(1).
3   Ibid, para 21(2).
4   Ibid, para 22(2).
5   Ibid, para 22(3).
6   Ibid, para 22(4).
7   Ibid, para 22(5).
8   Ibid, para 23.
9   Ibid, para 24(2).
10   Ibid, para 24(4).
11   Ibid, para 24(5).
12   Ibid, para 166.
13   Ibid, para 167.

Secret ballot

2.2.17   If the CAC decides to hold a secret ballot, it must be conducted by a qualified independent person appointed by the CAC and must take place within 20 working days of the person's appointment or within a longer period if the CAC so specifies.[1] The Secretary of State, by negative resolution procedure, may specify the criteria which the qualified person must satisfy to be appointed.[2] The ballot will either be conducted by post or will be a workplace ballot or a combination of both as the CAC decides and in making that decision the CAC must take into account the risk of unfairness or malpractice in a workplace ballot, costs, practicality and any other factors the CAC considers appropriate.[3] The ballot will normally be a workplace ballot or by post. The CAC cannot decide to hold a ballot which is a combination of the two unless there are special factors making that decision appropriate. Special factors include factors arising from the location of the workers or the nature of their work and any factors put to the CAC by the employer or union.[4] As soon as reasonably practicable after the CAC has decided to hold a ballot, it must inform the parties of the decision, the name of the qualified independent person conducting the ballot and the date of that person's appointment, the period within which the ballot must be held, whether it is a postal or workplace ballot and, if it is a workplace ballot, the workplace or workplaces where it will be conducted.[5] The employer has three duties when a ballot is held. First, is to co-operate generally in connection with the ballot with the union and with the person conducting it.[6] Secondly, to give the union or unions such access as is reasonable to the workers in the bargaining unit to enable the union to inform the workers of the object of the ballot and to seek their support and their opinions on the issues involved.[7] Thirdly, as far as it is reasonable to expect the employer to do so, to give the CAC, within 10 working days of being informed that the ballot will take place, the names and home addresses of the workers in the bargaining unit and, as soon as reasonably practicable, the names and home addresses of workers who join the unit after this but before the ballot and the name of any worker who leaves the unit.[8] This information must be passed on to the person conducting the ballot who, if requested to do so by the union or unions, must send information from the union to the people on the list.[9] The union must bear the cost of sending the information.[10] This means that the union can convey information to the workers without the union knowing the names and addresses of the workers. If the employer fails to comply with the above three duties and the ballot has not been held, the CAC may order the employer to take such reasonable steps as it may specify to rectify the failure within a specified time period.[11] If the employer fails to comply with the order, the CAC may issue a declaration that the union or unions are recognised,[12] in which case the ballot will be cancelled.[13] The costs of the ballot are borne 50:50 by the employer and the union (if there is only a single union). If there is more than one union, they shall share 50 per cent of the costs in equal proportions or such proportions as indicated by the person conducting the ballot.[14] Costs include the full costs of running the ballot incurred by the scrutineer and any other costs the parties agree to share.[15] The scrutineer shall issue a demand for payment which must be paid within 15 days.[16] The costs can be enforced by an order of a county court.[17] The CAC must inform the parties of the result of the ballot as soon as possible after the ballot. If recognition is supported by a majority of those who voted and at least 40 per cent of the workers constituting the bargaining unit, the CAC must declare the union to be recognised.[18] If there is a failure to meet this criteria, the CAC must issue a declaration that the union is not recognised.[19] The Secretary of State may alter the criteria for recognition by order subject to affirmative resolution procedure.[20]

---

1   TULR(C)A 1992, Sch A1, para 25(2) and (3).
2   Ibid, para 25(7) and (8). This is essentially the same arrangement as for independent scrutineers for trade union elections and industrial action ballots under ss 49 and 75 of the TULR(C)A 1992. Under those provisions solicitors, accountants and certain bodies such as the Electoral Reform Society are designated as qualified to act as scrutineers.
3   Ibid, para 25(4) and (5).
4   Ibid, para 25(6).
5   Ibid, para 25(9).
6   Ibid, para 26(2). Paragraph 26(8) gives the power to ask ACAS to draw up a Code of Practice under s 199 of TULR(C)A 1992 to give guidance on 'reasonable access'. Sub-paragraph 8 also gives this power to the Secretary of State under s 203 of TULR(C)A 1992.
7   Ibid, para 26(3).
8   Ibid, para 26(4).
9   Ibid, para 26(6).
10   Ibid, para 26(7).
11   Ibid, para 27(1).
12   Ibid, para 27(2).
13   Ibid, para 27(3).
14   Ibid, para 28(2) and (3).
15   Ibid, para 28(7).
16   Ibid, para 28(4) and (5).
17   Ibid, para 28(6).
18   Ibid, para 29(2) and (3).
19   Ibid, para 29(4).
20   Ibid, para 29(5), (6) and (7).

Consequences of recognition

2.2.18 If the CAC issues a declaration that the union or unions are recognised, the parties have 30 days, starting with the day after receipt of the declaration, to agree a method by which they will conduct collective bargaining. The 30-day period can be extended by the parties.[1] If no agreement is reached either party can ask the CAC for assistance.[2] The CAC must try to help the parties decide the method within the agreement period which is 20 days starting with the day the CAC receives the application for assistance.[3] The agreement period can be extended by the CAC with the consent of the parties.[4] If at the end of the agreement period the parties cannot agree a method of collective bargaining, the CAC must specify the method and any such method so specified shall have effect as a legally enforceable contract between the parties.[5] Any part of this may be altered by the parties in writing, including the method and the provision that the method is legally enforceable, and any alterations are also legally enforceable.[6] The remedy for breach of the method is specific performance.[7] The parties jointly can, at any time, ask the CAC to stop taking steps to assist them or specify a method.[8] The Secretary of State may, after consulting with ACAS and by order subject to negative resolution, specify a model method for collective bargaining which the CAC must take into account, but may vary in particular circumstances.[9]

1   TULR(C)A 1992, Sch A1, para 30(2) and (4).
2   Ibid, para 30(3).
3   Ibid, para 31(3) and 31(8)(a).
4   Ibid, para 31(8)(b).
5   Ibid, para 31(3) and (4).
6   Ibid, para 31(5).
7   Ibid, para 31(6).
8   Ibid, para 31(7).
9   Ibid, para 168.

Method not carried out

2.2.19   If the CAC issues a declaration that the union is recognised for collective bargaining purposes, the parties agree a method of collective bargaining and one or more of the parties fail to carry out the agreement, then the parties may apply to the CAC for assistance.[1] In this case the procedure in para 31 described above in **2.2.17** applies.[2]

1   TULR(C)A 1992, Sch A1, para 32(1) and (2).
2   Ibid, para 32(3).

2.3   VOLUNTARY RECOGNITION

Introduction

2.3.1   Generally, in respect of recognition, the Act has, as a policy, the promotion of agreement rather than imposed solutions as can be seen from the previous provisions which seek to get the parties to agree; only if this is unsuccessful will the CAC impose recognition. However, the Act intervenes where the employer seeks to avoid statutory recognition by agreeing to recognise voluntarily but then fails to observe the terms of the recognition agreement. In this situation, the Act establishes a process whereby either party, who believes the other party is not observing the terms of the agreement, can ask the CAC to determine the method by which collective bargaining should take place.

Agreement for recognition

2.3.2   The original proposals were fairly simple in respect of what constituted an agreement for recognition. The amendments, introduced at a fairly late stage,[1] went through with no debate and allow the CAC to decide whether there is an agreement for recognition within the definition laid down by the Act. By para 52 an agreement is an agreement for recognition if:

–   it is made in the permitted period between an employer and union in consequence of a request for recognition made under para 4 and which is valid within paras 5–9;

- the agreement recognises the union for the purposes of collective bargaining;
- at the time the agreement was made, the CAC had received an application under paras 11 or 12, and the parties have given notice to the CAC, before a declaration of recognition or before the end of the notification period, that they wish no further steps to be taken in respect of the application.[2]

The permitted period is the period which begins with the day on which the employer receives the request for recognition and ends with the first of the following:

- the union withdraws the request;
- the union withdraws an application under paras 11 or 12;
- the CAC gives notice of a decision under para 14(7) (two or more applications where both or neither satisfy the 10 per cent test) which precludes it from accepting the application;
- the CAC gives notice that the application is invalid;
- the parties give notice to the CAC that they want no further steps taken in respect of an application;
- the CAC issues a declaration of recognition;
- the parties inform the CAC they do not want a ballot to be held;
- the last day of the notification period ends;
- the CAC must cancel the application under para 51(3) (Competing applications).[3]

Collective bargaining means matters in respect of which the union is recognised as entitled to negotiate[4] except where the CAC specifies a method of collective bargaining, in which case this will only relate to pay, hours and holidays.[5]

---

1   HL Deb, vol 603, cols 1062 – 1064, 8 July 1999 (Lord McIntosh).
2   TULR(C)A 1992, Sch A1, para 52(2), (4) and (5).
3   Ibid, para 52(3).
4   Ibid, para 54(2) and (3).
5   Ibid, para 54(4).

Determination of type of agreement

2.3.3 Either party can apply to the CAC for a decision whether or not the agreement is an agreement for recognition. The CAC must give notice of the application to any parties to the agreement who are not part of the application and must make a decision within 10 working days starting with the day after it receives the application (the decision period).[1] When the CAC decides whether it is an agreement for recognition or not, it must make a declaration to that effect.[2]

---

1   TULR(C)A 1992, Sch A1, para 55(2) and (6).

2   Ibid, para 55(4).

Termination of the agreement

2.3.4   An agreement for recognition lasts for three years.[1] During that time the employer may not terminate the agreement, but the union may terminate at any time with or without the consent of the employer.[2] At the end of the three years the employer may terminate with or without the consent of the union.[3] The provisions on termination are subject to any provision in the agreement.[4] Once the agreement is terminated, any provision relating to the collective bargaining method ceases to have effect.[5]

1   TULR(C)A 1992, Sch A1, para 56(5).
2   Ibid, para 56(1) and (3).
3   Ibid, para 56(2).
4   Ibid, para 56(4).
5   Ibid, para 57(1).

Application to the CAC to specify method

2.3.5   If there is an agreement for recognition, the parties may, in the negotiation period, conduct negotiations to agree a method of collective bargaining.[1] The negotiation period is 30 working days starting with the day after the agreement was reached or such longer period as the parties agree.[2] If no agreement is reached, either the employer or the union or unions may apply to the CAC to specify the method of collective bargaining.[3] The parties may also apply to the CAC if the parties have agreed a method of collective bargaining but one or more of the parties fails to carry out the agreed method.[4] An application for assistance is admissible only if the following conditions are satisfied. The conditions are that the employer, taken with any associated employer, employs at least 21 workers on the day the application is made or employs an average of 21 workers in the 13 weeks ending on that day, and the union or unions have a certificate of independence.[5] The definition of associated employer, the form of application and the requirements of supporting documents and notices are the same as for statutory recognition.[6] The CAC must give notice of receipt of an application to the parties and within 10 working days (or longer if the CAC so specifies) decide whether the application is admissible.[7] If it is not admissible, the CAC must give notice to the parties and reject the application.[8] If the application is admissible, the CAC must accept the application and inform the parties of the acceptance.[9] As with the statutory recognition procedure, the CAC must try to help the parties reach an agreement within a 20-day agreement period[10] and, if they fail to do so, can specify the method which, as with the statutory recognition procedure, is a legally enforceable agreement with specific performance as the remedy.[11] The parties may vary the CAC method in writing, including the fact that it is legally enforceable and any changes are legally enforceable.[12] At any time before the CAC specifies the method, the parties may jointly apply to the CAC to stop taking steps and the CAC must comply with the request.[13] In other words, the procedure is the statutory procedure discussed above and, as with the statutory procedure, the Secretary of State, after consultation with ACAS, may specify a model collective bargaining method which the CAC must take into account although it may depart from the method to such extent as it thinks appropriate in the circumstances.[14]

---

1   TULR(C)A 1992, Sch A1, para 58(1) and (2).
2   Ibid, para 58(4) and (5).
3   Ibid, para 58(3).
4   Ibid, para 59.
5   Ibid, para 60(2), (3) and (4).
6   Ibid, paras 60(6), (7) and (8) and 61.
7   Ibid, para 62(1), (2) and (3).
8   Ibid, para 62(4).
9   Ibid, para 62(5).
10   Ibid, para 63(1) and (8).
11   Ibid, para 63(2), (3) and (5).
12   Ibid, para 63(4).
13   Ibid, para 63(7).
14   Ibid, para 168.

2.4   CHANGES AFFECTING THE BARGAINING UNIT

Introduction

2.4.1   These provisions were added to the original Bill at the Commons Committee stage. They provide for the situation where the employer's business has altered and where it is appropriate to alter the collective bargaining arrangements to reflect the changes in the business. Where recognition is purely voluntary, any changes in the collective bargaining arrangements will be by negotiation. Where, however, recognition has been imposed under Part I of the Schedule, or a bargaining method has been specified under Part II, Part III provides a procedure for altering collective bargaining arrangements.

Either party believes unit no longer appropriate

2.4.2   If the employer or union or unions believe that the original bargaining unit is no longer an appropriate bargaining unit, either or both may apply to the CAC for a decision as to what now is the appropriate bargaining unit.[1] Such an application is not admissible unless the CAC decides that it is likely that the original unit is no longer appropriate by reason of:

–   a change in the organisation or structure of the business carried out by the employer;
–   a change in the employer's activities;

− a substantial change in the number of workers employed in the original unit.[2]

The CAC must give notice to the parties of receipt of the application and, within 10 working days, or longer if the CAC so decides, the CAC must make a decision whether the application is admissible and inform the parties of its decision.[3] To be admissible, there must be evidence that the original unit is no longer appropriate by reference to the matters above and it must be made in the form specified by the CAC, along with any supporting documents, and whichever party applies must give the other party notice of the application and a copy of the application and supporting documents.[4]

1   TULR(C)A 1992, Sch A1, para 66(2).
2   Ibid, para 67.
3   Ibid, para 68(1), (2) and (6).
4   Ibid, para 92.

2.4.3 If the CAC accepts the application and, within 10 working days the parties agree a new bargaining unit, the CAC must issue a declaration that the union is recognised for the purposes of the new unit using the same method of collective bargaining used with the old unit, subject to such modifications which the CAC considers necessary.[1] The 10-working-day period may be extended by the parties and notified to the CAC.[2] If, in the CAC's opinion, the new unit contains at least one worker falling within an outside bargaining unit, it must take no further steps.[3] An outside unit is a bargaining unit which:

− is not the original unit;
− a union is recognised for collective bargaining purposes on behalf of the unit;
− the union is not a party which has applied to the CAC under these provisions.[4]

1   TULR(C)A 1992, Sch A1, para 69(1), (3) and (4)(a).
2   Ibid, para 69(4)(b).
3   Ibid, para 69(2).
4   Ibid, para 69(5).

2.4.4 If the parties do not agree at the end of the first 10-day period, the CAC has 10 working days (which can be extended) to decide whether the original unit is appropriate or whether another unit or units are appropriate and give the parties notice of its decision.[1] In deciding whether the original unit is appropriate, the CAC must have regard *only* to the factors listed above in **2.4.2**.[2] If the CAC decides that the original unit is no longer appropriate, when deciding whether another unit is appropriate and what the unit is, the CAC *must* take into account the need for the unit to be compatible with effective management and:

− the views of the employer and union or unions;
− existing national and local bargaining arrangements;

- the desirability of avoiding small, fragmented bargaining units in the undertaking;
- the characteristics of the workers within the original unit and of any other employees the CAC considers relevant;
- the location of workers.[3]

If the CAC decides that two or more bargaining units are appropriate, it must ensure that no worker falls within more than one of them.[4] The provisions envisage three different processes. First, if the CAC decides that the original unit is still appropriate, no further action will be taken.[5] In making that decision the CAC must have regard only to the factors in **2.4.2** above. Secondly, if it decides that the original unit is not appropriate the CAC can make a decision that another unit is appropriate under para 82. The third situation is that the parties agree a bargaining unit which is different from the original unit. If this occurs and para 69(2) does not apply (that is that the new unit does not contain at least one worker falling within an outside bargaining unit), then the bargaining arrangements continue unless one or more workers in the original unit falls outside the new unit. In this case the CAC must issue a declaration that the bargaining arrangements in respect of the workers now falling outside the new unit shall cease to have effect on a date specified in the declaration.[6]

1　　TULR(C)A 1992, Sch A1, para 70(1), (2) and (7).
2　　Ibid, para 70(3).
3　　Ibid, para 70(4) and (5).
4　　Ibid, para 70(6).
5　　Ibid, para 71.
6　　Ibid, para 73.

Employer believes unit has ceased to exist

2.4.5　Under the original Bill, the CAC could, if there was a change of bargaining unit, make a decision that no unit existed. After amendment, however, the CAC can make this decision only if the employer gives the union valid notice that he or she believes that the unit has ceased to exist and the union applies to the CAC for a decision on the matter. If the employer feels that the unit has ceased to exist and wishes to end the bargaining arrangements, the employer must give notice to the union with a copy to the CAC.[1] Such notice must identify the unit and the bargaining arrangements, be dated, state that the unit has ceased to exist and state that the bargaining arrangements will cease to have effect on a specified date which must be after the end of a 35-working-day period starting with the date of the notice.[2] The CAC, within the validation period, must decide if the notice complies with the Schedule.[3] The validation period is 10 working days starting with the day after the CAC receives a copy of the notice or longer if the CAC specifies.[4] If the CAC decides that the notice is not valid, it must tell the parties of its decision and the notice is treated as having not been given.[5] If the notice is valid the CAC must inform the parties and the bargaining arrangements will cease to exist on the day specified in the notice if the union does not apply to the CAC.[6] The union may make an application to the CAC, within 10 working days of receipt of the notice from the CAC, stating that the employer's notice is valid, to make a decision on:

- whether the original unit has ceased to exist;
- whether the unit is no longer appropriate by reason of any of the below, that is:
  - a change in the organisation or structure of the business carried out by the employer;
  - a change in the activities pursued by the employer in the course of the business carried on by the employer;
  - a substantial change in the number of workers employed in the original unit.[7]

---

1 TULR(C)A 1992, Sch A1, para 74(1).
2 Ibid, para 74(2).
3 Ibid, para 74(3).
4 Ibid, para 74(7).
5 Ibid, para 74(4).
6 Ibid, para 74(6).
7 Ibid, para 75.

2.4.6 The CAC must give notice to the parties of receipt of the union's application.[1] The CAC has 10 working days (or longer if it so decides)[2] to decide if the application is admissible. The 10 working days are called the decision period. To be admissible the application must be in the prescribed form, with supporting documents, and with notice and a copy of the application given to the employer.[3] If it decides that the application is not admissible, no further steps are taken apart from informing the parties.[4] If the application is admissible the CAC must accept the application and inform the parties of the acceptance.[5] In this case the CAC must give the parties the opportunity to put their views on the questions in relation to which the application was made and then decide the questions within a period of 10 working days or longer if it so decides.[6]

---

1 TULR(C)A 1992, Sch A1, para 76(1).
2 Ibid, para 76(6).
3 Laid down in para 92.
4 TULR(C)A 1992, Sch A1, para 76(4).
5 Ibid, para 76(5).
6 Ibid, para 77(1) and (5).

2.4.7 If the CAC decides that the original unit has ceased to exist, it must tell the parties and the bargaining arrangements cease on the termination date, that is the later date of the date specified in the employer's notice or the day after the last day of the decision period.[1] If the CAC decides that the original unit has not ceased to exist (using the factors in **2.4.5** above) and that it is not the case that the original unit is inappropriate, it must inform the parties and the employer's notice has no effect.[2] If the CAC decides that the original unit has not ceased to exist but is no longer appropriate (using the factors in **2.4.5**

above) the CAC must give notice of its decision to the parties.[3] The parties then have 10 working days (or longer if the parties agree and inform the CAC) to decide the new unit.[4] If at least one worker in the original unit does not fall within the new unit, the CAC must issue a declaration that the bargaining arrangements shall cease on a specified date in relation to such worker(s), but bargaining arrangements will continue for the remaining members of the new unit.[5] If the new unit contains at least one worker falling within an outside unit, no further steps are to be taken under the Schedule.[6] If neither of these apply then the CAC will issue a declaration that the union is recognised using the original collective bargaining method with any modifications the CAC considers appropriate.[7] An outside bargaining unit is one where there is a recognised union entitled to bargain on its behalf which is not the union making the application.[8] If the parties cannot agree, the CAC has 10 working days to decide what other unit or units are appropriate[9] taking into account the need for the unit or units to be compatible with effective management and taking into account:

- the views of the employer and union;
- existing national and local bargaining arrangements;
- the desirability of avoiding small, fragmented bargaining units within an undertaking;
- the characteristics of the workers falling within the original bargaining unit and of any other relevant employees of the employer;
- the location of the workers.[10]

If the CAC decides that two or more units are appropriate, one worker cannot fall within more than one of them.[11]

---

1   TULR(C)A 1992, Sch A1, para 77(2) and (6).
2   Ibid, para 77(3).
3   Ibid, para 77(4).
4   Ibid, para 78(1) and (4).
5   Ibid, para 81.
6   Ibid, para 78(2).
7   Ibid, para 78(3).
8   Ibid, para 78(5).
9   Ibid, para 79(1), (2) and (6).
10   Ibid, para 79(3) and (4).
11   Ibid, para 79(5).

CAC decides new bargaining unit

2.4.8   If the CAC decides the new bargaining unit or units, it must comply with the procedure laid out in paras 83–89 in respect of each unit.[1] If at least one worker in the new unit also falls within another bargaining unit for which a union is recognised by a declaration of the CAC (a statutory outside unit), the CAC must issue a declaration that the original bargaining arrangements and the arrangements in respect of the other bargaining unit shall cease to have effect with respect to the workers falling within the new unit on a date specified in the declaration.[2] The date specified must be a period of 65 working days starting with the day after the date of the declaration or, if the CAC believes that to maintain the relevant bargaining arrangements would be impracticable or contrary to the interests of good industrial relations, the date after the date of the declaration.[3] The union or unions may, of course, request recognition under Part I of the Schedule in respect of the new unit. If the new unit contains at least one worker falling within another outside unit where the union is recognised by virtue of an agreement with the employer (a voluntary outside unit) but no worker falling within a statutory outside unit, then the CAC must issue a declaration that the bargaining arrangements do not apply to those workers.[4] Again, the date at which the original arrangements cease to apply to those workers will be 65 working days after the date of the declaration or immediately if maintenance of the original bargaining arrangements are impracticable or contrary to the interests of good industrial relations.[5] If the new unit contains no workers covered by existing bargaining arrangements, the CAC must decide whether the difference between the original unit and the new unit is such that support for the union or unions needs to be assessed and inform the parties of its decision.[6] If the support does not need to be assessed, the CAC must declare the union as recognised for the new unit, with the original collective bargaining method, subject to any modifications the CAC deems necessary because of the change in the unit.[7]

---

1   TULR(C)A 1992, Sch A1, para 82(1) and (3).
2   Ibid, para 83(1)–(6).
3   Ibid, para 83(3).
4   Ibid, para 84(1) and (2).
5   Ibid, para 84(5).
6   Ibid, para 85(1).
7   Ibid, para 85(2).

2.4.9   If the support does need to be assessed, the CAC must decide whether the members of the relevant union or unions constitute at least 10 per cent of the new unit and whether the majority of the workers in the new unit would be likely to support recognition.[1] If the CAC decides that there is insufficient support, it must issue a declaration that recognition in respect of the workers falling within the new unit ceases on a specified date.[2] If the CAC is satisfied that at least 10 per cent of the workers are union members, the majority of the workers would support recognition and that the majority of the workers in the new unit are members of the union or unions, it must issue a declaration that the union or unions are recognised.[3] If, however, the CAC feels that a ballot should be held in the interests of good industrial relations, a significant number of the union members in the new unit inform the CAC that they do not want recognition or membership evidence is produced which leads the CAC to conclude that there are doubts whether a significant number of the union members in the new unit want recognition, the CAC shall arrange for a secret ballot to be held.[4] For these purposes, membership evidence is evidence about the circumstances in which the workers became union members and evidence of how long the workers have been union members.[5] Further, a ballot must be held even if 10 per cent of the new unit are union members and the majority support recognition if the majority of the new unit are not members of the union or unions.[6] The union or unions may, within 10 working days of receiving notice of the intention to hold a ballot, notify the CAC that they do not want a ballot conducted, in which case the CAC will issue a declaration that recognition ceases on the date specified in the declaration in respect of the workers falling within the new unit.[7] If the CAC does not receive such notification, it must arrange for the holding of a ballot which will be run in exactly the same way as in Part I, paras 24–29.[8] The CAC will then issue a declaration recognising or derecognising the union or unions depending on the outcome of the ballot.[9]

---

1   TULR(C)A 1992, Sch A1, para 86(1) and (2).
2   Ibid, para 86(3).
3   Ibid, para 87(1) and (2).
4   Ibid, para 87(3) and (4).
5   Ibid, para 87(5).
6   Ibid, para 88(1) and (2).
7   Ibid, para 89(1) and (2).
8   Ibid, para 89(3), (4) and (5).
9   Ibid, para 89(6) and (7).

Residual workers

2.4.10   If the CAC decides an appropriate bargaining unit or units and at least one worker falling within the original unit does not fall within the new unit or units, then the CAC must issue a declaration that the bargaining arrangements in respect of that worker or workers are to cease to have effect on a date specified in the declaration.[1] If the CAC has decided the unit or units on the basis that the original unit or units are now inappropriate, in accordance with the procedure laid down in paras 83–89 (**2.4.8** above), and has issued one or more declarations under para 83, the CAC must consider each declaration and, in relation to each declaration identify each statutory outside bargaining unit which contains at least one worker who also falls within the new unit to which the declaration relates.[2] Each statutory outside unit so identified will then be known as the parent unit for the purposes of para 91.[3] The CAC must then identify within each parent unit those workers who do not fall within the new unit and for the purpose of para 91 these are known as a residual unit.[4] In respect of each residual unit, the CAC must reaffirm the recognition of the outside union[5] although no declaration can be issued if the CAC has received an application under para 66 in relation to the parent unit (either party believes unit no longer appropriate) or para 75 (union applies to the CAC to determine whether original unit has ceased to exist).[6] These provisions ensure that the existing bargaining arrangements are reaffirmed with the old union unless there is a challenge as to whether the existing arrangements are now appropriate, given the changes that have taken place.

1   TULR(C)A 1992, Sch A1, para 90.
2   Ibid, para 91(1) and (2).
3   Ibid, para 91(2).
4   Ibid, para 91(3).
5   Ibid, para 91(4).
6   Ibid, para 91(5).

2.5   DERECOGNITION

Introduction

2.5.1   The statutory derecognition procedure set out in Part IV of the Schedule applies only where a declaration of recognition has been made under Parts I or III[1] or where a union has had a collective bargaining method specified by the CAC under Part II.[2] Applications for derecognition may be accepted only three years or more after the CAC's original decision.[3]

1   TULR(C)A 1992, Sch A1, para 96(1) and (3).
2   Ibid, para 96(3).
3   Ibid, para 97.

Employer employs fewer than 21 employees

2.5.2   The employer may give written notice to the union or unions (with a copy to the CAC) that the bargaining arrangements are to cease on the date given in the notice. The date shall be at least 35 days after the union is notified.[1] The employer may do so if, when taken with an associated employer, he or she employed an average of fewer than 21 employees in any period of 13 weeks when that period ends on or after the relevant date.[2] The relevant date is three years after the CAC declaration of recognition.[3] The notice must comply with the Schedule. That is it:

–   identifies the bargaining arrangements;
–   identifies the period of 13 weeks in question;
–   states the date on which the notice is given;
–   is given within a period of 5 working days starting with the day after the last day of the specified period of 13 weeks;
–   states that the employer together with an associated employer employed an average of fewer than 21 employees in a specified period of 13 weeks; and
–   states that the bargaining arrangements are to cease on a day specified in the notice and which is later than 35 working days starting with the day after that on which the notice is given.[4]

1   TULR(C)A 1992, Sch A1, para 99(2) and (3)(f).
2   Ibid, para 97.
3   Ibid, para 99(1).
4   Ibid, para 99(3).

2.5.3 Within 10 working days starting with the day after the CAC receives a copy of the notice or such longer period as the CAC specifies (the validation period) the CAC must decide if the notice complies with the Schedule.[1] If it does not, the CAC must inform the parties of its decision and the employer's notice is ineffective.[2] If the notice does comply with the Schedule, the CAC must inform the parties and the bargaining arrangements shall cease to have effect on the date specified in the notice.[3] The union or unions may make an application to the CAC within 10 working days starting with the day after the day on which the notice is given for a decision as to whether the employer has employed fewer than 21 workers in the specified 13-week period and whether the specified 13-week period ends on or after the relevant date.[4] Such an application is not admissible unless it is in a form specified by the CAC, is supported by any documents the CAC specifies,[5] and the union or unions have given the employer notice of the application together with a copy of the application and the documents supporting it.[6] An application is also inadmissible if a relevant application, which was accepted by the CAC and which relates to the same bargaining unit as the existing application, was made within the period of three years prior to the date of the application in question.[7] A relevant application means an application by the union under para 101 (that is the union has applied in the previous three years), an application by the employer under paras 106, 107 or 128 (**2.5.6** and **2.6.2** below) or by the worker or workers under para 112 (**2.5.7** below).[8] The CAC must give notice to the parties of receipt of an application[9] and decide if the application is admissible within 10 working days starting with the day after receipt of the application or such longer period as the CAC decides after informing the parties the reason for the extension (the decision period).[10] The CAC, when deciding if the application is admissible, must consider any evidence given to it by the employer or the union or unions.[11] If the CAC decides that the application is inadmissible, it must give notice of its decision to the parties and reject the application; the bargaining arrangements cease on the date given in the employer's notice.[12] If the CAC accepts the application, it must inform the parties and give the parties an opportunity to put their views as to whether the employer employed fewer than 21 employees in the specified 13-week period and whether the period ends on or before the relevant period.[13] The CAC must make a decision within 10 working days starting with the day after it gives notice of acceptance of the application, although the CAC can extend the period.[14] If the CAC finds that the employer has 21 or more employees in the specified period or that the period does not end on or after the relevant date, the employer's notice is treated as not having been given and the collective bargaining arrangements remain in place.[15] Otherwise the arrangements cease on the date specified in the notice or on the day after the end of the decision period, whichever is the later.[16]

---

1   TULR(C)A 1992, Sch A1, para 100(1) and (5).
2   Ibid, para 100(2). The calculation of 21 employees is found in para 100(4), (5) and (6).
3   Ibid, para 100(4).
4   Ibid, para 101(1).
5   Ibid, para 101(2).
6   Ibid, para 101(3).
7   Ibid, para 101(4).
8   Ibid, para 101(5).
9   Ibid, para 102(1).
10 Ibid, para 102(2) and (6).
11 Ibid, para 102(3).
12 Ibid, para 102(4).
13 Ibid, para 103(1)(a).
14 Ibid, para 103(4).
15 Ibid, para 103(3).
16 Ibid, para 103(2).

Employer's request to end arrangements

2.5.4 This statutory procedure is broadly similar to the procedure in paras 10 – 12 and 20 which deal with a request for recognition. If the union or unions are voluntarily recognised and the parties have agreed a bargaining method, this procedure does not apply and the employer can derecognise at any time although the union could apply under the statutory recognition procedure in Part I.

2.5.5 The employer may give a written request to the union or unions to agree to end the bargaining arrangements. The request must be in writing, be received by the union or unions, identify the bargaining arrangements and state that it is made under the Schedule.[1] If before the end of the first period (10 working days starting with the day after the union or the last of the unions receives the request)[2] the parties agree to end the arrangements, no further steps need be taken.[3] If before the end of 10 working days the union or unions inform the employer that they do not accept the request but are willing to negotiate, the parties may, in the second period (20 days or longer if the parties mutually agree),[4] conduct negotiations to end the bargaining arrangements.[5] The parties may ask ACAS to assist in the negotiations but there is no requirement to do so.[6] If the parties agree that the union should remain recognised, they need take no further action and the bargaining arrangements remain in place.

---

1   TULR(C)A 1992, Sch A1, para 104(2).
2   Ibid, para 105(6).
3   Ibid, para 105(1).

4   Ibid, para 105(7).
5   Ibid, para 105(3).
6   Ibid, para 105(5).

2.5.6   If before the end of the first period the union or unions fail to respond or the union or unions inform the employer that they do not accept the request and do not indicate a willingness to negotiate, the employer may apply to the CAC for the holding of a secret ballot to decide if derecognition should take place.[1] The employer may also apply for a secret ballot if the union has indicated a willingness to negotiate but no agreement is reached at the end of the second period[2] although no application by the employer for the holding of a secret ballot can be made if, within 10 working days after the union or unions have informed the employer that they are willing to negotiate, they propose that ACAS be requested to assist and the employer has rejected the proposal or fails to accept the proposal within 10 working days.[3] Any application to the CAC is inadmissible unless in the form specified by the CAC and supported by such documents as the CAC specifies.[4] The union or unions must be given notice of the application and a copy plus any supporting documents.[5] The application is also inadmissible if a relevant application was made within the period of three years prior to the date of the present application which related to the same bargaining unit and which was accepted by the CAC.[6] A relevant application is an application by the union under para 101, by the employer under paras 106, 107 or 128, or an application by a worker or workers under para 112.[7] Further, an application to derecognise is inadmissible unless the CAC decides that at least 10 per cent of the workers in the bargaining unit favour derecognition and the majority of the workers in the bargaining unit would be likely to favour derecognition[8] and the CAC must give reasons for its decision.[9] This is essentially the same test as for recognition applications. The CAC must decide whether or not the application is valid and admissible and therefore to proceed with the application, giving reasons, within 10 working days (or longer if the CAC so specifies to the parties, giving reasons for the extension) starting with the day after receiving the application.[10] If the request is not valid, is not made in accordance with paras 106 or 107, or is inadmissible, the CAC must not accept the application and no further steps are to be taken under the Schedule.[11] If the contrary is decided, the CAC must accept the application and give notice of acceptance to the parties.[12]

---

1   TULR(C)A 1992, Sch A1, para 106.
2   Ibid, para 107(1) and (2).
3   Ibid, para 107(3).
4   Ibid, para 108(1).
5   Ibid, para 108(2).
6   Ibid, para 109(1).
7   Ibid, para 109(2).
8   Ibid, para 110(1).
9   Ibid, para 110(2).
10   Ibid, para 111(2) and (6).
11   Ibid, para 111(4).
12   Ibid, para 111(5).

Workers' request to end arrangements

2.5.7 A worker or workers falling within the bargaining unit may apply after the relevant date (that is three years after the declaration of recognition) to the CAC to derecognise the union or unions.[1] The application is not admissible unless in the prescribed form with supporting documents and notice of the application plus a copy and the supporting documents, which must be given to the employer and the union or unions.[2] The application must be admissible, as outlined at **2.5.6** above. This means that, as well as being in the prescribed form and the correct notices given, there must not have been another relevant application within a period of three years prior to the date of the present application, which related to the same bargaining unit and which was accepted by the CAC.[3] As before, a relevant application is one by the union, employer, worker or group of workers.[4] The final test of admissibility, as above, is that the CAC cannot proceed with the application unless it decides that at least 10 per cent of the workers in the bargaining unit favour derecognition and the majority of workers in the bargaining unit would be likely to favour derecognition.[5] The CAC must decide whether the application is admissible within 10 working days (or longer if it so decides) starting with the day after receipt of the application[6] giving notice to the workers, union or unions and employer of its decision.[7] Before making that decision, it must consider any evidence given by the employer, the union or unions and any workers falling within the bargaining unit.[8] If the CAC decides that the application is admissible, it must inform the parties and proceed with the application.[9] There is then a negotiation period of 20 days[10] where the CAC must help the three parties with a view to the employer and union or unions ending the bargaining arrangements or the worker or workers withdrawing the application.[11] If no agreement is reached the CAC must hold a secret ballot as discussed below.[12]

---

1 TULR(C)A 1992, Sch A1, para 112(1).
2 Ibid, para 112(2) and (3).
3 Ibid, para 113(1).
4 Ibid, para 113(2).
5 Ibid, para 114.
6 Ibid, para 115(1) and (6).
7 Ibid, para 115(4) and (5).
8 Ibid, para 115(3).
9 Ibid, para 115(5).
10 Ibid, para 116(2).
11 Ibid, para 116(1).
12 Ibid, para 117(2) and (3).

Ballot on derecognition

2.5.8 If the CAC decides to proceed with either an employer's application or an application from a worker or group of workers where there has been no withdrawal of the application or agreement as to derecognition, it must arrange for the holding of a secret ballot of the workers constituting the bargaining unit.[1] The ballot must be conducted by a qualified independent person appointed by the CAC and must be conducted in the 20-day period after the scrutineer is appointed or a longer period if the CAC so decides.[2] The ballot may be a workplace ballot or by post at the CAC's preference, the CAC having to take into account the same matters as when deciding where to conduct a ballot on recognition.[3] The rest of the provisions regarding the ballot mirror the procedure for recognition ballots under paras 25–28.[4] As soon as is reasonably practicable after the CAC is informed of the result of the ballot, the CAC must inform the union or unions and the employer of the result.[5] If derecognition is supported by a majority of the workers voting and at least 40 per cent of the workers constituting the bargaining unit, the CAC must issue a declaration that the bargaining arrangements are to end at a date specified by the CAC in the declaration.[6] If the result is otherwise, the CAC must refuse the application.[7] The conditions for derecognition may be altered by the Secretary of State by order subject to affirmative resolution procedure.[8]

1   TULR(C)A 1992, Sch A1, para 117(1), (2) and (3).
2   Ibid, para 117(4) and (5).
3   Ibid, para 117(7).
4   The rest of para 117 and paras 118, 119 and 120.
5   TULR(C)A 1992, Sch A1, para 121(1) and (2).
6   Ibid, para 121(3).
7   Ibid, para 121(4).
8   Ibid, para 121(6), (7) and (8).

2.6 DERECOGNITION WHERE RECOGNITION AUTOMATIC

Introduction

2.6.1 In Part V, a different derecognition process applies in cases where a union or unions have been automatically recognised on the grounds of having a greater than 50 per cent membership in the bargaining unit and thus no ballot was held. This procedure applies where the union was recognised as a result of a CAC declaration under paras 22 or 87 and where a method of collective bargaining is in place, whether agreed by the parties under para 30(2), imposed by the CAC under para 31(3) or agreed as a variation on a CAC decision under para 31(5).[1] As before, applications for derecognition cannot be made until three or more years after the union or unions were recognised.[2]

1   TULR(C)A 1992, Sch A1, paras 122, 123 and 124.
2   Ibid, para 125.

Employer's request to end arrangements

2.6.2 The employer may contact the union or unions requesting an end to the arrangements.[1] The request must be in writing, be received by the union or unions, identify the bargaining arrangements, state that it is made under the Schedule, and state that fewer than half the workers in the bargaining unit are members of the union or unions.[2] The parties may negotiate to end the arrangements within a period of 10 working days which starts to run from either the day the union receives the request or the last day any of the unions received the request.[3] This period may be extended by the parties. If before the end of the negotiation period the parties agree to end the arrangements, no further action is taken under the Schedule.[4] If an agreement is not reached during the negotiation period, the employer may apply to the CAC for the holding of a secret ballot to decide on derecognition.[5] As before, an application is not admissible unless in the prescribed form with supporting documents; notice of the application and a copy of the application and documents must be given to the union or unions.[6] Further, the application is inadmissible if there has been a relevant application by the union, employer or a worker or group of workers, relating to the same bargaining unit, made within a period of three years prior to the present application, and which was accepted by the CAC.[7] An application is also inadmissible unless the CAC is satisfied that fewer than half the workers in the bargaining unit are members of the union or unions.[8] Within the acceptance period (10 working days starting with the day after the CAC receives the application or longer if the CAC so specifies)[9] the CAC must give notice to the parties of receipt of the application and decide whether the application is valid and admissible taking into account evidence from the parties.[10] If the CAC decides the application is invalid or inadmissible, it must give notice to the parties and the bargaining arrangements will remain in place.[11] If it decides that the application is valid and admissible, it must accept the application and give notice of acceptance to the parties.[12] Once an application has been accepted the CAC must conduct a secret ballot using the same derecognition ballot procedure as in Part IV.[13]

---

1   TULR(C)A 1992, Sch A1, para 127(1).
2   Ibid, para 127(2).
3   Ibid, para 127(3).
4   Ibid, para 128(1).
5   Ibid, para 128(2).
6   Ibid, para 129(1) and (2).
7   Ibid, para 130.
8   Ibid, para 131.
9   Ibid, para 132(6).
10   Ibid, para 132(1), (2) and (3).
11   Ibid, para 132(4).
12   Ibid, para 132(5).
13   Ibid, para 133.

2.7 DERECOGNITION WHERE UNION NOT INDEPENDENT

Introduction

2.7.1 Part VI provides that workers can apply to the CAC for the derecognition of a union or unions which do not have a certificate of independence but which have been voluntarily recognised by the employer.[1] This is the sole exception to the principle that if the CAC did not declare recognition or specify a bargaining method the statutory derecognition procedure does not apply. The definition of collective bargaining within s 178(1) does not apply to this part of the Schedule.[2] In other words, an agreement between the parties to negotiate on anything on behalf of a group of workers will be construed as collective bargaining for the purposes of this part. Note that in the statutory recognition procedures, collective bargaining is restricted to pay, hours and holidays unless the parties agree to include other matters. It is clear, therefore, that this part of the Schedule is intended to apply to a much wider range of negotiations.

---

1   TULR(C)A 1992, Sch A1, para 134.
2   Ibid, para 135.

Workers' application to end arrangements

2.7.2 A worker or workers from the bargaining unit may apply to the CAC to have the bargaining arrangements ended.[1] As before, there are various conditions laid down for the application to be admissible. First, the application must be in the prescribed form with supporting documents; notice and a copy of the application and documents must be given to the employer and union or unions.[2] Secondly, the application is inadmissible if any of the unions has a certificate of independence.[3] Thirdly, the application is inadmissible unless the CAC decides that at least 10 per cent of the workers in the bargaining group favour derecognition and a majority of workers in that group would be likely to favour derecognition.[4] Fourthly, the application is inadmissible if any of the unions has applied to the Certification Officer for a certificate of independence and the Certification Officer has not yet reached a decision.[5] The CAC must decide within 10 working days starting with the day after receipt of the application (or longer if the CAC so decides) whether the application is admissible taking into account evidence put forward by the employer, the union or unions and workers from the bargaining unit.[6] If the application is not admissible the CAC must give notice to the parties and the bargaining arrangements remain.[7]

---

1   TULR(C)A 1992, Sch A1, para 137(1).
2   Ibid, para 137(2) and (3).
3   Ibid, para 138.

4   Ibid, para 139.
5   Ibid, para 140.
6   Ibid, para 141(2), (3) and (4).
7   Ibid, para 141(4).

2.7.3   If the CAC decides that the application is admissible, it must accept the application and inform the parties.[1] If the CAC accepts the application in the 20-day period after its decision, it must help the employer, union or unions and worker or workers with a view to their agreeing to end the arrangements or the worker or workers withdrawing the application.[2] If, during the 20-day negotiation period, the CAC is satisfied that before the workers put in their application for derecognition any of the unions had applied for a certificate of independence and the Certification Officer has not yet made a decision, and the parties have not reached an agreement on derecognition, then the CAC is no longer under a statutory duty to help the parties reach an agreement.[3] If, subsequently, the Certification Officer awards a certificate of independence, the CAC must inform the parties and the workers' application for derecognition is treated as if it had not been made.[4] If, conversely, the Certification Officer decides that the union or unions are not independent, the CAC must inform the parties and there is a further negotiation period of 20 working days, starting with the day after which the CAC informs the parties, where the CAC must help the parties to reach an agreement as to derecognition or the workers withdrawing their application.[5] If either the first or second negotiation period begins and before there is:

(a)   an agreement to end recognition;
(b)   a withdrawal of the application by the workers; or
(c)   a ballot has been held and the CAC has been informed of the result by the scrutineer, and the CAC is satisfied that a certificate of independence has been granted to the union or unions,

the CAC must inform the parties and the workers' application is treated as if it had never been made.[6] Should none of these situations apply and an agreement has not been reached the CAC must hold a derecognition ballot under paras 118–121 (**2.5.8** above).[7]

1   TULR(C)A 1992, Sch A1, para 141(5).
2   Ibid, para 142.
3   Ibid, para 143.
4   Ibid, para 144.
5   Ibid, para 145.
6   Ibid, para 146.
7   Ibid, para 147.

Derecognition in other cases

2.7.4 The final paragraph of Part VI deals with the situation where there has been a successful application for derecognition but the employer has re-recognised the non-independent union for substantially the same bargaining unit. It allows an independent union to apply under para 35 within 3 years of the derecognition. If the application is successful, the CAC must issue a declaration that the bargaining arrangements with the non-independent union shall cease to have effect on a date specified.[1] In other words, the statutory procedure pre-empts the employer voluntarily recognising a recently derecognised, non-independent union.

---

1   TULR(C)A 1992, Sch A1, para 148.

2.8   LOSS OF INDEPENDENCE

Introduction

2.8.1   Part VII of the Schedule applies when the CAC has issued a declaration that a union or unions are entitled to conduct collective bargaining on behalf of a bargaining unit or there has been voluntary recognition and the CAC has specified the method of collective bargaining which the parties have not replaced,[1] and the Certification Officer withdraws the certificate of independence from the union or unions so recognised under s 7 of TULR(C)A 1992. In such a case the bargaining arrangements shall cease to have effect on the day after (or the day after the last day if there is more than one union and the withdrawals happen on different days) of the withdrawal of the certificate and the parties shall be taken to agree that the union is recognised for the purpose of collective bargaining on behalf of the unit concerned.[2] In other words, the recognition becomes entirely voluntary as does the method of collective bargaining with the attendant consequences in respect of derecognition. If, however, the union or unions appeal against withdrawal of the certificate of independence under s 9 of TULR(C)A 1992 and, as a result, the certificate or certificates are re-issued, then on the day after the re-issue the original bargaining arrangements shall be effective again.[3]

---

1   TULR(C)A 1992, Sch A1, paras 149 and 150.
2   Ibid, para 152.
3   Ibid, para 153.

2.9 PROTECTION FOR WORKERS

Detriment

2.9.1 Part VIII provides protection for workers who take action or who refuse to take action in respect of recognition or derecognition. A worker has a right not to suffer a detriment by any act or deliberate failure to act by his or her employer[1] if the act or failure to act is because:

- the worker acted with a view to obtaining or preventing recognition of the union or unions by the employer under the Schedule;
- the worker indicated that he or she supported or did not support the recognition of a union or unions by the employer under the Schedule;
- the worker acted with a view to securing or preventing the ending of bargaining arrangements under the Schedule;
- the worker indicated that he or she supported or did not support the ending of bargaining arrangements under the Schedule;
- the worker influenced or sought to influence the way in which votes were to be cast by other workers in a ballot arranged under the Schedule;
- the worker influenced or sought to influence other workers to vote or to abstain from voting in such a ballot;
- the worker voted in such a ballot;
- the worker proposed to do, failed to do, or proposed to decline to do any of the things referred to above.[2]

The worker is not protected, however, if the action is an unreasonable act or omission by the worker.[3] Originally the sub-paragraph also excluded protection where the act by the employee constituted a breach of contract on the part of the worker. This phrase was removed, however, to prevent employers inserting into a contract of employment a requirement that the employee should not campaign about recognition and therefore negate the protection afforded by the provision.[4] It also makes the provision consistent with other provisions on detriment, for example s 44 of ERA 1996, which do not contain a reference to breaches of contract. The wording of this provision makes it clear that the Act is overruling the House of Lords' decision in *Associated Newspapers Ltd v Wilson* and *Associated British Ports v Palmer*[5] where their lordships decided that on interpretation of s 146 of the TULR(C)A 1992 (action short of dismissal on grounds related to union membership or activities) that, having regard to the legislative history of the provision, 'act' and 'action' did not include omissions to act.[6] The clarification is to be welcomed, and brings the definition in line with similar provisions in ERA 1996.[7] Further, the Act specifically states that para 156 does not apply where the worker is an employee and the detriment is dismissal.[8] This is because such a dismissal would be unfair by virtue of para 161 below. On the wording, it would appear that if a worker is dismissed then this does constitute a detriment for the purposes of the Schedule.[9]

1   TULR(C)A 1992, Sch A1, para 156(1).
2   Ibid, para 156(2).
3   Ibid, para 156(3).
4   HL Deb, vol 603, col 1072, 8 July 1999 (Lord McIntosh).
5   [1995] 2 All ER 100.
6   See Lord Bridge at 104 – 109. This is despite the fact that s 298 provides that 'act or action each includes omission and references to doing an act or taking action shall be construed accordingly'.
7   In Part V.
8   TULR(C)A 1992, Sch A1, para 156(4).
9   This would appear to be a logical interpretation from the wording of para 156(4) and is supported by para 156(6) which states that a worker has a right of complaint on the basis of having been subjected to a detriment but no other remedy for infringement of that right, that is the worker cannot claim unfair dismissal. See also the discussion in **2.9.2** below.

2.9.2   The remedy for infringement of the provision is complaint to an employment tribunal.[1] Such complaint must be presented within three months of the act or failure to act complained of.[2] Where the act extends over a period the three months start to run from the last day of that period and where there is a failure to act it shall be treated as done when it was decided upon.[3] A tribunal has the usual discretion to hear a complaint out of time.[4] In the absence of evidence to the contrary, an employer is taken to have decided on a failure to act when that employer does an act inconsistent with doing the failed act or, if the employer has not acted inconsistently, when the period expires within which he or she might reasonably have been expected to do the failed act if it was to be done.[5] The burden is on the employer to show why the employer acted or failed to act.[6] On finding the complaint well-founded the tribunal shall make a declaration to that effect and may make an award of compensation which it considers just and equitable having regard to the infringement and to any loss sustained by the complainant.[7] Loss includes expenses reasonably incurred and any loss of benefit the complainant might reasonably be expected to have but for the act or failure to act.[8] The complainant is under a duty to mitigate any loss and an award will be reduced for contributory conduct.[9] If the detriment complained of is the termination of the complainant's contract and that contract is not a contract of employment, any compensation awarded must not exceed the limit of the basic award the complainant would receive had he or she been an employee who had been unfairly dismissed, together with any compensatory award.[10] This provision gives unfair dismissal rights to workers who are not employees within the normal legal definition, if they are dismissed in relation to activities relating to recognition or derecognition. This reflects other legislation such as the National Minimum Wage Act 1998 and the Working Time Regulations 1998 and the Government's view in *Fairness at Work* that some employment protection rights should be extended to those who work for another and not only those who work under a contract of employment.[11]

---

1 TULR(C)A 1992, Sch A1, para 156(5).
2 Ibid, para 157(1)(a).
3 Ibid, para 157(2).
4 Ibid, para 157(1)(b).
5 Ibid, para 157(3).
6 Ibid, para 158.
7 Ibid, para 159(1) and (2).
8 Ibid, para 159(3).
9 Ibid, para 159(4) and (5).
10 Ibid, para 160.
11 *Fairness at Work*, para 3.18.

Dismissal

2.9.3 There are new unfair dismissal rights. Paragraph 161 provides that the dismissal of an employee shall be regarded as unfair for the purposes of ERA 1996[1] if the reason or main reason for the dismissal was one of the grounds relating to recognition or derecognition stated in **2.9.1** above.[2] As before, if the act is an unreasonable act or omission by the employee, there is no protection.[3] The selection of an employee for redundancy is also unfair if the reason or principal reason for the employee's selection was a reason in **2.9.1** above.[4] Neither the normal continuity period nor upper age limit applies to an unfair dismissal under these provisions[5] and any waiver provision in a fixed-term contract is void for these purposes.[6] This latter provision is transitional as the Act prohibits such waivers in respect of unfair dismissal.[7]

---

1 TULR(C)A 1992, Sch A1, para 161(1) and Part X of ERA 1996.
2 Ibid, para 161(2).
3 Ibid, para 161(3).
4 Ibid, para 162.
5 Ibid, para 164. The qualifying period for unfair dismissal is one year as set out in s 108 of ERA 1996 (as amended on 1 June 1999). The upper age limit is in s 109 of ERA 1996 which provides that s 94 (the right not to be unfairly dismissed) does not apply if the employee has reached the normal retirement age for an employee holding that position or, in any other case, 65.
6 TULR(C)A 1992, Sch A1, para 163.
7 ERA 1999, s 18.

Power to amend procedures and issue guidance

2.9.4 Part IX of the Schedule contains general provisions relating to powers to amend paras 22 or 87 and to give guidance. If the CAC makes representations to the Secretary of State that the automatic recognition procedure in para 22 or the provisions on the CAC deciding a new bargaining unit in para 87 do not work, the Secretary of State may amend the procedures by statutory instrument subject to affirmative resolution.[1] The amendments do not have to be those proposed by the CAC.[2] The Secretary of State may also issue guidance to the CAC on how to exercise its functions under paras 22 or 87, in other words how to decide the three questions in paras 22(4) or 87(4) in deciding whether to hold a secret ballot.[3] Again, such guidance is subject to the affirmative resolution procedure[4] and the CAC must take into account such guidance when exercising its functions under paras 22 or 87, although the guidance will not apply to any application made to the CAC before the guidance was issued.[5] The Secretary of State may also issue guidance to the CAC on the method for collective bargaining it should impose under paras 31(3) and 63(2) after consultation with ACAS.[6] Such guidance is subject to the negative resolution procedure and the CAC must take such guidance into account when specifying a method, although it may depart from the guidance if it feels it is appropriate to do so in the circumstances.[7] Further, where the CAC has two or more relevant applications in relation to the same bargaining unit, under paras 101, 106, 107, 112 or 128, none of which it has yet accepted, the Secretary of State may make directions as to the order in which the CAC must decide the admissibility of the applications.[8] Such directions may include provision to deal with a case where a relevant application is being made while the CAC is still considering the admissibility of another application relating to the same bargaining unit.[9] Finally, the CAC, when it issues a declaration, is under a duty to notify the parties of the declaration and its contents[10] and, when exercising its functions under Sch A1, it must have regard to the 'object of encouraging and promoting fair and efficient practices and arrangements in the workplace, so far as having regard to that object is consistent with applying other provisions of [the] Schedule in the case concerned'.

---

1 TULR(C)A 1992, Sch A1, para 166(3) and (4).
2 Ibid, para 166(2).
3 Ibid, para 167(1).
4 Ibid, para 167(4).
5 Ibid, para 167(3).
6 Ibid, para 168(1).
7 Ibid, para 168(2) and (3).
8 Ibid, para 169(1) and (2).
9 Ibid, para 169(3).
10 Ibid, para 170.

2.10 DETRIMENT RELATED TO TRADE UNION MEMBERSHIP

Introduction

2.10.1 The original s 146 of TULR(C)A 1992 prohibited discrimination by a positive act taken on the grounds of trade union membership, non-membership or activities but not by omission on the same grounds. In other words, if the employer took action which conferred a benefit to non-union members but omitted to confer the same benefit to union members this did not amount to action short of dismissal. This was the interpretation of the House of Lords in *Associated Newspapers v Wilson* and *Associated British Ports v Palmer* above.

Detriment

2.10.2 Section 2 of ERA 1999 gives effect to Sch 2. The Schedule amends s 146(1) and (3) by substituting for the original words 'action short of dismissal taken against him' the new phrase 'be subjected to any detriment as an individual by any act, or any deliberate failure to act, by his employer if the act or failure takes place'.[1] Section 146(4) is amended so that the phrase 'action short of dismissal taken against him' is substituted by 'be subjected to any detriment as an individual by an act of his employer taking place'[2] and s 146(5) has been amended by the substitution of 'action has been taken against him' for 'he has been subjected to a detriment'.[3] In addition, a new sub-section (6) states that detriment means detriment short of dismissal.[4] The amendments bring the definition of detriment in line with the definition in para 156 in the new Sch A1 and with comparable provisions in ERA 1996.

---

1   ERA 1999, Sch 2, para 2(2) and (3) amending s 146(1) and (2) of TULR(C)A 1992.
2   Ibid, para 2(4) amending s 146(4). The reason why the substituted words do not include a failure to act on the part of the employer is because s 146(4) deals specifically with deductions from pay.
3   Ibid, para 2(5) amending s 146(5). This sets out the ground on which an employee may present a complaint to an employment tribunal.
4   Ibid, para 2(6).

Time-limit for proceedings

2.10.3 Subsequent amendments are made to the rest of the relevant provisions of TULR(C)A 1992. Section 147 is amended to include an act or failure to act[1] by the insertion of a new sub-section 1.[2] A new sub-section (2) provides that, where an act extends over a period, the three-month time-limit for presentation of a complaint begins on the last day of that period and a failure to act shall be treated as done when it was decided on.[3] Further, in the absence of evidence to the contrary, an employer shall be taken to decide on a failure to act when the employer does an act which is inconsistent with doing the failed act, or, if there is no inconsistent act, when the period expires within which the employer might reasonably have been expected to do the failed act if it was to be done.[4] These provisions are identical to the provisions relating to detriment and recognition or derecognition in Sch A1, para 157.

---

1   ERA 1999, Sch 2, para 3(3).
2   Ibid, para 3(2).
3   Ibid, para 3(4).
4   Ibid, inserting a new s 147(3) into TULR(C)A 1992.

2.10.4 The remainder of Sch 2 amends ss 148,[1] 149[2] and 150;[3] the original phrases in those sections have been amended so that action taken against the complainant also includes a failure to act. There are no other changes made.

---

1   ERA 1999, Sch 2, para 4.
2   Ibid, para 5.

2.11   BLACKLISTS

Introduction

2.11.1   Under ss 137 and 138 of TULR(C)A 1992, refusal of employment (or in the case of employment agencies refusal of service) on the grounds of trade union membership is unlawful. The original legislation, however, did not prevent the compilation of blacklists of workers. This was particularly damaging to prospective employees as the protection against discriminatory recruitment lies only in respect of trade union membership and not in respect of trade union activities – a deliberate omission by the previous Government.[1] There have been organisations which maintain such lists.[2]

---

1   See *Removing Barriers to Employment* (Cm 655) (London: HMSO, 1989) ch 2.
2   For example, the Economic League. See Hollingsworth M and Tremayne C *The Economic League: The Silent McCarthyism* (London, National Council for Civil Liberties, 1989).

2.11.2   The present Government in *Fairness at Work* proposed to prohibit the blacklisting of trade union members.[1] It does this by s 3 which gives the Secretary of State the power to make regulations, subject to affirmative resolution under s 42(2), prohibiting the compilation of lists which contain details of members of trade unions or persons who have taken part in the activities of trade unions which are compiled with a view to being used by employers or employment agencies for the purposes of discrimination in relation to recruitment, or in relation to the treatment of workers.[2] Regulations may prohibit the use of blacklists and the sale or supply of blacklists.[3] The section further provides that the regulations may, inter alia, confer jurisdiction upon employment tribunals and the Employment Appeal Tribunal; include provision for compensation; include provision permitting a trade union to take action on behalf of members in specified circumstances; protect an employee against dismissal where the principal reason for the dismissal is that the employee's name is on a blacklist; create criminal offences; and extend liability for a criminal offence to a person who aids the commission of an offence or to a person who is an agent, principal, employee, employer or officer of a person who commits the offence.[4] Regulations may not provide for an offence created under the section to be punishable by imprisonment or by a fine in excess of level 5 on the standard scale in the case of an offence triable summarily only, or a fine in excess of the statutory maximum in the case of summary conviction for an offence triable either way.[5] 'List', within the section, includes one held in electronic form.[6]

---

1   *Fairness at Work*, para 4.25.
2   ERA 1999, s 3(1).
3   Ibid, s 3(2).

4   Ibid, s 3(3).
5   Ibid, s 3(4).
6   Ibid, s 3(5).

2.12   NOTICE RELATING TO INDUSTRIAL ACTION

Introduction

2.12.1   Sections 226–235 of TULR(C)A 1992 give details of the law relating to industrial action ballots and required notices. These provisions are complex and in *Fairness at Work* the Government invited suggestions as to how the requirements could be simplified.[1] Section 4 of ERA 1999 gives effect to Sch 3 which incorporates some of the suggestions received.

1   *Fairness at Work*, para 4.26. The Government stated that the rules were unnecessarily complex and rigid and that one study suggested that three-quarters of the legal actions brought against trade unions concern the ballot and notice provisions. The Government stated that these actions were damaging to business efficiency as well as to trade unions.

Informing employers of the ballot result

2.12.2   Section 231A of TULR(C)A 1992 requires unions to inform employers of the result of an industrial action ballot involving their employees. Where the action involves employees of a number of employers, the union must inform all of those employers and a failure to do so renders any subsequent action unlawful even in respect of employers who were informed. Schedule 3 amends s 231A so that any subsequent action will still be unlawful in respect of those employers who were not informed of the result of the ballot, but will be lawful in respect of those employers who were informed.[1]

1   ERA 1999, Sch 3, para 2(3).

Notice to employers of ballots and the taking of industrial action

2.12.3   When a union decides to call on its members to take or continue industrial action, it has no immunity from legal liability unless it holds a properly conducted secret ballot in advance of the industrial action. By ss 226A and 234A of TULR(C)A 1992, unions are required to give the employer advance notice in writing both of the ballot and of any industrial action which may result. The original provisions stated that the ballot notice had to describe, so that the employer could readily ascertain them, the employees who it was reasonable for the union to believe would be entitled to vote;[1] likewise the notice of official industrial action had to describe, so that the employer could readily ascertain them, those employees the union intended should take part in the industrial action.[2] The House of Lords in *Blackpool and Fylde College v*

National Association of Teachers in Further and Higher Education[3] interpreted these provisions as meaning that the union was required, in certain circumstances, to give the employer the names of the employees balloted or who were called upon to take industrial action.

---

1   The original s 226A(2)(c) of TULR(C)A 1992.
2   Ibid, the original s 234A(3)(a).
3   [1994] ICR 982. Their lordships affirmed the judgment of the Court of Appeal ([1994] ICR 648) which concluded that while Parliament had not required the union to name the employees who were to be balloted, it did require that the employer could readily ascertain them, thus Parliament had allowed for the possibility that there would be occasions when a union could identify employees by category rather than by name.

2.12.4   The present Government in *Fairness at Work* stated that trade unions are reluctant to give names to the employer because some members may not wish the trade union to disclose their names.[1] Schedule 3 amends the original s 226A(2)(c) (notice of ballot) by substituting the original phrase that the ballot notice is notice in writing 'describing (so that he can readily ascertain them) the employees of the employer' for the phrase 'containing such information in the union's possession as would help the employer to make plans and bring information to the attention of those of his employees'.[2] Further, a new s 226A(3A) provides that if a union possesses information as to the number, category or workplace of the employees concerned, a notice must contain at least that information, but the fact that the notice does not name employees shall not be grounds for holding that the union has failed to comply with its legal obligations under the section.[3] It should be noted that the amended s 226A(2)(c) talks of the information in the union's possession, although the new s 226A(3A) is unclear as to whether, if the union has more information than the number, category or workplace of the employees, it is under a legal obligation to disclose that additional information, or whether it has complied with its obligations by giving the employer the minimum required. In the *Blackpool and Fylde College* case above, the National Association of Teachers in Further and Higher Education (NATFHE) specified in its notice to the employer that it would be balloting 'all our members in your institution'. The college had been told by the branch secretary some time earlier that around one-third of its staff (288) were union members but only 109 had their union dues debited directly from their salaries. Whether the notice in that case would satisfy the amended requirements has yet to be seen. Given that only academic staff are members of NATFHE, it is arguable that the union had identified both the category and the workplace. If the notice had also mentioned the number which had been given to the employer some time earlier, it could be argued it had given sufficient information to comply with s 226A(3A). Schedule 3 also amends the original s 234A(3)(a) (notice relating to industrial action) in the same way, again requiring the union to give, as a minimum, information to the employer as to the number, category or workplace of those intended to take part in industrial action, if such information is in its possession.[4] Whether the union is under a legal duty to give any other information it has which would help the employer to make plans, again, has yet to be seen.

---

1   *Fairness at Work*, para 4.27A.
2   ERA 1999, Sch 3, para 3(2) amending s 226A(2)(c) of TULR(C)A 1992.
3   Ibid, para 3(3) inserting s 226A(3A).
4   Ibid, para 11(1), (2) and (3) amending s 234A(3)(a) and inserting a new s 234A(5A).

Requirement to send sample voting papers to employers

2.12.5   Section 226A(1) of TULR(C)A 1992 requires the union or unions to send sample voting papers to all employers whose employees will be entitled to vote in the ballot. The effect of this section is that, if the union uses different voting papers for different employees, the union is obliged to send all the samples to all the employers whether the voting paper is to be used by the employer's employees or not. The Schedule inserts a new s 226A(3B) into TULR(C)A 1992 so that the union has to send to an employer only a sample voting paper which will be sent to that employer's employees and not the papers which will be sent to employees of another employer who is involved in the same action.[1]

---

1   ERA 1999, Sch 3, para 3(3).

Inducing members to take industrial action

2.12.6   Section 227(1) of TULR(C)A 1992 gives an entitlement to vote in an industrial action ballot to all members who, at the time of the ballot, it is reasonable for the union to believe will be induced to take part in the industrial action. No other member has an entitlement to vote. Further, s 227(2) provides that the requirements are not satisfied (and thus the action loses immunity) if a person who was a member of the union at the time of the ballot and was denied an entitlement to vote is subsequently induced by the union to take action. The effect of these provisions has meant that, whilst a union could induce members who joined the union after the ballot,[1] it could not induce existing members who were not entitled to vote at the time of the ballot but who, by the time the action was due, had become part of the relevant workforce because, for example, they had changed jobs. Schedule 3 repeals s 227(2).[2] Further, the Schedule inserts a new s 232A into TULR(C)A 1992.[3] This new section retains immunity for the action where a member is induced to take action or induced to continue to take action but was not balloted *unless* it was reasonable at the time of the ballot for the union to believe that the member would be induced to take part or induced to continue to take part. This should cover the situation of members changing jobs after the ballot but before the action. Consequential amendments are also made to s 226.[4]

---

1   See, for example, *London Underground v RMT* [1995] IRLR 636.
2   ERA 1999, Sch 3, para 4.
3   Ibid, para 8.
4   Ibid, para 2(2).

Separate workplace ballots

2.12.7   Paragraph 5 of the Schedule tidies up the original complex provisions of s 238 regarding separate workplace ballots. It also inserts a new s 238A into TULR(C)A 1992. Essentially, this relieves the union of the duty to hold separate ballots in each workplace and allows the union to hold a single ballot if one of the following applies:

- if the workplace of each member entitled to vote is the workplace of at least one member who is affected by the dispute;[1]
- if entitlement to vote is accorded to and limited to all members who according to the union's reasonable belief have a common occupation and are employed by a common employer or number of employers with whom the union is in dispute;[2]
- if entitlement to vote is accorded to and limited to all the union members employed by a particular employer or number of employers with whom the union is in dispute.[3]

For the purposes of s 238A members of the union affected by a dispute means members of the union affected by items listed in s 244(1)(a), (b) and (c).[4] Members affected by a dispute which relates to a matter listed in s 244(1)(d) are those whom the matter directly affects.[5] Members affected by a dispute which relates to a matter listed in s 244(1)(e) are those persons whose membership or non-membership is in dispute[6] and members affected by a dispute which relates to a matter in s 244(1)(f) are officials of the union who have used or would use the facilities concerned in the dispute.[7]

---

1   TULR(C)A 1992, s 228A(2).
2   Ibid, s 228A(3).
3   Ibid, s 228A(4).
4   Ibid, s 228A(5)(a). Section 244(1)(a) covers terms and conditions of employment or the physical conditions in which any workers are required to work. Section 244(1)(b) covers engagement or non-engagement, termination or suspension of employment or the duties of employment. Section 244(1)(c) covers the allocation of work or the duties of employment between workers or groups of workers.
5   Ibid, s 228A(5)(b). Section 244(1)(d) covers matters of discipline.
6   Ibid, s 228A(5)(c). Section 244(1)(e) covers a worker's membership or non-membership of a trade union.
7   Ibid, s 228A(5)(d). Section 244(1)(f) covers facilities for officials of trade unions.

Overtime and call-out bans

2.12.8 Section 229(2) provides that the ballot paper must contain either or both of the following questions. Is the voter prepared to take part in a strike? Is the voter prepared to take part in industrial action short of a strike? The position in regard to overtime bans and call-out bans has been unclear. Is such action a strike or is it other industrial action? Such a definition is crucial. If this form of action is a strike, the union is protected if it only asks the first question above. If, however, the union has only asked the first question, and the action is not classed as a strike, the union has not conducted an appropriate ballot and the action will not have statutory immunity. For the purposes of clarity, Sch 3 defines both call-out bans and overtime bans as industrial action short of a strike.[1] In addition, the Schedule amends s 229(4) of the TULR(C)A 1992. This provision requires that the voting paper should contain a statement saying that by taking part in a strike or other industrial action the employee may be in breach of the contract of employment; now the voting paper must also contain a statement that any dismissal for taking part in official industrial action which is otherwise lawful will be unfair if it takes place fewer than eight weeks after the employee started taking part and may be unfair if the dismissal takes place later.[2]

---

1   ERA 1999, Sch 3, para 6(2) inserting s 229(2A) into TULR(C)A 1992.
2   Ibid, para 6(3) inserting additional statement at the end of s 229(4).

Conduct of ballot – merchant seamen

2.12.9 Paragraph 7 amends s 230(2A) and (2B). Essentially this gives a merchant seaman the right to vote in a ballot if the trade union reasonably believes the seaman will be employed on a ship at some time in the period during which votes may be cast.[1] The original provision entitled merchant seamen to vote only if they were employed on a ship throughout the period during which votes may be cast. Therefore, if the ship left Great Britain during the vote period, the seamen on that ship lost their entitlement.

---

1   Substituted s 230(2A) of TULR(C)A 1992.

Disregard of certain minor breaches and accidental failures

2.12.10 Schedule 3 tries to mitigate the harshness of the previous law when a small error could invalidate a ballot and thus render the union subject to legal action. Where there are small accidental failures to comply with the statutory requirements, these are to be disregarded if they are on a scale which is unlikely to affect the outcome of the ballot.[1] The accidental failures which can be disregarded are failures to meet the requirements of s 227(1) (entitlement to vote), s 230(2) (the requirement that the ballot paper be sent to a member's home address and the member be given the opportunity to vote by post) and s 230(2A) (special provisions on voting in respect of merchant seamen).[2] These provisions are likely to cause some problems in interpretation given that it appears that the burden will be on the union to not only show that the failure or failures were accidental but also that they are unlikely to affect the outcome of the ballot. Presumably, the section will have a cumulative effect and, whereas a number of failures taken individually may not, on their own, affect the result of the ballot, their cumulative effect may well do.

---

1   ERA 1999, Sch 3, para 9 inserting a new s 232B(1) into TULR(C)A 1992.
2   Ibid, para 9 inserting s 232B(2).

Ballots for industrial action: periods of effectiveness

2.12.11   Section 233 of TULR(C)A 1992 provides that industrial action does not have the support of a ballot unless it is called by a specified person, there is no call for industrial action before the date of the ballot, and any call for industrial action must take place before the ballot ceases to be effective under s 234.[1] The original s 234(1) provided that a ballot ceased to be effective at the end of a period of four weeks beginning with the day of the ballot, or, if votes were cast on more than one day, on the last of those days.[2] Section 234(1) has now been amended so that the union and the members' employer can agree a longer period than four weeks not exceeding eight weeks from the date of the ballot;[3] this is to avoid the situation where the union has to organise industrial action within the four-week period before the ballot becomes ineffective, even though the parties feel that a settlement might be achieved by further negotiation. Where more than one employer is involved, the extension must be negotiated with each employer, so that one employer may agree an extension but another may not.

---

1   TULR(C)A 1992, s 233(3).
2   Ibid, s 246.
3   ERA 1999, Sch 3, para 10 inserting a new s 234(1).

Suspension of industrial action

2.12.12   Section 234A requires the union to send written notice to the employee's employer informing the employer that the union intends to induce all or some of the employees to take industrial action. Such notice must be received seven days before the commencement of the action and must specify the date of commencement of the action and whether the action is continuous or discontinuous.[1] Further, where action which is continuous ceases to be authorised or endorsed by the union but then later is authorised or endorsed, the original notice to the employer does not cover the later action.[2] This discourages the union to suspend industrial action for the purposes of negotiating with the employer because, if the action is suspended and negotiations fail, the union must give another seven days' notice before the action can recommence, otherwise the union will lose its immunity. In order to encourage unions to suspend action in order to negotiate, the Schedule introduces a new s 234A(7A) and (7B).[3] These new subsections provide that the union and employer can agree that the action will cease to be authorised or endorsed with effect from a date specified in the agreement (the suspension date) and it will resume authorisation or endorsement at a date specified in the agreement (the resumption date). This means that the parties can agree to suspend the action so that they can negotiate but, should negotiations fail, there will be no need for the union to issue a fresh notice to the employer. Although the new sections do not state that there is no such need to re-issue the notice, the employer will, of course, be aware of the date of resumption of industrial action for the whole of the period of the negotiation as the parties will have agreed this date before the negotiations begin.

---

1   TULR(C)A 1992, s 234A(3) and (4).
2   Ibid, s 234A(7).
3   By Sch 3, para 11(5) of ERA 1999.

2.13 TRAINING

Introduction

2.13.1   Section 1 of ERA 1999 inserts Chapter VA into Part I of TULR(C)A 1992. The new s 70A of TULR(C)A 1992 inserts Sch A1. The new ss 70B and 70C provide new rights to recognised trade unions to consult on the employer's policy and plans for training and report on training which has been undertaken.

2.13.2   Where a union or unions are recognised under the procedure set out in Sch A1 to TULR(C)A 1992[1] and the CAC has specified a method for collective bargaining under para 31(3) of the Schedule which the parties have not agreed should not be legally binding under para 31(5) of the Schedule,[2] the employer must from time to time invite union representatives to a meeting for the purposes of:

–   consulting about the employer's policy on training for workers within the bargaining unit;
–   consulting about the employer's plans for training those workers during the period of six months starting with the date of the meeting; and
–   reporting about training provided for those workers since the previous meeting.[3]

Note that the duty applies only in respect of workers within the bargaining unit. The first meeting must be held within six months of the CAC imposing a method of collective bargaining and further meetings must be held within six months of previous meetings.[4] The employer is obliged to provide the union, two weeks in advance of the meeting, with information without which the representatives would be to a material extent impeded in participating in the meeting and which would be in accordance with good industrial relations practice to disclose.[5] The employer is not required to disclose any information the employer does not have to disclose by s 182(1) of TULR(C)A 1992.[6] The employer is under a duty to take account of any written representations about matters raised at the meeting given by the union or unions within a period of four weeks after the date of the meeting.[7] Where more than one union is recognised, each trade union has the same rights.[8]

---

1   TULR(C)A 1992, s 70B(1)(a).
2   Ibid, s 70B(1)(b).
3   Ibid, s 70B(2).
4   Ibid, s 70B(3).
5   Ibid, s 70B(4).
6   Ibid, s 181 provides that an employer who recognises an independent trade union must disclose information for collective bargaining purposes. The employer is not under a duty to disclose information which falls within s 182(1). Section 182(1) provides:
     'An employer is not required by s 181 to disclose information –
     (a)   the disclosure of which would be against the interests of national security, or
     (b)   which he could not disclose without contravening a prohibition imposed by or under an enactment, or
     (c)   which has been communicated to him in confidence, or which he has otherwise obtained in consequence of the confidence reposed in him by another person, or
     (d)   which relates specifically to an individual (unless that individual has consented to its being disclosed), or
     (e)   the disclosure of which would cause substantial injury to his undertaking for reasons other than its effect on collective bargaining, or
     (f)   obtained by him for the purpose of bringing, prosecuting, or defending any legal proceedings.'
7   Ibid, s 70B(6).
8   Ibid, s 70B(7).

2.13.3   A trade union may present a complaint to an employment tribunal that an employer has failed to comply with obligations under s 70B.[1] Such a failure could consist of a failure to hold meetings or to supply information. It could also apply to a failure to take account of written representations but, it is submitted, it may be difficult to show that an employer has not taken such representations into account. A complaint must be presented within three months beginning with the date of the alleged failure, with the normal discretion on the part of the tribunal to extend that period.[2] Should the tribunal find the complaint well-founded, it must make a declaration to that effect and it may make an award of compensation of a maximum of two weeks' pay to each member of the bargaining unit.[3] This is subject to the statutory limit of one week's pay imposed by s 227 of ERA 1996.[4] Only an individual within the bargaining unit can take action to enforce payment. The union cannot do so on behalf of its members.[5]

---

1   TULR(C)A 1992, s 70C(1).
2   Ibid, s 70C(2).
3   Ibid, s 70C(3) and (4).

4   Ibid, s 70C(5). The current limit for a week's pay is £220: ERA 1996, s 227 as substituted
     by SI 1998/924, arts 3, 4, Schedule.
5   Ibid, s 70C(6).

2.14   UNFAIR DISMISSAL CONNECTED WITH RECOGNITION: INTERIM RELIEF

Introduction

2.14.1   Interim relief is provided for by ss 128–132 of ERA 1996. It may be awarded by a tribunal if it is applied for within seven days of the employee being dismissed. The original provision allowed for interim relief where the reason or principal reason for the dismissal is that the employee was a health and safety representative and carried out or proposed to carry out relevant duties or functions,[1] the employee was the trustee of an occupational pension scheme and performed or proposed to perform duties as such,[2] or the employee was an employee representative or a candidate in an election for such a post and performed or proposed to perform the relevant duties[3] and where the tribunal considers that it is likely to find that the dismissal was unfair. The effect of interim relief is that the employer must re-employ the employee on terms which are not less favourable than those before the dismissal and therefore the employee will continue to be paid. The amount paid to the employee is offset against any compensation awarded.[4]

1   ERA 1996, s 100(1)(a) and (b).
2   Ibid, s 102(1).
3   Ibid, s 103.
4   Ibid, s 130(5).

2.14.2   Section 6 of ERA 1999 amends s 128(1)(b) and s 129(1) of ERA 1996 and inserts 'or in paragraph 161(2) of Schedule A1 to the Trade Union and Labour Relations (Consolidation) Act 1992' into those sections. The effect of this is that interim relief is now available to an employee who has been dismissed in connection with recognition or derecognition.

Chapter 3

LEAVE FOR FAMILY AND DOMESTIC REASONS

3.1 MATERNITY LEAVE

Introduction

3.1.1 Section 7 gives effect to Part I of Sch 4, which provides basic rights and regulation-making powers relating to maternity and parental leave and which replace Part VIII of ERA 1996. The new provisions provide a coherent package of maternity and parental-leave rights, extending the existing maternity rights for women and introducing a new right to parental leave for both men and women. Employees also have protection from detriment or dismissal for exercising the new rights. The old maternity rights were considered complex and have been criticised.[1] The new provisions aim to simplify the scheme by providing a basic framework in primary legislation with details in a single set of regulations. A new Chapter 1 of Part VIII of ERA 1996 sets out the amended rights to maternity leave. It provides for three periods of leave: ordinary maternity leave; compulsory maternity leave; and additional maternity leave.

---

1   See, for example, House of Commons, Session 1994–95, Employment Committee First Report *Mothers in Employment* vol 1, Report and Proceedings of the Committee, 15 February 1995 and the judgment of Browne-Wilkinson J in *Lavery v Plessey Communications* [1982] IRLR 180.

Ordinary maternity leave

3.1.2 A new s 71 in ERA 1996 gives the right to all employees, regardless of length of service, to ordinary maternity leave. This right, like that which it replaces, implements the requirements of the Pregnant Workers Directive.[1] During such leave the employee is entitled to the benefit of all the terms of her contract excluding pay,[2] is bound by any obligations arising under those terms and conditions[3] and is entitled to return from leave to the job in which she was employed before her absence.[4] The right to return is a right to return with her seniority, pension rights and similar rights as they would have been if she had not been absent and on terms and conditions not less favourable than those which would have applied had she not been absent.[5] The Secretary of State may make regulations prescribing conditions for the qualification for this right.[6] It is expected that the requirements will be no more than that the employee tells her employer she is pregnant and the date the baby is due.

---

1   Council Directive 92/85/EEC.
2   ERA 1996, s 71(4)(a) and (5).
3   Ibid, s 71(4)(b).
4   Ibid, s 71(4)(c).

5   Ibid, s 71(7).
6   Ibid, s 71(2) and s 75(2).

3.1.3   The length of ordinary maternity leave has been extended from the old 14 weeks to 18 weeks.[1] This is in line with the Government's proposal in *Fairness at Work* which was to bring maternity leave into line with statutory maternity pay which is payable for 18 weeks.[2] Employees may choose, as they did under the old law, when to start maternity leave, subject to restrictions laid down by the Secretary of State.[3] It is likely that similar restrictions which existed under the old provisions will be set and that women can start maternity leave any time from the eleventh week before the expected week of the birth. Maternity leave will start, automatically if the woman is absent from work with a pregnancy-related illness in the six weeks prior to the birth and at the latest when the baby is born. The Secretary of State is further empowered to make regulations specifying what is meant by remuneration.[4] It is intended that remuneration should be defined as the monetary element of the woman's wages. This should clarify the position in regard to mortgage subsidies etc.

1   ERA 1996, s 71(3)(a).
2   *Fairness at Work,* para 5.14.
3   ERA 1996, s 71(3)(b).
4   Ibid, s 71(6).

Compulsory maternity leave

3.1.4   The new s 72 replaces the Maternity (Compulsory Leave) Regulations 1994[1] which implemented the health and safety requirement of the Pregnant Workers Directive. This requires that there should be a minimum period of at least two weeks after the birth when the woman must not work. The new provisions are intended to have a similar effect to the old regulations. Section 72 gives the Secretary of State the power to issue regulations subject to negative resolution procedure, to prescribe the minimum length of compulsory maternity leave (which must be at least two weeks) during which the employer shall not permit the employee to work,[2] and the fact that the compulsory leave must fall within an ordinary maternity-leave period.[3] The onus is on the employer not to allow the woman to return to work during the period and contravention of the provision is a criminal offence and subject to a fine not exceeding level 2 on the standard scale for fines for summary offences.[4] Under the previous law, when maternity leave was 14 weeks, it would be possible, if the baby was late and the woman had started her maternity leave 11 weeks before the expected date of birth, that her maternity leave ran out before the birth. It will be more difficult for this to occur now that the ordinary maternity leave has been increased to 18 weeks.

1   SI 1994/2479.
2   ERA 1996, ss 72(1) and 72(3)(a).
3   Ibid, s 72(3)(b).

4   Ibid, s 72(5).

Additional maternity leave

3.1.5   The new s 73 and the proposed regulations replace ss 79–84 of ERA 1996. Under s 73 and the regulations, there is a right to additional maternity leave distinct from the right to ordinary maternity leave. The old law was silent as to whether there was a contract of employment during maternity absence and so the new provisions clarify this by creating a right to leave rather than a right to return thus making it clear that the contract continues.[1] As with ordinary maternity leave the woman is entitled (subject to regulations) to the benefit of the terms and conditions of employment (excluding remuneration) which would have applied had she not been absent and is bound by any obligations arising under those terms and conditions.[2] However, unlike ordinary maternity leave, where she is entitled to return to the job in which she was employed before her absence, after additional maternity leave she is only entitled to return to a job 'of a prescribed kind'.[3] The intention is for regulations to allow employers flexibility where it is not reasonably practicable to allow a woman to return to her old job.[4] The Secretary of State has the power to prescribe by regulation who will qualify for the right and make provision in relation to the right to return in respect of seniority, pension rights and similar rights and the terms and conditions of employment on return.[5] *Fairness at Work* proposed that those with one year's service will qualify for additional maternity leave.[6] In addition, regulations will specify the duration and timing of maternity leave.[7] The additional maternity leave is intended to be taken at the end of ordinary maternity leave and, it is thought, will end 29 weeks after the birth. This means that the total length of maternity leave will remain the same as the old law (ie 40 weeks) but more women will benefit because of the shorter qualifying period.

1   ERA 1996, s 73(1) and s 73(4)(a) and (b).
2   Ibid, s 73(4)(a) and (b) and s 73(5).
3   Ibid, s 73(4)(c).
4   Ibid, s 235 defines a job 'in relation to an employee, means the nature of the work which he is employed to do in accordance with his contract and the capacity and place in which he is so employed'.
5   Ibid, s 73(1) and (7).
6   *Fairness at Work*, para 5.19.
7   ERA 1996, s 73(2) and (3).

Redundancy and dismissal

3.1.6   By a new s 74 the Secretary of State may make provision in regulations about the treatment of an employee during ordinary or additional maternity leave when a redundancy situation occurs, or where there is a dismissal for reasons other than redundancy.[1] Such regulations may include a provision requiring the employer to offer suitable alternative employment and provision for the consequences of failure to comply with the regulations which may include provision for a dismissal to be treated as unfair for the purposes of Part X.[2]

Regulations may also make provision about dismissal other than by reason of redundancy during ordinary or additional maternity leave.[3] It is thought that this provision has been inserted so that the right to return can be disapplied where a woman is dismissed during maternity leave for reasons other than pregnancy or maternity, for example because of conduct prior to maternity leave. It is also thought that the new regulations will replicate the old provisions in that an employer who employs five or fewer employees will not have to take the woman back after additional maternity leave if it is not reasonably practicable to offer her either her old job back or a suitable alternative job.[4]

1   ERA 1996, s 74(1) and (2).
2   Ibid, s 74(3).
3   Ibid, s 74(2).
4   Ibid, s 74(4).

Supplemental

3.1.7 A new s 75 prescribes the scope of the power of the Secretary of State to make regulations in respect of all three types of maternity leave. The Secretary of State may make regulations on the following:

–   provision about notices to be given, evidence to be produced and other procedures to be followed by employees and employers;
–   provision for the consequences of failure to give notices, to produce evidence or to comply with other procedural requirements;
–   provision for the consequences of a failure to act in accordance with a notice given under (a);
–   special provision for cases where an employee has a right under her contract of employment or otherwise, which corresponds to the rights conferred by the regulations;
–   provision modifying the calculation of a week's pay in relation to an employee who is or who has been absent from work on ordinary or additional maternity leave;
–   provision applying, modifying or excluding an enactment, in such circumstances as may be specified and subject to any conditions specified, in relation to a person entitled to ordinary compulsory or additional maternity leave;
–   different provision for different cases or circumstances.[1]

Under the old law, there were a number of different notification procedures required before maternity leave, after the birth if required by the employer and before the return to work. In *Fairness at Work* the Government stated that those rules were complex and could be simplified[2] and is out to consultation on what the procedures should be. The old law also provided that a failure to comply with any of the procedural requirements meant that a woman lost her right to return. This is a harsh penalty for a technical infringement, particularly if the employer is aware of the woman's intentions. The new provisions allow the Secretary of State to allow for smaller and less harsh penalties to be imposed. The regulations may make provision in the case where a woman has both statutory and contractual rights. It is thought that the old law will be enacted allowing the woman to choose the better of those rights. Further, the regulations can make provision that for the purposes of redundancy and unfair dismissal compensation, one week's pay is calculated on the employee's normal pay rather than the pay she receives while on maternity leave. Finally, the regulations will allow flexibility for different circumstances, for example where there is a very late birth which may mean that, even with 18 weeks' maternity leave, the leave still runs out before the end of the compulsory maternity-leave period.

---

1   ERA 1996, s 75(1). The paragraphs above relate to the paragraphs in the subsection.
2   *Fairness at Work*, para 5.17.

3.2   PARENTAL LEAVE

Introduction

3.2.1   In addition to the amended maternity rights, Part I of Sch 4 inserts a new Chapter 11 of Part VIII into ERA 1996, following on after the maternity-leave provisions. These new rights implement the Parental Leave Directive.[1]

---

1   Council Directive 96/34/EC.

Entitlement

3.2.2   A new s 76 provides that the Secretary of State must make regulations entitling a person who satisfies conditions in respect of duration of employment and who is having or expecting to have responsibility for a child to be absent from work on parental leave for the purposes of caring for that child.[1] The amount of leave must be a minimum of three months.[2] Regulations may also prescribe the extent of an employee's entitlement to parental leave and when that leave may be taken,[3] what happens when a person ceases to satisfy any qualifying criteria[4] and whether parental leave can be transferred.[5] In particular, the regulations will set the maximum age of a child in respect of whom parental leave may be taken (which, following consultation on *Fairness at Work*, is likely to be below eight years of age, the upper limit in the Directive)[6] and specify a period of leave starting from a specified event.[7] This will enable the regulations to apply to adoptive parents, a proposal contained in *Fairness at Work*.[8] The Government does not intend, however, to give adoptive mothers rights equivalent to maternity leave.[9] The Government, in *Fairness at Work* did however intend to align parental-leave and maternity-leave rights in respect of continuity requirements so that the right to additional maternity leave and the right to parental leave would apply after one year's service[10] and it is thought that this will be the qualifying period for parental leave. The regulations may also:

–   specify things which are or are not to be taken as done for the purposes of caring for a child;
–   require parental leave to be taken as a block in all or some cases;
–   require parental leave to be taken as a series of periods of absences in some or all cases;
–   require all or some leave to be taken at specified times (eg a proportion taken in the child's first year);
–   make provision about the postponement by an employer of a period of parental leave;
–   specify a minimum or maximum period of absence which may be taken as part of a period of parental leave;
–   specify a maximum aggregate of periods of parental leave which may be taken during a specified period of time.[11]

---

1   ERA 1996, s 76(1).
2   Ibid, s 76(3). Three months is the minimum amount of leave under the Directive.
3   Ibid, s 76(2).
4   Ibid, s 76(3)(a).
5   Ibid, s 76(3)(b).
6   Ibid, s 76(4)(a).
7   Ibid, s 76(4)(b).
8   *Fairness at Work*, para 5.23.
9   Ibid.
10   *Fairness at Work*, para. 5.19. This is the qualifying period under the Directive.
11   ERA 1996, s 76(5).

Rights during and after parental leave

3.2.3   As for additional maternity leave, regulations will specify that the employment contract is to continue during parental leave and the terms and conditions of employment (excluding remuneration) continue to apply.[1] Likewise the employee is bound by any obligations arising under the terms and conditions of employment.[2] The employee is also entitled to return to a job of such a kind as the regulations may specify and this will also apply when the employee has a period of absence attributable partly to maternity leave and partly to parental leave.[3] As with the maternity-leave provisions, the regulations may make provision on the exercise of the right to return in respect of seniority, pension rights and similar rights and terms and conditions on return.[4] Again, as for maternity leave, regulations may make provision about redundancy or dismissal for a reason other than redundancy during a period of parental leave, requiring the employer to offer alternative employment in a redundancy situation or treating a dismissal as unfair in some circumstances.[5] However, unlike the provisions on maternity leave, the regulations may provide for an employee to be entitled to exercise all or part of his parental leave requiring the employer to provide the option of part-time working over a longer period, albeit limited to particular circumstances[6] and permitting parental leave to be transferred between parents.[7] In respect of this latter provision, the Act talks of a transfer to another employee, but does not specify whether that is an employee employed by the same employer. Presumably, the regulations will clarify this. Again, as with maternity leave, the regulations may provide that specified provisions will not apply if the employee's contract of employment specifies, either expressly or by the incorporation of a collective agreement, an entitlement to parental leave.[8] While the Act is not specific, it is assumed that the regulations will only not apply if the contractual right is at least equivalent to that provided by the legislation.

---

1   ERA 1996, s 77(1)(a) and 2(b).
2   Ibid, s 77(1)(b).
3   Ibid, s 77(1)(c) and s 78(6).
4   Ibid, s 77(4).
5   Ibid, s 78(1) and (2).
6   Ibid, s 78(3) and (4).
7   Ibid, s 78(5).
8   Ibid, s 78(7).

Supplemental

3.2.4 A new s 79 provides the scope of the Secretary of State's regulation-making powers. It provides that regulations may make provision about:

- notices to be given, evidence to be produced by employees to employers, employers to employees and employers to employers (this may suggest an intention that parental leave can be transferred to another employer);
- requiring employers or employees to keep records;
- other procedures to be followed by either party;
- specifying the consequences of failing to comply with the procedural requirements including the creation of criminal offences;
- specifying the consequences of a failure to act in accordance with a notice given (see first item of list);
- where there is a contractual right, allowing the employee to take the better right;
- make consequential amendments;
- make different provision for different cases.[1]

Regulations can also modify the calculation of a week's pay[2] and ensure that the Secretary of State can make any other provision which may be necessary or expedient to implement the Parental Leave Directive.[3]

---

1   ERA 1996, s 79(1).

2   Ibid, s 79(2).
3   Ibid, s 79(3).

Complaint to an employment tribunal

3.2.5   An employee can present a complaint to an employment tribunal that the employer has unreasonably postponed a period of parental leave or has prevented or attempted to prevent an employee taking parental leave.[1] The complaint must be presented within three months of the date or the last date of the matters complained of with the usual discretion to extend that period.[2] If the tribunal finds the complaint well-founded, it shall make a declaration to that effect and may award compensation.[3] The amount of compensation shall be what the tribunal considers just and equitable having regard to the employer's behaviour and any loss sustained by the employee.[4]

1   ERA 1996, s 80(1).
2   Ibid, s 80(2).
3   Ibid, s 80(3).
4   Ibid, s 80(4).

3.3   TIME OFF FOR DEPENDANTS

Introduction

3.3.1   The original Bill gave an employee the right to take reasonable unpaid time off to deal with a domestic incident. This provision was intended to implement the rest of the Parental Leave Directive not implemented by the parental-leave provisions. The Directive gives a right to unpaid time off for urgent family reasons, but this was not the original wording used in the new provision. The explanatory notes to the Bill, however, stated that the intention behind the right was to allow employees time off to deal with an urgent problem where it was reasonable in the circumstances to do so. Furthermore, the question of whether the time off was reasonable would be linked to the amount of time necessary to deal with a short-term problem or make longer-term arrangements, the needs of the business and the impact of the employee's absence on it. For time off to be justifiable, the explanatory note stated that the employee's attendance would have to be crucial to the resolving of the problem or, where the incident affected someone other than the employee, to the welfare and/or recovery of that person.[1]

1   House of Commons, Explanatory Note, Employment Relations Bill 1999, para 167 at http://www.parliament.the-stationery-office.co.uk.

3.3.2   It was clear from the House of Lords' debate that the original provisions were thought to be too wide and there was concern that the substance of the right would be contained in regulations. It was stated that 'the Bill as published provide[d] a wide right to time off for domestic incidents . . . The provisions were never intended to allow employees time off to get their washing machines mended, for example . . . the statutory right will be limited to urgent cases of real need'.[1] As a result, the provision was totally rewritten and the rights are now stated in the Act, removing the need for regulations.

---

1   HL Deb, vol 603, col 1084, 8 July 1999 (Lord Sainsbury).

Dependants

3.3.3   Section 8 and Part II of Sch 4 insert a new s 57A into ERA 1996 and create the right to reasonable time off during working hours, to take action which is necessary:

–   to provide assistance on an occasion when a dependant falls ill, gives birth or is injured or assaulted;
–   to make provision for the care of a dependant who is ill or injured;
–   to deal with the consequences of the death of a dependant;
–   to make provision because of the unexpected disruption or termination of arrangements for the care of a dependant;
–   to deal with an incident which involves the child of the employee and which occurs unexpectedly in a period during which an educational establishment which the child attends is responsible for him.[1]

A 'dependant' means, in relation to the employee, a spouse, a child, a parent or a person who lives in the same household as the employee, otherwise than by reason of being an employee, tenant, lodger or boarder.[2] In addition to these classes of person, in respect of the need to take action or make arrangements because of illness, birth, injury or assault, the definition of dependant is expanded to include any person who reasonably relies on the employee;[3] for the purposes of the unexpected disruption or termination of arrangements for the care of a dependant, the definition of dependant includes a person who reasonably relies on the employee to make such arrangements.[4] Illness or injury includes mental illness or injury.[5] While the definition is wide in some circumstances (it will, for example, include unmarried partners who share a home and neighbours who rely on the employee), the provisions are considerably more restricted than originally drafted. When the Bill was first published and proposed the right to time off to deal with domestic incidents, the Explanatory Note stated that it would include time off to deal with a domestic emergency involving the employee's property.[6] It is clear from both the House of Lords' debate and the redrafted provisions that this was not the intention of the Government and the new s 57A will not give a right to time off in these circumstances. Any time off is unpaid. While this does not appear to be explicit in the Act, it is when read with the other time-off provisions in ERA 1996. In the case of some of the time-off provisions, there is a following section providing that the time off shall be with pay, whereas in others there is no such following provision.[7] In respect of time off for dependants, there is no following provision providing that this time off shall be paid.

1　　ERA 1996, s 57A(1).
2　　Ibid, s 57A(3).
3　　Ibid, s 57A(4).
4　　Ibid, s 57A(5).
5　　Ibid, s 57A(6).
6　　House of Commons, Explanatory Note, Employment Relations Bill 1999, para 168 at
　　　http://www.parliament.the-stationery-office.co.uk.
7　　For example, s 50 of ERA 1996 gives a right to reasonable time off for public duties, but
　　　this is not followed by a provision stating that the time off shall be with pay. By contrast,
　　　s 55 (right to time off for ante-natal care) is followed by s 56 giving a right of
　　　remuneration when the right under s 55 is exercised.

3.3.4 While the original drafting of the Bill gave the Secretary of State power to make regulations laying down notice provisions, evidence required, and factors to be considered when deciding if the time allowed off is reasonable, the Act only provides a skeleton, which will give employment tribunals a great deal of discretion. There is nothing on the face of the Act giving guidance to tribunals to aid them in respect of how much time is reasonable. The Government decided not to set a limit which 'could be seen as a minimum, which employees might well consider an entitlement to be added to their annual leave . . . In all cases, the right will be limited to the amount of time which is reasonable in the circumstances of a particular case'.[1] An example given, however, is that if a child falls ill with chicken pox, a reasonable time would be one or two days to sort out longer-term arrangements but not the fortnight while the child is in quarantine.[2] The Act is also not proscriptive in respect of notice to be given to the employer. It merely states that the employee should tell the employer the reason for absence as soon as reasonably practicable and should tell the employer when he or she intends to return.[3] The employee will lose the right to time off if the employee fails to comply with these provisions unless he or she cannot comply with them until he or she has returned.[4]

1　　HL Deb, vol 603, col 1085, 8 July 1999 (Lord Sainsbury).
2　　Ibid.
3　　ERA 1996, s 57A(2).
4　　Ibid.

3.3.5 An employee has a right of complaint to an employment tribunal if the employer unreasonably refused to permit the employee to exercise the right. Such a complaint must normally be brought within three months of the failure, with the normal discretion to extend this period and, if the tribunal finds the complaint well-founded, it must make a declaration to that effect and may make an award of compensation.[1] The amount of compensation shall be what is just and equitable in the circumstances having regard to the employer's default in failing to permit the time off to be taken by the employee and any loss sustained by the employee.[2]

1   ERA 1996, s 57B(1), (2) and (3)
2   Ibid, s 57B(4).

Right not to suffer a detriment

3.3.6   Section 9 gives effect to Part III of Sch 4 which sets out changes resulting from the provisions on maternity leave, parental leave and time-off rights for dependants. The consequential amendments implement the Parental Leave Directive, fulfil proposals in *Fairness at Work* and replace previous provisions. A new s 47C of ERA 1996 gives employees the right not to suffer a detriment, by any act or deliberate failure to act, for reasons set out in regulations to be drawn up by the Secretary of State, that is: pregnancy, childbirth or maternity; ordinary, compulsory or additional maternity leave; parental leave or time off for dependants.[1] The regulations will also protect against an employee suffering a detriment for exercising a right in relation to parental leave or time off contained in a collective or workforce agreement.[2] Until the passing of s 47C, although there was a right not to be dismissed for reasons relating to pregnancy and maternity, there was no specific right not to suffer a detriment on these grounds, although less favourable treatment would be sex discrimination.[3] The inclusion of pregnancy and maternity merely brings it in line with the new parental-leave and time-off rights, therefore, rather than creating additional rights.

1   ERA 1996, s 47C(1) and (2).
2   Ibid, s 47C(3).
3   Sex Discrimination Act 1975 (SDA 1975), s 1(1)(a) and (b). See, in particular, cases such
     as *Dekker v Stichting Vormingscentrum Voor Jonge Volwassenen (VJV Centrun) Plus* [1991] IRLR
     27 and *Webb v EMO Air Cargo (UK) Ltd (No 2)* [1995] IRLR 645.

Dismissal

3.3.7   The old s 99 of ERA 1996, which made dismissal for reasons connected with pregnancy and maternity unfair, has been replaced by a new s 99. The new section provides that a person who is dismissed shall be regarded as unfairly dismissed if the reason or principal reason for the dismissal is of a prescribed kind or the dismissal takes place in prescribed circumstances, both of which will be laid down in regulations. Those regulations will state that a prescribed reason or set of circumstances will relate to: pregnancy, childbirth or maternity; ordinary, compulsory or additional maternity leave; parental leave or time off for dependants and it may also relate to redundancy or other factors.[1] As before, regulations will also protect an employee against dismissal for exercising rights to parental leave or time off for domestic incidents under the provisions of a collective or workforce agreement which is part of the employee's contract of employment.[2] As these rights are being brought into an amended s 99, this means that in respect of all of them the normal qualifying period in s 108 will not apply and neither will the upper age limit in s 109 of ERA 1996.

---

1   ERA 1996, s 99(1), (2) and (3).
2   Ibid, s 99(4).

Chapter 4

OTHER RIGHTS OF INDIVIDUALS

4.1 RIGHT TO BE ACCOMPANIED IN DISCIPLINARY AND GRIEVANCE HEARINGS

Introduction

4.1.1 The ACAS Code of Practice No 1 on *Disciplinary Practice and Procedures in Employment* states that disciplinary procedures should 'give individuals the right to be accompanied by a trade union representative or by a fellow employee of their choice'.[1] While the Code has no legal force,[2] it must be taken into account by employment tribunals when hearing unfair dismissal cases where it appears to be relevant[3] and a failure to allow representation may result in a finding of unfair dismissal.[4] Whilst there is no statutory duty to have disciplinary or grievance procedures, ERA 1996[5] requires employers to give all employees details of the person to whom a grievance can be taken and requires employers who employ more than 20 employees to give those employees details of any disciplinary rules applicable to them.[6]

---

1   Paragraph 10(g).
2   TULR(C)A 1992, s 207(1).
3   Ibid, s 207(2).
4   See, for example, *Rank Xerox (UK) Ltd v Goodchild & Ors* [1979] IRLR 185 where the Employment Appeal Tribunal held that a dismissal was unfair where the employer refused to allow the employee to be accompanied by an official of a union the employer did not recognise and where the employer had agreed to the employee's solicitor being present on condition that the solicitor did not participate in the proceedings.
5   ERA 1996, s 3(1)(b)(ii). See also *WA Goold (Pearmak) Ltd v McConnell* [1995] IRLR 516 where the Employment Appeal Tribunal held that given employers were under a duty to provide employees with a grievance procedure and that such a duty was a fundamental one, failure to do so constituted a constructive dismissal.
6   ERA 1996, s 3(1)(a) and 3(3)(a).

4.1.2 By s 10, where a worker is required or invited by the employer to attend a disciplinary or grievance hearing and the worker reasonably requests to be accompanied at the hearing, the employer must permit the worker to be accompanied by a single companion (who must be employed by a trade union of which he or she is an official,[1] or an official of a trade union whom the union has reasonably certified in writing as having experience of, or as having received training in, acting as a worker's companion at a disciplinary or grievance hearing, or another of the employer's workers).[2] The employer must allow the worker to choose the companion and that companion is to be permitted to address the hearing and confer with the worker but cannot ask questions on behalf of the worker.[3] For these purposes, a disciplinary hearing is a hearing which could result in the administration of a formal warning by the employer, the taking of some other action against the worker by the employer or the confirmation of a warning issued or action taken.[4] A grievance hearing is a hearing which concerns the performance of a duty by an employer in relation to a worker.[5] If the worker's chosen companion is not available at the time proposed and the worker proposes an alternative time which is reasonable and falls within a period of five working days after the day on which the worker was informed of the original hearing date, the employer must hold the hearing at that time.[6] An employer must allow the companion time off during working hours to accompany a worker.[7] Such time off should be paid.[8]

1   For the definition of a 'trade union' see s 1 of TULR(C)A 1992. For the definition of 'trade union official' see s 119 of the same Act.
2   ERA 1999, s 10(3).
3   Ibid, s 10(2).
4   Ibid, s 13(4).
5   Ibid, s 13(5).
6   Ibid, s 10(4) and (5).
7   Ibid, s 10(6).
8   Ibid, s 10(7). Entitlement to paid absence is defined by reference to s 168(3) and (4), s 169, s 171 and s 172 of TULR(C)A 1992 which state an employer's obligation to allow officials of recognised trade unions to paid time off for trade union duties. Section 10, however, does not require an official who accompanies a worker at a disciplinary or grievance hearing to be an official of a recognised trade union and the right to paid time off applies equally where the companion is not a trade union official.

4.1.3   These provisions are a significant change from the original. Section 13 now clearly defines what is meant by disciplinary and grievance hearing and in particular ensures that a worker has a right to be accompanied when a serious issue is to be addressed. This is particularly the case in respect of grievance hearings which must be in respect of the performance of a duty by the employer. This presumably means some legally imposed duty, whether contractual or statutory, and will prevent a worker from requesting a grievance hearing for a trivial matter. One thing which is clear, however, is that the Act does not require the employer to hold such hearings as the right to be accompanied arises only when the worker is required or invited to such a hearing by the employer. A failure to have such hearings may, however, affect the decision of a tribunal as stated above. The definition of an appropriate companion for the worker has been through a variety of changes. The final version attempts to address concerns that outsiders would become involved with internal matters and the risks of using persons who are inexperienced at representation to the detriment of the worker. Section 10(3) does not meet all of these criticisms as, by virtue of s 10(3)(a), a union official employed by the union may not have the relevant experience of representation. The section also appears to place a burden on trade unions to put in place training for representatives. This issue was raised in the House of Lords' debate. In response, it was stated that most unions already provide training for their lay representatives.[1] It was also stated in the debate that ACAS has agreed to draw up a code of practice setting out in detail how the right to be accompanied will apply.[2]

1   HL Deb, vol 604, col 561, 15 July 1999 (Lord Simon).
2   HL Deb, vol 603, col 1098, 8 July 1999 (Lord Simon).

4.1.4. For the purposes of ss 10, 11 and 12 discussed below, 'worker' is defined as a worker under the meaning of s 230(3) of ERA 1996,[1] an agency worker, a home worker, a person within Crown employment within the meaning of s 191(3)[2] of ERA 1996 other than a member of the naval, military, air or reserve forces of the Crown, or employed as a relevant member of the House of Lords or Commons staff within the meaning of s 194(6) or s 195(5)[3] of ERA 1996.[4] 'Agency worker' is defined as an individual who is supplied by an agent to a principal, who is not in a contract of employment or a contract to personally provide work or services with the principal.[5] For the purposes of ss 10–12, both the agent and the principal are employers of the agency worker, meaning both must afford the agency worker the right to be accompanied.[6] 'Home worker' is defined as an individual who contracts with a person, for the purposes of that person's business for work to be done at a place which is not under the person's control or management where the person is the home worker's employer.[7] For the purposes of the right to be accompanied the person contracting with the home worker is the home worker's employer.[8]

1   ERA 1996, s 230(3) provides:
        'In this Act "worker" (except in the phrases "shop worker" and "betting worker") means an individual who has entered into or works under (or, where the employment has ceased, worked under) –
        (a)   a contract of employment, or
        (b)   any other contract, whether express or implied
        and (if it is express) whether oral or in writing, whereby the individual undertakes to do or perform personally any work or services for another party to the contract whose status is not by virtue of the contract that of a client or customer of any profession or business undertaking carried out by the individual.'
2   Ibid, s 191(3) provides:
        'In this Act "Crown employment" means employment under or for the purpose of a government department or any officer or body exercising on behalf of the Crown functions conferred by a statutory provision.'
3   Ibid, s 194(6) provides:
        'In this section "relevant member of the House of Lords staff" means any person who is employed under a contract of employment with the Corporate Officer of the House of Lords.'
    Section 195(5) provides:
        'In this section "relevant member of the House of Commons staff" means any person –
        (a)   who was appointed by the House of Commons Commission or is employed in the refreshment department, or
        (b)   who is a member of the Speaker's personal staff.'
4   ERA 1999, s 13(1).
5   Section 13(2).
6   Ibid.

7   ERA 1999, s 13(3).
8   Ibid.

4.1.5   A worker may present a complaint to an employment tribunal that his or her employer has failed or threatened to fail to allow the worker to be accompanied or that his or her employer has refused or threatened to refuse to reconvene a hearing because the companion cannot come at the original time allocated.[1] A complaint must be presented within three months of the failure or threat with the tribunal having the normal discretion to extend that time.[2] If the tribunal finds the complaint well-founded, it shall order the employer to pay compensation to the worker not exceeding two weeks' pay.[3] One weeks' pay is calculated in accordance with Chapter 11 of Part XIV of the ERA 1996 and for the purposes of that Chapter the calculation date depends on the nature of the tribunal complaint. If the claim for a breach of s 10(2) or s 10(4) is part of a claim for unfair dismissal, the calculation date is the date on which the employer's notice was given or, if there was no notice, the effective date of termination of employment. In all other cases the calculation date is the date on which the hearing was or should have taken place.[4] The award is subject to the upper limit on one week's pay in s 227(1) of ERA 1996[5] and no compensation will be awarded for a breach of the right to be accompanied, if, in an unfair dismissal complaint, the tribunal makes a supplementary award of compensation under s 127A(2) of ERA 1996 where the employer provided a procedure for appealing against dismissal but prevented the employee from using it.[6] In other words, the employee cannot get double compensation for essentially the same breach.

1   ERA 1999, s 11(1).
2   Ibid, s 11(2).
3   Ibid, s 11(3).
4   Ibid, s 11(4).
5   Ibid, s 11(5).
6   Ibid, s 11(6).

Detriment and dismissal

4.1.6   A worker has the right not to be subjected to a detriment by any act or deliberate failure to act on the grounds that the worker exercised or sought to exercise his or her rights to be accompanied or that he or she accompanied or sought to accompany a worker at a disciplinary or grievance hearing whether the person who was accompanying the worker is employed by the same employer as the worker or not.[1] A worker has a right under s 48 of ERA 1996 to complain to an employment tribunal that he or she has been subjected to a detriment on these grounds[2] and a tribunal, if it finds the complaint well-founded, shall make a declaration to that effect and may make an award of compensation.[3] The amount of compensation shall be what is just and equitable in the circumstances having regard to the infringement to which the complaint relates and any loss attributable to the act or failure to act.[4] The tribunal can reduce any compensation on the basis of contributory conduct of the complainant.[5] This creates an anomaly in that the previous sections of ERA 1996[6] which give protection against being subjected to a detriment protect only employees, whereas protection under the new provisions is much wider in that it protects workers. This again appears to be giving effect to the intention of the Government to extend certain employment protection rights to anyone who works for someone else and not only to those employed under a legally defined contract of employment[7] as it has already done with the National Minimum Wage Act 1998 (NMWA 1998) and the Working Time Regulations 1998. It does, however, create the strange situation that, whereas some but not all of the new provisions protect workers,[8] previous employment protection which is still current protects a much more restricted group.

---

1   ERA 1999, s 12(1).
2   Ibid, s 12(2).
3   ERA 1996, s 49(1).
4   Ibid, s 49(2).
5   Ibid, s 49(5).
6   Ibid, s 44–47.
7   *Fairness at Work*, para 3.18.
8   See, for example, the provisions relating to detriment and dismissal in respect of recognition and derecognition which protect workers (**2.9** above). However, s 16 and Sch 5 to ERA 1999, inserting s 238A into ERA 1996 (dismissal for taking part in official industrial action), only applies to employees, despite the Schedule being entitled 'Unfair Dismissal of Striking Workers'.

4.1.7   A worker who is dismissed shall be regarded as unfairly dismissed if the reason or principal reason for dismissal was that the worker exercised or sought to exercise the right to be accompanied or that the worker accompanied or sought to accompany a worker at a disciplinary or grievance hearing.[1] Such a dismissal is automatically unfair and the normal qualifying period of employment[2] and upper age limit[3] do not apply to such dismissals.[4] Further, a worker is entitled to interim relief under s 128(1)(b) of ERA 1996[5] and any reference to employee in Chapter 11 of Part X of that Act (remedies for unfair dismissal) shall be taken as a reference to worker for the purposes of this section.[6] Any provision in an agreement purporting to restrict or exclude a worker's right to complain to a tribunal is void, subject to the exceptions in s 203 of ERA 1996 in respect of a properly written compromise agreement or conciliation by a conciliation officer.[7]

---

1   ERA 1999, s 12(3).
2   ERA 1996, s 108.
3   Ibid, s 109.
4   ERA 1999, s 12(4).

5   Ibid, s 12(5).
6   Ibid, s 12(6).
7   Ibid, s 14.

National security

4.1.8   Section 15 of ERA 1999 provides that the rights to be accompanied do not apply in relation to a person employed for the purposes of the Security Service, the Secret Intelligence Service or the Government Communications Headquarters. This was a late addition to the Act and has been brought in because of the sensitive information which may be revealed at such hearings. In introducing the new provision, Lord Simon stated that the intention behind the provision is to prevent a representative from outside these agencies gaining access to sensitive information and that all three agencies already have internal procedures which allow for an employee to be accompanied by a fellow worker, from within the relevant agency, at disciplinary and grievance hearings.[1] The difference, however, between giving a statutory right to such workers to be accompanied and internal procedures giving such a right, is that the statutory right can be enforced in an employment tribunal, whereas a right under an internal procedure cannot be enforced in a tribunal unless it is contractual. Given the new provisions introduced in Sch 8 to the Act in respect of tribunal hearings and national security (discussed in Chapter 6) it would have been possible to create a statutory right to be accompanied at disciplinary and grievance hearings by, in the case of employees of the three agencies, restricting the class of representative to a fellow worker employed by the agency, who may or may not be a union official. This would have given those employees employed by the three agencies a right which could be enforced, while national security could be protected if the provisions in Sch 8 applied. The Government, however, refused to make this amendment, preferring to allow the internal procedures to offer protection.

1   HL Deb, vol 603, col 1101, 8 July 1999 (Lord Simon).

4.2   UNFAIR DISMISSAL OF STRIKING WORKERS

Introduction

4.2.1   Employees who take most forms of industrial action are in breach of their contracts of employment. A strike is a fundamental breach on the part of the employee which would allow an employer to treat the breach as repudiatory and dismiss the employee. The original provisions of TULR(C)A 1992 gave limited protection against the common-law principles. First, by s 237 an employee has no right to complain of unfair dismissal if at the time of dismissal the employee is taking part in unofficial industrial action unless it is shown that the reason or principal reason for dismissal was one of those specified in ss 99(1)–(3), 100 or 103 of ERA 1996 (dismissal on the grounds of maternity or the activities of a health and safety or employee representative). This provision remains untouched by the amendments and there is still no protection where the action is unofficial. Unofficial action is action which has not been authorised or endorsed by the union, or action which was originally authorised or endorsed but the union has later repudiated that authorisation.[1] The original s 238 of TULR(C)A 1992 gave a right of complaint of unfair dismissal to an employee taking part in official industrial action if one or more of the relevant employees[2] was not dismissed or one of the relevant employees was offered re-engagement within three months of the complainant's dismissal and the complainant had not been offered re-engagement. In other words, an employee was protected only if there had been selective dismissals and the employer could avoid liability by re-engaging selectively three months and one day after the original dismissals.

---

1   TULR(C)A 1992, ss 20 and 21. By s 20(2) action shall be taken as authorised or endorsed by the union if it was authorised or endorsed by a person empowered by the rules to authorise or endorse the acts in question; by the principal executive committee, the president or the general secretary; or by any other committee of the union or any other official of the union (whether employed by it or not). By s 21(1), (2) and (3) an act is repudiated by the union if it is repudiated by the executive, president or general secretary and where written notice in the prescribed form is given to the committee or official who authorised the action, and to all members taking part in the action and their employer. Such repudiation will be ineffective if after the repudiation the executive, president or general secretary behave in a way which is inconsistent with the repudiation (s 21(5)).

2   'Relevant employee' was defined in s 238(3) of TULR(C)A 1992 as:
    '(a)   in relation to a lock out, employees who were directly interested in the dispute in contemplation or furtherance of which the lock out occurred, and
    (b)   in relation to a strike or other industrial action, those employees at the establishment of the employer at or from which the complainant works who at the date of his dismissal were taking part in the action'.
    For an interpretation of this provision see, for example, *H Campey & Sons Ltd v Bellwood* [1987] ICR 311, *Coates v Modern Methods and Materials Ltd* [1982] ICR 763 and *P & O Ferries (Dover) Ltd v Byrne* [1989] ICR 779. Both this section and s 238(2) (selective dismissals) are not repealed by ERA 1999 and thus will apply where the new protection discussed below does not.

4.2.2 The Employment Relations Act 1999, Sch 5, introduces s 238A into TULR(C)A 1992 which gives additional rights to employees to complain of unfair dismissal in specified circumstances. It has the effect that an employee who takes part in protected industrial action, where one of the following set of circumstances applies and who is dismissed, will be regarded as being unfairly dismissed if the reason or principal reason for the dismissal was that the employee was taking part in protected industrial action. The circumstances are:

–   if the dismissal takes place within a period of eight weeks beginning with the day on which the employee started to take protected industrial action, whether or not at the date of dismissal the employee is still engaged in such action;[1]

–   if the dismissal takes place after the period of eight weeks has elapsed, but the employee had ceased to take protected industrial action before the eight-week period ended;[2] or

– if the dismissal takes place after the eight-week period and the employee is continuing the protected industrial action, the dismissal will be unfair if the employer has not taken such procedural steps as would have been reasonable for the purposes of resolving the dispute to which the protected industrial action relates.[3]

In deciding whether the employer had taken reasonable procedural steps regard shall be had, in particular, to:

– whether procedures established by a collective agreement, or any other agreement, had been complied with by the employer or union;
– whether either party offered or agreed to negotiate or resume negotiations after the start of the protected action;
– whether the employer or union unreasonably refused after the start of the protected action a request for conciliation services to be used;
– whether the employer or union unreasonably refused, after the start of the protected action, a request that mediation services be used in relation to the procedures to be adopted for resolving the dispute.[4]

In looking at the factors above no regard is had to the merits of the dispute.[5] Protected industrial action is action which under s 219 of TULR(C)A 1992 the union has lawfully organised and which is therefore protected from liability in tort for inducement to break or interfere with contracts.[6]

---

1   TULR(C)A 1992, s 238A(3).
2   Ibid, s 238A(4).
3   Ibid, s 238A(5).
4   Ibid, s 238A(6).
5   Ibid, s 238A(7).
6   Ibid, s 238A(1). Section 219 provides that action is protected if it is not to enforce union membership (s 222), taken because of dismissal during unofficial industrial action (s 223), is not secondary action (s 224) and is not pressure to impose union recognition (s 225). In addition, the union must have complied with the complex balloting provisions in s 226 and have given the required notice to the employer under s 234A.

4.2.3 Section 238A also deals with union repudiation of the action and provides that if the union repudiate the action under s 21 so that the action becomes unofficial, if employees continue the action they lose their entitlement to claim unfair dismissal on the second working day following the repudiation. That is, if the union repudiates on a Wednesday, protection will be lost if the action continues on or after Friday.[1] Schedule 5 to ERA 1999 amends s 239 of TULR(C)A 1992 (supplementary provisions relating to unfair dismissal) to include the new dismissal rights in s 238A.[2] Furthermore, the normal qualifying period and age limit do not apply to dismissals under s 238A.[3] Employment tribunals also have the jurisdiction to hear complaints of unfair dismissal under s 238A while the protected industrial action is continuing, but may not make an order for re-instatement or re-engagement under s 113 until the conclusion of the dispute.[4] There is also a power to issue regulations under s 7 of the Employment Tribunals Act 1996 (ETA 1996) to require tribunals to adjourn and renew applications in specified cases[5] and under s 9 of ETA 1996 to require tribunals to conduct pre-hearing reviews in specified cases.[6] The explanatory notes state that it is envisaged that a pre-hearing review will be required in all s 238A, dismissals and tribunals will be required to adjourn proceedings where an employer or another is bringing proceedings in a court challenging the lawfulness of the industrial action.[7] Section 105 of ERA 1996 is similarly amended so that it is an unfair dismissal to select for redundancy on the basis of participation in protected industrial action.[8]

---

1   TULR(C)A 1992, s 238A(8).
2   ERA 1996, Sch 5, para 4(2) amending s 239(1) of TULR(C)A 1992.
3   Ibid, para 4(3) amending s 239(1).
4   Ibid, para 4(5) inserting s 239(4)(a).
5   Ibid, para 4(5) inserting s 239(4)(b).
6   Ibid, para 4(5) inserting s 239(4)(c).
7   House of Lords, Explanatory Note, Employment Relations Bill 1999, para 193 at http://www.parliament.the-stationery-office.co.uk.
8   ERA 1996, Sch 5, para 5.

4.3   COLLECTIVE AGREEMENTS: DETRIMENT AND DISMISSAL

4.3.1   In the Foreword to *Fairness at Work* the Prime Minister stated that one of the canons of fairness which was a matter of course elsewhere in Europe was rights against discrimination for making a free choice of being a trade union member. The implementation of this canon of fairness can be seen in various sections of ERA 1999 such as the change in the definition of detriment in relation to trade union membership, the prohibition of blacklists and protection from detriment and dismissal in connection with recognition or derecognition of a union. The Act also gives the Secretary of State the power to make regulations, subject to affirmative resolution procedure, to give protection to a worker who is subjected to a detriment or dismissal on the grounds that he or she refuses to enter into a contract which includes terms which differ from the terms of a collective agreement which applies to him or her.[1] The Act only uses the words detriment and dismissal without specifying that detriment means an act or a deliberate failure to act, although presumably, in line with the other amendments discussed earlier (at **2.9.1** and **4.1.6**), the regulations will make this specific. The Act does, however, specify that the payment of higher wages, rates of pay, bonuses or the provision of any other benefit having a monetary value to other workers employed by the employer shall not constitute a detriment to a worker not receiving the same, provided that there is no inhibition in the contract of the worker receiving the higher payments from being a member of a union and the higher payments are in accordance with the terms of a contract of employment and reasonably relate to the services provided by the worker under that contract.[2] This was a late amendment introduced in the House of Lords.[3] It was introduced with some controversy in that the Government in *Fairness at Work* stated: 'As under existing law, individual employees will continue to have the right, should they wish, to agree terms with their employer'[4] but also stated its intention to 'make it unlawful to discriminate by omission on the grounds of trade union membership, non-membership or activities'[5] having stated that the House of Lords in *Associated Newspapers v Wilson* and *Associated British Ports v Palmer*[6] had ruled that the old provisions allowed an employer to discriminate by omission on the grounds of trade union membership, non-membership or activities.[7] Given that in *Wilson* and *Palmer* the omission was a failure to pay a 4.5 per cent rise to those who refused to move from a collectively bargained contract to an individual one, *Fairness at Work* appeared to suggest that a worker should have the right to negotiate a higher rate of pay than that contained in a collective agreement as long as the price of that pay rise was not loss of trade union membership. The new provision is intended to implement this. It specifically applies only in the context of collective agreements and pay, and does not relate to other provisions in respect of detriment and trade union membership or activities contained in s 146 of TULR(C)A 1992.[8] The regulations may also make provision which applies only in specified cases, make different provision for different circumstances and make supplementary, incidental and transitional provision.[9] 'Collective agreement' under this section has the meaning given in s 178(1) of TULR(C)A 1992 and 'employer' and 'worker' have the same meaning as in s 296 of the same Act.[10]

1　　ERA 1999, s 17(1).
2　　Ibid, s 17(4).
3　　HL Deb, vol 602, col 354, 16 June 1999 (Baroness Miller).
4　　*Fairness at Work*, para 4.20.
5　　*Fairness at Work*, para 4.25.
6　　[1995] 2 AC 454.
7　　*Fairness at Work*, para 4.24.
8　　The original amendment did also relate to s 146 but this part was later removed. HL Deb, vol 604, col 1363, 26 July 1999 (Baroness Miller).
9　　ERA 1999, s 17(2).
10　Ibid, s 17(3).

4.4　AGREEMENT TO EXCLUDE DISMISSAL RIGHTS

Introduction

4.4.1　In *Fairness at Work* the Government stated that 850,000 people in the UK have contracts for a fixed term, of whom 160,000 have a contract for over two years.[1] Under the original legislation, employees on fixed-term contracts of one year or more could waive their rights to unfair dismissal,[2] except in the case of a shop or betting-shop worker where the reason for the dismissal was a refusal to work on Sundays.[3] Employees could also waive their rights to redundancy if the fixed-term contract was for two years or more.[4] The Government in the White Paper felt that while such waivers allow flexibility in that employers can take on employees for fixed-term projects without fear of claims for unfair dismissal or redundancy, some employers force employees to accept fixed-term contracts and waive employment rights for open-ended jobs.[5] The Government therefore proposed amendments which did not remove flexibility from genuine employers but which would deter unscrupulous employers. These are contained in s 18 of ERA 1999.

---

1   *Fairness at Work*, para 3.11.
2   ERA 1996, s 197(1). For an interpretation of 'fixed-term contract' see, for example, *Dixon v BBC* [1979] QB 546. On renewal of fixed-term contracts, see *Mulrine v University of Ulster* [1993] IRLR 545 and *BBC v Kelly-Phillips* [1998] ICR 587.
3   ERA 1996, s 197(2).
4   Ibid, s 197(3).
5   *Fairness at Work*, para 3.11.
6   Ibid, para 3.13.

4.4.2 Section 18(1) of ERA 1999 repeals s197(1) and (2) of ERA 1996 so removing the ability of anyone on a fixed-term contract to waive rights to unfair dismissal. The section further amends the original ss 44(4), 46(2), 47(2), 47A(2) and 47B(2) of ERA 1996. These sections cover the right not to suffer a detriment in certain cases[1] and originally allowed an employee who had waived rights to unfair dismissal to claim that he or she had suffered a detriment when dismissed, although providing that in all other cases detriment did not include dismissal. These special provisions are no longer necessary now any such waiver is void. Similar amendments to provisions on working time in s 45A of ERA 1996, s 23(4)(a) of NMWA 1998 and Sch 3, para 1 to the Tax Credits Act 1999 are also made as, again, they are now superfluous.[2]

---

1   ERA 1999, s 18(2). The relevant circumstances where there is a right not to suffer a detriment are an employee's actions in relation to health and safety cases (s 44); as a trustee of an occupational pension scheme (s 46); as an employee representative (s 47); exercising the right to take time off for study or training (s 47A) or making a protected disclosure under the Public Interest Disclosure Act 1998 (s 47B).
2   ERA 1999, s 18(3), (4) and (5).

4.5 PART-TIME WORK

Introduction

4.5.1 Section 19 requires the Secretary of State to issue regulations to ensure that part-time workers are treated no less favourably than full-time workers. These regulations will implement the Directive on Part-Time Work[1] which in turn implements a Framework Agreement between the European social partners. The Directive and Framework Agreement aim to end discrimination against part-time workers and improve the quality of part-time work. The terms of the Agreement on Social Policy, under which the Framework Agreement and the Directive were brought forward, state that Directives which implement

Framework Agreements cannot cover pay. The Government, however, feels that pay should be covered and as the powers in the European Communities Act 1972 do not allow regulations to go beyond the scope of a Directive, a power is specifically needed in ERA 1999 to implement the Government's proposals.[2] The regulations will be subject to the affirmative resolution procedure.[3]

---

1   Council Directive 97/81/EC.
2   House of Lords, Explanatory Note, the Employment Relations Bill 1999, paras 199 and 200, http://www.parliament.the-stationery-office.co.uk.
3   ERA 1999, s 42.

4.5.2   The section states the issues which may be covered by the regulations. They may give a statutory definition of what is full- and part-time work.[1] This will be a default provision because the section also allows for specified agreements to have effect in place of the regulations and such agreements may themselves define part-time work.[2] The regulations may also specify circumstances which are defined as less favourable treatment[3] and exclude certain classes of worker from the definition.[4] Jurisdiction will be given to employment tribunals with an appeal to the Employment Appeal Tribunal.[5] The regulations may also create criminal offences in relation to specified acts or omissions by employers, employers' organisations, trade unions and professional bodies and extend liability to a person who aids the commission of an offence.[6] Such offences shall be triable summarily only and cannot be punishable by imprisonment or a fine in excess of level 5 on the standard scale.[7] Further, the regulations can exclude certain obligations or offences in particular circumstances and make different provision for different cases or circumstances.[8] The regulations will also provide for information and evidence to be produced to aid a complainant in the claim[9] and there is a general power to make any provision necessary to implement the Part-Time Work Directive or the Framework Agreement.[10]

---

1   ERA 1999, s 19(2)(a) and (b).
2   Ibid, s 19(3)(g).
3   Ibid, s 19(2)(c).
4   Ibid, s 19(2)(d).
5   Ibid, s 19(3)(a).
6   Ibid, s 19(3)(b) and (c). See, for example, s 42(4) of SDA 1975 which makes it a criminal offence to knowingly or recklessly make a false or misleading statement.
7   Ibid, s 19(5).
8   Ibid, s 19(3)(d) and (i).
9   Ibid, s 19(3)(e). The questionnaire procedure under s 56 of DDA 1995 is an example.
10   Ibid, s 19(4).

4.5.3   Section 20 provides for the Secretary of State to issue Codes of Practice to give guidance for the purposes of eliminating discrimination against part-time workers in employment, facilitating the development of opportunities for part-time work, facilitating flexible working time and to deal with any other matter within the framework agreement.[1] The section specifically states that breach of the Code (as is the case with other Codes of Practice) will not give rise to legal proceedings but is admissible in evidence before a tribunal and shall be taken into account in proceedings before the tribunal.[2] Section 21 creates a legal duty on the Secretary of State to consult before publishing the Code or any revisions and the Code and revisions must be laid before both Houses of Parliament which must approve the Code before its issue.[3]

---

1   ERA 1999, s 20(1).
2   Ibid, s 20(3) and (4).
3   Ibid, s 21(1), (2) and (3).

4.6   EXEMPTION FROM THE NATIONAL MINIMUM WAGE

4.6.1   Section 22 seeks to exclude residential members who live in intentional religious and other communities, and who work for the community, from the minimum wage by inserting s 44A into NMWA 1998. The new s 44A provides that:

–   a community is a charity or established by a charity;
–   a purpose of the community is to practise or advance a belief of a religious or similar, nature; and
–   all or some of a community's members live together for that purpose.[1] The section does not apply to independent schools or to a community which provides a course of further or higher education.[2] The provision was inserted on the recommendation of the Low Pay Commission and is intended to exempt some 1,000 members of communities who 'share living accommodation and tasks with the purpose of advancing a common religious or spiritual aim'[3] such as the Ioana Community and the Society of Mary and Martha. There were concerns expressed in the Commons debate that the provision would exempt workers for such communities and would create a loophole because of the phrase 'a belief of a religious or similar nature'.[4] However, on the *ejusdem generis* rule 'or similar nature' will be constrained by 'religious' and the exemption will only apply to members of the community who reside there. Even workers who live in the community should not be covered by the provision if they do not share the views of that community, although it remains to be seen if this is how the provision is interpreted.

---

1   NMWA 1998, s 44A(2).
2   Ibid, s 44A(3).
3   HL Deb, vol 603, col 1114, 8 July 1999 (Lord Sainsbury).

4   HC Deb, vol 335, col 1274–1290, 21 July 1999.

4.7   POWER TO CONFER RIGHTS ON INDIVIDUALS

Introduction

4.7.1   Employment protection rights have been developed piecemeal over a number of years. It has already been noted that, whilst more recent legislation such as NMWA 1998 applies to workers, earlier legislation restricts employment protection rights to employees, that is persons who work under contracts of employment. This obviously creates anomalies as well as leading to litigation to establish whether a person is an employee within the legal definition.[1]

1   See, for example, *Nethermere (St Neots) Ltd v Taverna and Another* [1984] IRLR 240 on the position of home workers, *O'Kelly v Trust House Forte plc* [1983] IRLR 369 on the position of casual workers and *McMeechan v Secretary of State for Employment* [1995] ICR 365 on the position of agency workers.

4.7.2   The Government in *Fairness at Work* stated that it intended to consult on the idea of extending the coverage of some or all of the existing employment protection rights to workers rather than just employees.[1] Section 23 gives the Secretary of State the power, by order subject to affirmative resolution,[2] to extend employment rights under TULR(C)A 1992, ERA 1996 and ERA 1999 and any instrument made under s 2(2) of the European Communities Act 1972 to all workers, ensuring that only the genuinely self-employed do not have protection.

1   *Fairness at Work*, para 3.18.
2   ERA 1999, s 42.

Chapter 5

CAC, ACAS, COMMISSIONERS AND THE CERTIFICATION OFFICER

5.1 CENTRAL ARBITRATION COMMITTEE

Introduction

5.1.1 The CAC was established by the Employment Protection Act 1975 (EPA 1975).[1] Until the passing of ERA 1999, its functions were to determine statutory claims from trade unions relating to the disclosure of information for collective bargaining purposes[2] and to provide arbitration in trade disputes, where both parties consent, on a reference from ACAS.[3] In the three years 1995–97, the CAC received 70 applications under its disclosure of information jurisdiction but no requests to arbitrate in a trade dispute.[4] Section 1 of ERA 1999 inserts Sch A1 into TULR(C)A 1992 which, inter alia, confers new jurisdiction on the CAC in respect of statutory trade union recognition and derecognition.

---

1   Now s 259 of TULR(C)A 1992.
2   The rights to information for collective bargaining purposes are in ss 181–5 of TULR(C)A 1992.
3   Ibid, s 212(1).
4   House of Lords, Explanatory Note, Employment Relations Bill 1999, para 216 at http://www.parliament.the-stationery-office.co.uk.

CAC members

5.1.2 The appointment of CAC members is covered by s 260 of TULR(C)A 1992. Section 24 of ERA 1999 amends s 260(1)–(3). Previously all members were appointed by the Secretary of State after nomination by ACAS, apart from the chairman. The amended section gives power of appointment to the Secretary of State after consultation with ACAS and any other relevant persons, this includes the chairman and deputy chairmen.[1] Further, the previous legislation provided that members should be appointed from persons nominated by ACAS as experienced in industrial relations and there was a requirement that some should have experience as representatives of employers and workers. The ERA 1999 amendment strengthens this and provides that the Secretary of State can appoint only persons experienced in industrial relations and still includes the requirement that some must have experience as employer or worker representatives.[2]

---

1   TULR(C)A 1992, s 260(1), (2) and (3A) as amended.
2   Ibid, s 260(3) as amended.

CAC proceedings

5.1.3 The functions of the CAC are contained in s 263 of TULR(C)A 1992. The new functions in relation to trade union recognition and derecognition are incorporated by a new s 263(7) and a new s 263A.[1] The additional provisions deal only with the new CAC functions and do not affect its previous functions which it still retains. When the CAC is discharging its functions under Sch A1, the chairman of the Committee shall establish a panel or panels each consisting of three persons – the chairman or a deputy chairman who will act as chair, a member who is experienced as an employer representative and a member who is experienced as a worker representative.[2] A panel may sit in private at the discretion of its chair where it appears expedient to do so.[3] If the panel cannot reach a unanimous decision but reaches a majority decision, the majority decision is the decision of the panel.[4] Where there is no majority decision, the chairman shall decide the question.[5] Apart from this, the panel shall determine its own procedure.[6]

---

1   Inserted by s 25 of ERA 1999.
2   TULR(C)A 1992, s 263A(1) and (2).
3   Ibid, s 263A(4).
4   Ibid, s 263A(5).
5   Ibid, s 263A(6).
6   Ibid, s 263A(7).

5.2   ACAS

Introduction

5.2.1 The Advisory, Conciliation and Arbitration Service (ACAS) came into existence in 1974 and was placed on a statutory footing by EPA 1975. It consists of a Council which comprises a chairman and up to nine members appointed by the Secretary of State. Three are appointed after consultation with employers' organisations, three after consultation with workers' organisations and three are independent members. ACAS has a variety of functions. It may provide advice, on request or by its own volition, to employers or workers or their organisations on any matter concerned with, or likely to affect, industrial relations.[1] It can conciliate where a trade dispute exists or is apprehended, again on its own volition or at the request of any party,[2] and conciliates when a claim is presented by an individual to an employment tribunal.[3] It can also, with the consent of the parties, refer a trade dispute to arbitration, either to an arbitrator or to the CAC where the parties have exhausted all agreed procedures unless there is a special reason why those procedures should not be followed.[4] In addition, ACAS may inquire into industrial relations generally, or any particular industry or undertaking[5] and ACAS is one of the bodies empowered to issue Codes of Practice.[6]

1   TULR(C)A 1992, s 213.
2   Ibid, s 210.
3   Ibid, s 211.
4   Ibid, s 212.
5   Ibid, s 214.
6   Ibid, s 199. There are three ACAS Codes currently in force covering disciplinary powers and procedures, disclosure of information for collective bargaining purposes and time off for trade union duties and activities.

General duty

5.2.2   The general duty of ACAS is found in s 209 of TULR(C)A 1992. When first established, ACAS was given the general duty to promote 'the improvement of industrial relations, and in particular the duty of encouraging the extension of collective bargaining and the development and, where necessary, reform of collective bargaining machinery'. This general duty was amended by the Trade Union Reform and Employment Rights Act 1993 (TURERA 1993) which removed all references to collective bargaining and created the duty to 'promote the improvement of industrial relations in particular by exercising its functions in relation to the settlement of trade disputes'. Section 209 is now in its third iteration. ERA 1999 amends s 209 so that the general duty of ACAS is now simply 'to promote the improvement of industrial relations'.[1] Thus, the duty is much wider in that legislation no longer gives a specific focus on how this duty is to be performed. Presumably, however, given the new functions of the CAC in respect of recognition and in particular the power to specify a method of collective bargaining, this old function of ACAS is unlikely to be exercised to the same extent as it was under its original powers in 1975.

1   Amended by s 26 of ERA 1999.

5.3   ABOLITION OF COMMISSIONERS

Introduction

5.3.1   The Employment Act 1988 and TURERA 1993 created two new commissioners – the Commissioner for the Rights of Trade Union Members (CRTUM)[1] and the Commissioner for Protection Against Unlawful Industrial Action (CPAUIA).[2] The nature of the former post is to assist trade union members who wish to take certain legal action against their union. Such action includes a failure to comply with balloting provisions in respect of industrial action, election of officers, or the use of the political fund, action in relation to the use of funds or property and actions on disciplinary or expulsion proceedings taken against a member.[3] The CPAUIA had the power to assist any party who wished to take proceedings on the basis that the supply of goods or services to that party as an individual had been prevented or delayed by unlawful industrial action or that the quality of the goods or services had been affected.[4] Since the creation of the CRTUM, an average ten applications per year have been assisted; the CPAUIA has had one application to date.[5]

---

1   TULR(C)A 1992, original s 266.
2   Ibid.
3   Ibid, original s 109.
4   Ibid, original s 235B.
5   House of Lords, Explanatory Note, the Employment Relations Bill 1999, para 225 at
     http://www.parliament.the-stationery-office.co.uk.

5.3.2   ERA 1999 abolishes these two posts[1] by repealing ss 266–271 and ss 235B and 235C of TULR(C)A 1992.[2] In some respects, the essence of the functions of the CRTUM pass to the Certification Officer as described below. The functions of the CPAUIA cease to exist although ERA 1999 does not repeal s 235A of TULR(C)A 1992. In other words, an individual still has a right to complain to the High Court that unlawful industrial action has prevented or delayed the supply of goods or services to him or her or reduced the quality of goods or services supplied. The abolition of the CPAUIA means that the individual will have to meet the legal costs of such action.

---

1   ERA 1999, s 28(1).
2   Ibid, s 28(2) of ERA 1999.

5.4   THE CERTIFICATION OFFICER

Introduction

5.4.1   The Certification Officer (CO) is a post originally created by EPA 1975.[1] The original functions in respect of trade unions included:

–   maintaining lists of trade unions ensuring they comply with statutory requirements concerning membership and accounting records;
–   auditing accounts;
–   annual returns;
–   financial affairs;
–   political funds; and
–   procedures for amalgamations and transfers of engagements.[2]

In addition the CO determines whether unions meet the statutory test of independence and issues certificates of independence[3] and deals with complaints from union members concerning breaches by unions of their statutory duties in relation to the election of senior officials.[4] The amendments discussed below give the CO similar powers to those held by the court under the original 1992 provisions in respect of failures by the union to comply with statutory requirements. These powers give an applicant an alternative route to the court and not an additional route.

---

1   Now s 254 of TULR(C)A 1992.
2   TULR(C)A 1992, ss 25, 26, 45C and 80.
3   Ibid, s 8.
4   Ibid, s 55.

5.4.2   Section 29 of ERA 1999 gives effect to Sch 6 which amends the statutory powers of the CO set out in TULR(C)A 1992. The effect of the amendments is to widen the role of the post to enable trade union members to make complaints to the CO concerning breaches of trade union provisions in the Act or trade union rules. In other words, it establishes the CO as an alternative dispute resolution to the court. This is not passing the functions of the old post of CRTUM over to the CO as that post could only offer assistance where trade union members wished to take action against the union in specified cases. The new functions of the CO include order-making powers (previously there was only a power to issue declarations) and extending the power to issue declarations and make orders where previously no such power existed.

Register of members

5.4.3   By s 24 of TULR(C)A 1992, unions are under a requirement to compile and maintain a register of the names and addresses of their members. Section 24A requires unions to impose a duty of confidentiality on scrutineers and independent persons not to reveal the names and addresses of members except in specified circumstances.[1] Sections 25 and 26 provide a remedy for an individual through the courts or the CO for breaches of the statutory provisions. Paragraphs 2 and 3 of Sch 6 to ERA 1999 repeal the provisions in ss 24 and 24A which allow the complainant to apply to the court after making an application in respect of the same breach or breaches to the CO. The amendment removes the sentence 'The making of an application to the Certification Officer does not prevent the applicant, or any other person, from making an application to the court in respect of the same matter'.[2] This could suggest that, if an applicant has first made an application to the court, he or she is not prevented from also making an application to the CO. However, this is not the interpretation which will be placed on these sections. This is for two reasons. First, the removal of the above sentence now leaves both sections stating that: 'The remedy for failure to comply with the requirements of this section is by way of application under section 25 (to the Certification Officer) *or* section 26 (to the court)' (italics provided). This would suggest that it is an either/or situation. Second, a new s 25(11)(a) provides that, if a person applies to the court under s 26 in respect of a failure, that person may not apply under s 25 in respect of the same failure.[3]

---

1   By s 24A(4) of TULR(C)A 1992 disclosure of a member's name and address is permitted when:
     (a)   the member consents;

(b) it is requested by the CO for the purpose of the discharge of any of his functions or of the functions of an inspector appointed by him;

(c) it is required by the scrutineer or independent person for the discharge of their functions;

(d) it is required for the purposes of the investigation of crime or of criminal proceedings.

2 Ibid, ss 24(6) and 24A(6).
3 Inserted by Sch 6, para 4(4) to ERA 1999.

5.4.4 The Schedule makes considerable amendments to s 25. It requires the CO in all cases to give an opportunity to both sides to be heard.[1] The previous provision allowed both sides to be heard if the CO considered it appropriate to do so. The amendment gives the CO no discretion. The CO must make an enforcement order (unless the CO considers it inappropriate to do so) requiring the union to remedy a declared failure to comply with the law on membership records within a specified period and abstain from acts which could lead to a recurrence of the breach in the future.[2] Any member of the union who was a member at the time of the declared failure has the right to apply to the court to enforce the order from the CO.[3] Any declaration or enforcement order from the CO has the effect of a court order or declaration[4] and if another person has taken action in the court for the same failure the CO on the application shall have due regard to any declaration, order, observations or reasons made or given by the court regarding that failure which are brought to the attention of the CO.[5] The obvious limit on this is that the burden is on the party who wishes to rely on the court decision to ensure it is brought to the attention of the CO.

---

1 Amended by Sch 6, para 4(2) ERA 1999.
2 Ibid, para 4(3) inserting s 25(5)A into TULR(C)A 1992.
3 Ibid inserting s 25(5)B.
4 Ibid, para 4(4) inserting s 25(9) and (10).
5 Ibid, inserting s 25(11)(b).

5.4.5 Section 26 is similarly amended to prevent parallel proceedings where an application has been made to the CO[1] and requiring the court, on an application by another person in respect of the same failure, to have due regard to any declaration, order, observations or reasons given by the CO regarding that failure and brought to the court's notice.[2] The comments noted above in **5.4.4** also apply to this amendment.

---

1 ERA 1999, para 5(3) inserting s 26(8)(a) into TULR(C)A 1992.
2 Ibid, inserting s 26(8)(b).

Accounting records

5.4.6 Schedule 6, para 6 to ERA 1999 amends s 31 of TULR(C)A 1992, which gives a remedy to a union member if the union fails to give the member access to the union's accounting records, as required by s 30.[1] Whereas the original s 31 only gave a right of complaint to the court, the amended section gives an alternative right to apply to the CO.[2] The CO has the power to make any enquiries the CO thinks fit and must give the applicant and the union the opportunity to be heard.[3] If the CO finds the complaint well-founded, the CO may make an order in the same terms as the court, that is, an order allowing the applicant to inspect the records, allowing the applicant to be accompanied by an accountant and allowing the applicant to take copies or extracts of the record.[4] The CO must determine any claim within six months of an application being made as far as reasonably practicable.[5] The CO may request any information be supplied and specify a time by which the information should be supplied. The CO may, however, determine the complaint where the information has not been supplied by the specified date if the CO feels that it is appropriate to do so.[6] Any order made by the CO is enforceable as if it were a court order.[7] Further amendments prevent parallel applications so that the applicant may apply to the court or the CO but not both.[8]

---

1   By s 30 of TULR(C)A 1992, a member and any accountant accompanying the member, have a right to inspect the accounting records and take copies or extracts within 28 days of making a request.

2   ERA 1999, Sch 6, para 6(2) amending s 31(1) of TULR(C)A 1992.

3   Ibid, para 6(4) inserting subsection 2A into s 31.

4   Ibid, inserting subsection 2B into s 31.

5   Ibid, inserting subsection 2C into s 31.

6   Ibid, para 6(6) inserting a new s 31(4).

7   Ibid, inserting a new s 31(5).

8   Ibid, inserting a new s 31(6) and (7).

Offenders

5.4.7 Schedule 6, para 7 amends s 45C of TULR(C)A 1992 which provides a remedy for a union member where the union has failed to comply with the duty under s 45B to ensure that certain disqualified individuals do not hold senior positions in the union.[1] Under the original provisions, the CO could issue declarations but could not issue orders. Section 45C is amended in a similar way to s 31 above. The CO can make enquiries, must allow both sides the opportunity to be heard and can request information within a specified time but make a determination without that information if it is not supplied in that time.[2] The CO may make an order requiring the union to take steps to rectify the failure within a specified time.[3] Any declaration or order made by the CO is enforceable as if it were a court order[4] and parallel applications are prevented[5] although, where there has been an application in respect of the same failure to the court, the CO must have regard to any declaration, order, observations or reasons given by the court which are brought to the CO's attention and vice versa in respect of an application to the court where the CO has heard an application by another applicant in respect of the same failure.[6] An appeal lies to the Employment Appeal Tribunal on a point of law in respect of any of the new powers of the CO under ss 25, 31 or 45C.[7]

---

1   By s 45(1) of TULR(C)A 1992, failing to keep accounting records, failure to allow such records to be inspected, failure to allow a member to inspect the accounts, failure to submit an annual return and failure to keep a separate fund for members' superannuation are all criminal offences. Section 45A lists the penalties and prosecution time-limits for such offences and s 45B allows for the disqualification of offenders from union office (that is a member of the executive, the president or the general secretary) for a period of up to ten years.

2   ERA 1999, Sch 6, para 7(2), (3) and (7) amending s 45C(2) and inserting a new s 45C(7) of TULR(C)A 1992.

3   Ibid, para 7(5) inserting a new s 45C(5A).

4   Ibid, para 7(7) inserting a new s 45C(8) and (9).

5   Ibid, para 7(5) inserting a new s 45C(5B)(a) and s 45C(5C)(a).

6   Ibid inserting a new s 45C(5B)(b) and s 45C(5C)(b).

7   Ibid, para 8 inserting a new s 45D.

Elections

5.4.8   Paragraphs 9–12 of Sch 6 further amend the powers of the CO in respect of complaints of breaches by the union of the law relating to trade union elections. Again, under the original legislation, the CO could only issue declarations. As with the previous amendments, the Schedule amends the existing legislation to prevent parallel applications in the court[1] and requiring the CO to hear both parties to the complaint.[2] In line with the other amendments to the CO's powers where there has been an application by another person in respect of the same breach heard in the court, the CO must have regard to any declaration, order, observations or reasons given by the court and brought to the CO's attention and vice versa.[3] Where the CO finds the complaint well-founded and makes a declaration the CO must also make an enforcement order unless the CO considers it inappropriate to do so.[4] The order can require the union, within a stated time, to secure the holding of the election in accordance with the order, take the specified steps in the order to remedy the failure, or abstain from any specified acts to secure that the failure does not occur in the future.[5] The CO may also order the union to hold a fresh election, which complies with the provisions of the legislation and any other provisions laid out in the order.[6] Where an enforcement order is made, any member of the union who was a member at the time the order was made or anyone who was a candidate in the election can apply to the court to force the union to comply with the order.[7] An appeal lies to the Employment Appeal Tribunal on a point of law against the decision of the CO.[8]

---

1   ERA 1999, para 9 amending s 54 of TULR(C)A 1992.

2   Ibid, para 10(1) amending s 55(2)(b).

3   Ibid, para 10(4) inserting a new s 55(10)(b) and para 11 inserting a new s 56(8)(b).

4   Ibid, para 10(3) inserting a new s 55(5A).

5   Ibid.

6   Ibid, para 10(3) inserting a new s 55(5B).

7   Ibid, para 10(3) inserting a new s 55(5C).
8   Ibid, para 12 inserting a new s 56A.

Application of funds for political objects

5.4.9 A new s 72A in TULR(C)A 1992 allows a member of a union to apply for a declaration from the CO that the union has applied its funds in breach of s 71.[1] The CO shall make any enquiries the CO sees fit, shall give the applicant and the union the right to be heard, shall determine the application, as far as reasonably practicable, within six months, shall give written reasons for making or refusing the declaration and may make written observations on any matter arising from or connected with the proceedings.[2] If the CO makes a declaration the CO must specify the provisions of s 71 which have been breached and the amount of funds applied in the breach and if the CO is satisfied that the union has taken or agreed to take steps to remedy the breach or ensure it does not recur, the CO must specify those steps in the declaration.[3] If the CO makes a declaration the CO may make any order necessary for remedying the breach.[4] As with other amended provisions, if the CO requests information in connection with enquiries, to be furnished by a specified date, the CO can proceed with the determination of the application notwithstanding that the information has not been given, unless the CO feels that it is inappropriate to do so.[5] Any member of the union who was a member when the order was made can apply to the court for enforcement of the order.[6] As before, a declaration by the CO may be relied on as if it were a declaration of the court and an order may be enforced in the same way as an order of the court.[7] Again, parallel applications are prevented.[8]

1   ERA 1999, Sch 6, para 13. TULR(C)A 1992, s 71 allows the funds of a trade union to be
      used for the furtherance of political objects as long as there is in force a political
      resolution approving the furtherance of those objects and there are rules in force
      allowing the payment out of a separate fund to further those objects and allow the
      exemption of any member who objects to contributing to the fund.
2   Paragraph 13 inserting a new s 72A(2) of TULR(C)A 1992.
3   Ibid, para 13 inserting a new s 72A(3) and (4).
4   Ibid, para 13 inserting a new s 72A(5).
5   Ibid, para 13 inserting a new s 72A(6).
6   Ibid, para 13 inserting a new s 72A(8).
7   Ibid, para 13 inserting a new s 72A(7) and (9).
8   Ibid, para 13 inserting a new s 72A(10) and (11).

Political ballot rules

5.4.10   Schedule 6, paras 14 and 15 extend the CO's powers under ss 79 and 80 of TULR(C)A 1992 which gives the CO powers when hearing complaints about breaches of the statutory requirements, by the union, in respect of political fund ballots. By s 74, a ballot on a political resolution must be held by the union in accordance with its rules, and approved by the CO. Once a fund has been established, a ballot must be held every ten years to retain the fund and the approval of the CO must be sought for each ballot.[1] Under the original legislation, the CO could make or refuse declarations for alleged failures to comply with the approved rules.

---

1   TULR(C)A 1992, s 74(2).

5.4.11   Section 79 of TULR(C)A 1992 is amended so that parallel applications to the court and the CO are precluded.[1] In respect of the further powers, again the powers of the CO replicate the original powers of the court to a large extent. Where there is a complaint, the CO must hear both sides.[2] If the CO makes a declaration, the CO must also, unless the CO feels that it is inappropriate to do so, make an enforcement order requiring the union, within a time period, to secure the holding of a ballot in accordance with the order, to take steps specified in the order to remedy the failure or to abstain from acts to secure a failure will not recur.[3] The CO may also order the union to conduct a fresh ballot, complying with the union's political ballot rules and any other provisions the CO requires.[4] Where such an order has been made, any union member who was a member at the time of the order is entitled to enforce the order.[5] Again, any declaration or order is enforceable as if made by the court[6] and if another person has applied in respect of the same failure to the court, the CO must have regard to any declaration, order, observations or reasons given by the court and brought to the CO's attention and vice versa.[7]

---

1   ERA 1999, Sch 6, para 14.
2   Ibid, para 15(2) amending s 80(2)(b) of TULR(C)A 1992.
3   Ibid, para 15(3) inserting a new s 80(5A).
4   Ibid, para 15(3) inserting a new s 80(5B).
5   Ibid, para 15(3) inserting a new s 80(5C).
6   Ibid, para 15(4) inserting a new s 80(8) and (9).
7   Ibid, para 15(4) inserting a new s 80(10) and para 16 inserting a new s 81(8).

Political fund

5.4.12   Section 82 of TULR(C)A 1992 gives a union member the right to complain to the CO about breaches of statute in relation to the political fund maintained by the union. ERA 1999 has strengthened these powers by enabling the CO to make such enquiries as the CO sees fit[1] and enabling the CO to seek information from interested parties within a specified time period.[2] The CO may still make a determination notwithstanding that the information was not given by the specified date.[3]

---

1   ERA 1999, Sch 6, para 17(2) inserting a new s 82(2A) of TULR(C)A 1992.
2   Ibid, para 17(3) inserting a new s 82(3A).
3   Ibid.

Amalgamations or transfer of engagements

5.4.13   ERA 1999 again strengthens the powers of the CO in this area. The statutory requirements are in ss 99–103 of TULR(C)A 1992. The powers of the

CO in s 103 are enhanced by giving the CO the power to make enquiries and request information, although, again, the CO can make a determination if the information is not supplied by the specified time.[1] Further, any declaration or order made by the CO has the same effect as if made by the court[2] and a union member who was a member at the time the order was made is entitled to enforce obedience to the order.[3]

---

1   ERA 1999, Sch 6, para 18(2) inserting a new s 103(2A) and para 18(3) inserting a new s 103(6) of TULR(C)A 1992.
2   Ibid, para 18(3) inserting a new s 103(7) and (9).
3   Ibid, para 18(3) inserting a new s 103(8).

5.5   BREACH OF UNION RULES

Introduction

5.5.1   The original legislation gave trade union members the right to complain to the court about breaches of the rules of the union; ERA 1999 adds to these rights by providing an alternative right of complaint to the CO. It does this by adding a new Chapter VIIA into TULR(C)A 1992.[1]

---

1   By Sch 6, para 19 to ERA 1999.

5.5.2   The new Chapter VIIA comprises three new sections. By s 108A(1) of TULR(C)A 1992, a person who claims that there has been a breach or a threatened breach of the rules of the union in respect of certain matters may apply to the CO for a declaration. Rules of the union include the rules of any branch or section of the union.[1] The matters are:[2]

–   the appointment or election of a person to, or removal of a person from, office;
–   disciplinary proceedings by the union (including expulsion);
–   balloting of members on an issue other than industrial action;[3]
–   the constitution or proceedings of any executive committee or of any decision-making meeting;[4]
–   any other such matters specified in an order made by the Secretary of State.[5]

The applicant must have been a member of the union at the time of the alleged breaches[6] and no application can be made in respect of the dismissal of an employee of the union or disciplinary proceedings against an employee of the union.[7] There is an additional prohibition against parallel applications in the sense that an applicant who is entitled to apply under s 80 (failure to comply with political ballot rules) cannot apply under s 108A.[8] An application must be made within six months of the date of the alleged breach, unless an internal complaints procedure is invoked, in which case the application must be made to the CO within six months after consideration of the complaint under the procedure ended or 12 months after the procedure was invoked, whichever is the sooner.[9] These procedures are an alternative to the original right to apply to the court and thus the Act prevents parallel applications.[10]

---

1   TULR(C)A 1992, s 108A(8).
2   Ibid, s 108A(2).
3   Defined in s 108A(9) as a strike or other industrial action by persons employed under contracts of employment.
4   Defined in s 108A(10), (11) and (12).
5   By s 108A(13), such an order must be made by the affirmative resolution procedure.
6   Ibid, s 108A(3).
7   Ibid, s 108A(5).
8   Ibid, s 108A(4).
9   Ibid, s 108A(6) and (7).
10   Ibid, s 108A(14) and (15).

5.5.3 The CO may refuse an application unless satisfied that the applicant has taken all reasonable steps to resolve the claim through the internal complaints procedure of the union.[1] If the CO hears the complaint, the CO must give the applicant and the union an opportunity to be heard, ensure that as far as reasonably practicable the CO determines the case within six months and the CO must give reasons for the decision in writing.[2] The CO may also make such enquiries as the CO sees fit and request interested parties to supply information within a specified time, although the CO can determine the complaint if that information is not supplied within the time period.[3] The CO can issue an enforcement order requiring the union to take steps to remedy the breach or withdraw the threat of a breach or abstain from acts with a view to preventing a recurrence of the breach.[4] The CO may place a time-limit on any such requirement.[5] Any declaration or order has the effect as if made by the court[6] and any union member may enforce the order if a member when it was made.[7] The Secretary of State may add to the matters in respect of which an application may be made to the CO.[8] There is an appeal to the Employment Appeal Tribunal on a point of law in respect of a decision made by the CO under Chapter VIIA.[9]

---

1   TULR(C)A 1992, s 108B(1).
2   Ibid, s 108B(2).
3   Ibid and s 108B(5).
4   Ibid, s 108B(3).
5   Ibid, s 108B(4).
6   Ibid, s 108B(6) and (8).
7   Ibid, s 108B(7).
8   Ibid, s 108B(9).
9   Ibid, s 108C.

Employers' associations

5.5.4 Schedule 6, paras 20 and 21 cover employers' associations. The paragraphs amend ss 132 and 133 of TULR(C)A 1992 in order to leave unchanged the original arrangements whereby the CO hears complaints about breaches of statute in respect of the use of funds for political purposes and employers' association amalgamations. These amendments are necessary because the original provisions cross-referred to the provisions on trade unions.

Procedure before the Certification Officer

5.5.5   The procedure that the CO must follow is in s 256 of TULR(C)A 1992. This is now amended so that the CO must normally disclose the name of the applicant unless there are good reasons for not doing so.[1] This means that the union will know the identity of the applicant whether the application is made to the court or the CO. The CO may also refuse to entertain an application made by a vexatious litigant.[2] A vexatious applicant is defined as a person who is the subject of:

–   an order under s 33(1) of the Employment Tribunals Act 1996 which is in force;
–   a civil proceedings order or an all proceedings order which is made under s 42(1) of the Supreme Court Act 1981 which is in force;
–   an order which is made under s 1 of the Vexatious Actions (Scotland) Act 1898; or
–   an order which is made under s 32 of the Judicature (Northern Ireland) Act 1978.[3]

---

1   Amended by Sch 6, para 22 to ERA 1999.
2   Ibid, para 23 inserting a new s 256A of TULR(C)A 1992.
3   Ibid, para 23 inserting a new s 256A(4).

Chapter 6

MISCELLANEOUS PROVISIONS

6.1 PARTNERSHIPS AT WORK

6.1.1 In *Fairness at Work* the Government stated that the best modern companies had some things in common:

'–   they seek to harness the talents of their employees in a relationship based on fairness and through a recognition that everyone involved in the business has an interest in its success;

–   they ensure that everyone understands the business so that change is readily accepted and implemented, not feared;

–   they set clear objectives for employees but also encourage them to exercise their initiative and to contribute their ideas to the development of the business; and

–   they develop the workforce through training and work experience to respond to and lead change.'[1]

While the Government recognised that such relationships with employees are not easy, it also recognised the returns from effective partnerships:

'–   where they have an understanding of the business, employees recognise the importance of responding quickly to changing customer and market requirements;

–   where they are taken seriously, employees at every level come forward with ways to help the business innovate, for example by developing new products; and

–   where they are well prepared for change, employees can help the company to introduce and operate new technologies and processes, helping to secure employment within the business.'[2]

---

1   *Fairness at Work*, 1998, Cm 3968, para 2.2.
2   Ibid, para 2.4.

6.1.2 The Government recognised that partnerships at work develop in different ways depending on the organisation. In some ways the partnerships are between employers and trade unions and, given that freedom of choice should apply to both employers and employees, the Government has introduced the procedures on recognition seen in Chapter 2, so that, where employees wish the union to represent them, the employer must comply with this wish. This is, however, only part of the equation and the Government noted in *Fairness at Work* the need to disseminate good practice from the best organisations to the rest.[1] As such, the Government stated its intention to carry out research into work-based partnerships and make funds available to contribute to the training of managers and employee representatives in order to assist and develop partnerships at work.[2]

1   *Fairness at Work*, para 2.7.
2   Ibid.

6.1.3   The proposals above are, in part, implemented by s 30 of ERA 1999. This section gives the Secretary of State the authority to make funding available for the purpose of encouraging and helping employers or their representatives and employees or their representatives to improve the way they work together.[1] The funds may be provided in such way as the Secretary of State thinks fit, whether as grants or otherwise and whether repayable or otherwise.[2] It should be noted that this provision is extremely wide. The Government in *Fairness at Work* stated that it intended to review the work of ACAS and see how that body could do more to promote such partnerships.[3] A late House of Lords amendment was intended to restrict the power given to the Secretary of State by limiting the funds which could be used to £100,000 per year with any increase subject to the approval of both Houses of Parliament. Further, the amendment proposed that recipients of such funding should produce audited accounts and that the Secretary of State be required to produce an annual report to both Houses of the allocation of the funding and the reports received from the recipients. The amendments, however, were not adopted.

1   ERA 1999, s 30(1).
2   Ibid, s 30(2).
3   *Fairness at Work*, para 2.8.

6.2   EMPLOYMENT AGENCIES

Regulations

6.2.1   The Government stated its intention, in *Fairness at Work*, to review the rules governing the conduct of employment agencies.[1] Agency work is covered by the Employment Agencies Act 1973 (EAA 1973) and the Conduct of Employment Agencies and Employment Businesses Regulations 1976.[2] Section 31 gives effect to Sch 7 which amends EAA 1973 by redefining 'employment agency'[3] and extending the power of the Secretary of State, contained in s 5(1) of EAA 1973, to make regulations.[4] It should be noted that the new regulations and amendments to EAA 1973 relate to the conduct of agencies but do not clarify the position of the person who is taken on by an agency. Whilst it is clear that the hirer of the person supplied by the agency has certain responsibilities in respect of compliance with anti-discriminatory legislation[5] and duties under the Health and Safety at Work Act 1974,[6] it is less clear whether the hirer incurs obligations to the agency worker under the common-law duty of care and the employment relationship between the person and the agency is still a matter for the common law. Whilst income tax and National Insurance legislation treat the agency as the employer of such persons for the purposes of liability for income tax and National Insurance contributions,[7] for the purposes of employment protection, the common law tests as to status are applied and thus in most cases the agency worker is deemed to be self-employed,[8] although there have been cases when the court has held that there is sufficient mutuality of obligations and control by the agency that the relationship is one of employer/employee.[9] The new rights, for employees to be accompanied at disciplinary and grievance hearings and not to suffer a detriment or dismissal because those rights were exercised, apply to agency workers (see Chapter 2) and s 23 gives the Secretary of State a general power to confer rights on individuals, yet, at the time of writing, the employment status of agency workers has not been clarified, a situation which some may regard as unfortunate.

---

1   *Fairness at Work*, para 3.18.
2   SI 1976/715.
3   ERA 1999, Sch 7, para 7 amending s 13(2) of EAA 1973.
4   Ibid, Sch 7, para 2 amending s 5(1).
5   SDA 1975, s 9; Race Relations Act 1976 (RRA 1976), s 7; *BP Chemicals v Gillick* [1995] IRLR 128.
6   Health and Safety at Work Act 1974, s 3(1).
7   Income and Corporation Taxes Act 1988, s 134; Social Security (Categorisation of Earners) Regulations 1978, SI 1978/1689.
8   *Wickens v Champion Employment Agency Ltd* [1984] ICR 365.
9   *McMeechan v Secretary of State for Employment* [1995] ICR 444.

6.2.2   'Employment agency' has been redefined so that for every place where the definition mentions 'workers' this is now changed to 'persons'.[1] This means that the definition now includes the supply of services to companies as well as to individuals, in line with the definition of employment business activity in s 13(3). The amendments to EAA 1973 also extend the power of the Secretary of State to make regulations.[2] It does this by specifying that the Secretary of State may make regulations:

'(ea) restricting the services which may be provided by persons carrying on such agencies and businesses;
(eb) regulating the way in which and the terms on which services may be provided by persons carrying on such agencies and businesses;
(ec) restricting or regulating the charging of fees by persons carrying on such agencies and businesses'.[3]

The above amendments allow the Secretary of State to restrict and regulate both the provision of services in respect of any worker or employer[4] (the former provisions only allowed for regulation of the provision of services in respect of persons seeking employment outside the UK, those ordinarily resident outside the UK and seeking employment here and in respect of workers under the age of 18 or in full-time education,[5] and removes the former prohibition in respect of regulations regulating or restricting the charging of fees.[6] The explanatory note gives examples of what the regulations might include such as:

- restricting the ability of agencies to unilaterally vary contracts with workers or hirers;
- restricting the ability of agencies to make payment to a worker conditional upon the worker doing other work;
- preventing agencies from purporting to enter into contracts on behalf of workers which charge workers for finding them work or having binding contracts giving them authority to enter into such contracts;
- restricting the ability of agencies to impose terms which seek to prevent or discourage employers from dealing with workers supplied by the agency or referring such workers to other employers who may employ them.

Such restrictions may also limit the charges an agency may make or abolish charges in these situations altogether.[7] The Government intends to consult on draft regulations.

---

1   ERA 1999, Sch 7, para 7 amending s 13(2) of EAA 1973.
2   Ibid, Sch 7, para 2 amending s 5(1).
3   Ibid.
4   The new s 5(1)(ea)–(ec) and a new s 5(1A) inserted by Sch 7, para 2(3).
5   The old s 5(1)(f)–(g).
6   Ibid.
7   House of Lords, Explanatory Note, para 266 at
      http://www.parliament.the-stationery-office.co.uk.

Charges

6.2.3   Schedule 7 substitutes s 6(1) of EAA 1973 (restriction on demand or receipt of fees for finding or seeking to find employment). Whereas the old provision prevented a person carrying on an employment agency from directly or indirectly receiving a fee from a person for the provision of information or the provision of services for the purpose of finding that person employment,[1] the new provisions are much more far reaching. The amended section makes it clear that it is unlawful for a person carrying on an employment business to receive a fee directly or indirectly from a person already under contract with the employment business for the purposes of finding or seeking to find employment for that person[2] and also prevents the employment business charging persons who will be under a contract with the business once they have agreed to undertake an assignment with a hirer.[3] There remains, however, the power of the Secretary of State to exempt certain classes of case where fees can be charged.[4] The explanatory note suggests that exceptions may include:

- the provision of employment agency services to entertainers, models and certain other classes of persons where it is the norm for an agent to be engaged to represent the worker, except where the agent charges the hirer;

- the provision of information about people seeking work in publications made available to employers and potential employers; and
- the provision of information about work opportunities to persons seeking work where no other provisions are offered and where the charge is within prescribed limits.[5]

1   Old s 6(1) of EAA 1973.
2   ERA 1999, Sch 7, para 3 inserting a new s 6(1)(b) into EAA 1973.
3   Ibid, Sch 7, para 3 inserting a new s 6(1)(c) into EAA 1973.
4   EAA 1973, s 6(1).
5   House of Lords, Explanatory Note, para 270 at
     http://www.parliament.the-stationery-office.co.uk.

Inspection

6.2.4   Schedule 7, para 4 amends the inspection powers contained in s 9 of EAA 1973. The range of premises which may be entered is extended. The old provisions allowed entry to any premises used or to be used for or in connection with an employment agency or business or any premises the officer had reasonable cause to believe were used for or in connection with the business.[1] The Schedule amends s 9(1)(a) by simply giving a power to enter any relevant business premises;[2] however 'business premises' is now defined by a new s 9(1B).[3] In addition to premises which under the old provision could be entered, 'business premises' is now extended to include premises which have been used in connection with an employment agency or business, those premises which an officer has reasonable cause to believe are used or have been used as such and any other premises, if an officer has reasonable cause to believe that records or other documents relating to the business are kept there and the premises are used by a person who is or who used to carry on an employment agency or business.[4] Officers now have extended powers. Under the old s 9(1)(b), officers could only inspect records or documents;[5] this power has been extended to allow officers to take copies of anything inspected.[6] Further, if any records, documents or other information are not kept at the premises being inspected, the officer may require a person on the premises to inform him or her where and by whom the information is kept and make arrangements, if it is reasonably practicable to do so, for the information to be inspected by or furnished to the officer at a time the officer specifies.[7] To take into account new technology, 'document' within the section includes information recorded in any form and information is kept at premises if it is accessible from them.[8]

1   The old s 9(1)(a) of EAA 1973.
2   ERA 1999, Sch 7, para 4(2)(a).
3   Ibid, inserted by Sch 7, para 4(3).
4   New s 9(1B)(a), (b) and (c) of EAA 1973.
5   Ibid, the old s 9(1)(b).
6   Ibid, new s 9(1)(d).
7   Ibid, new s 9(1A).
8   Ibid, new s 9(1C).

Self-incrimination

6.2.5   The original s 9(2) of EAA 1973 has been replaced to take into account the judgment of the European Court of Human Rights in *Saunders v United Kingdom.*[1] The substituted provisions provide that a person is not required to produce, provide access to or make arrangements for the production of anything which the person could not be compelled to produce in civil proceedings.[2] Further, although a statement made by a person in compliance with s 9 may be used in criminal proceedings,[3] except in proceedings for an offence under s 5 of the Perjury Act 1911 (false statements made otherwise than on oath) no evidence relating to the statement may be adduced and no question relating to it may be asked by or on behalf of the prosecution unless evidence relating to it has been adduced or a question relating to it has first been asked by or on behalf of the person who made the statement.[4] The offences of obstructing an officer in the exercise of the officer's powers of inspection and failing, without reasonable excuse, to comply with a requirement to furnish the officer with information for the purpose of ascertaining whether the provisions of EAA 1973 or any regulations are being complied with[5] have been extended to include obstruction under the new s 9(1)(d) and failure without reasonable excuse to comply with a requirement under s 9(1A).[6] The original s 9(4)(a)(iv) has also been amended so that any information obtained under the powers in s 9(1) can be used for criminal proceedings other than those brought under EAA 1973.[7] Officers, however, have no power to inspect documents and information other than those required to be kept under EAA 1973 or any regulations made pursuant to the Act, nor can they require the production of such information other than to ascertain whether EAA 1973 or any regulations have been complied with or to enable the Secretary of State to discharge the relevant functions under the Act.[8]

---

1   [1997] 23 EHRR 313.
2   New s 9(2) EAA 1973.
3   Ibid, new s 9(2A).
4   Ibid, new s 9(2B).
5   Ibid, old s 9(3).
6   Inserted by Sch 7, para 4(5) to ERA 1999.
7   Ibid, extended by Sch 7, para 4(6).
8   EAA 1973, s 9(1)(c).

Offences

6.2.6   Section 11 of EAA 1973 is amended to extend the time-limit in which an offence under the Act, prosecuted by the Secretary of State, may be tried. The amended s 11 covers all offences except those in s 9(3).[1] Notwithstanding s 127(1) of the Magistrates' Courts Act 1980 and s 136 of the Criminal Procedure (Scotland) Act 1995, any information relating to a relevant offence may be tried if it is laid at any time:

- within 3 years after the date of the commission of the offence; and
- within 6 months after the date on which evidence sufficient in the opinion of the Secretary of State or Lord Advocate to justify proceedings came to his or her knowledge.[2]

A certificate from the Secretary of State or Lord Advocate as to the date on which the evidence came to his or her knowledge is conclusive.[3] Further, a new s 11B allows a court, where there is a conviction, to award the costs of the investigation to the Secretary of State.[4]

---

1   ERA 1999, Sch 7, para 5.
2   New s 11A(2) and (3) of EAA 1973.
3   Ibid, new s 11A(4).
4   Inserted by Sch 7, para 5 to ERA 1999.

6.2.7 Paragraph 6 of the Schedule deals with the procedure for making regulations under EAA 1973. Regulations made under the amended s 5 (relating to the conduct of employment agencies or businesses) and the amended s 6 (charging persons seeking employment) are subject to the affirmative resolution procedure.[1] Regulations under s 13(7)(i) (exemptions) shall be subject to the negative resolution procedure.[2]

---

1   ERA 1999, Sch 7, para 6 substituting a new s 12(5) of EAA 1973.
2   Ibid, inserting a new s 12(6).

6.3   COMPENSATION

Unfair dismissal: special and additional awards

6.3.1 Under the old provisions, a tribunal could award an additional award where re-instatement or re-engagement was ordered and the employer failed to comply with the order. The additional award was between 13 and 26 weeks' pay[1] but where the dismissal involved discrimination on the grounds of sex, race or disability, the additional award was between 26 and 52 weeks' pay.[2] In addition, in certain cases of unfair dismissal, a tribunal could award a special award, in place of an additional award where the employee had asked for re-instatement or re-engagement, even if the tribunal did not order it. This was where the dismissal was due to membership or non-membership of a trade union, the activities of the employee as an employee representative or as an occupational pension scheme trustee or because of certain actions taken by the employee on health and safety grounds.[3] To simplify this area, s 33 of ERA 1999 replaces the special awards with additional awards and repeals the special award provisions in s 117(4)(b), s 118(2) and (3) and s 125 of ERA 1996 and ss 157 and 158 of TULR(C)A 1992. Section 33(2) provides that all additional awards will now consist of between 26 and 52 weeks' pay.[4] Whilst this simplifies compensation considerably, it has to be noted that the old provisions relating to special awards were more generous in that, where the tribunal had not ordered re-instatement or re-engagement but the employee had requested it, the award was 104 weeks' pay, subject to statutory minimum and maximum amounts.[5] Where the tribunal had ordered re-instatement or re-engagement and the employer had disobeyed the order, the special award was a minimum of 156 weeks' pay.[6] While the increase in the compensatory award discussed below will no doubt mitigate some of the consequences of this change, it will still mean that in some cases the employer will benefit from the simplification of the rules.

---

1   ERA 1996, s 117(5)(b).
2   Ibid, s 117(5)(a) and (6).
3   Ibid, ss 117(4)(b) and 118(2) and (3).
4   By amending s 117(3)(b).
5   Ibid, s 125(1).
6   Ibid, 1996, s 125(2).

Indexation of amounts

6.3.2   Until ERA 1999 came into force, various tribunal awards were required to be reviewed every year, for example the amount of a week's pay for the basic award in unfair dismissal and redundancy pay.[1] The Act still requires that awards will change every year but the limits on such awards will now be index-linked.[2] Index-linking applies to guarantee payments;[3] the minimum basic award which must be made where the dismissal is for membership or non-membership of a trade union, trade union activities, activities as an employee representative, activities as an occupational pension scheme trustee or certain activities on health and safety grounds;[4] the compensatory award in unfair dismissal;[5] the maximum an employee can claim on the employer's insolvency;[6] the calculation of a week's pay for statutory compensation purposes[7] and the compensation payable for exclusion or expulsion from a trade union.[8] The changes to these awards will be linked to the retail prices index in September each year and will be changed by order as soon as reasonably practicable after the index is published.[9] The Act requires that the limits of the awards should go up or down by the same percentage as the amount of the increase or decrease of the index.[10] In the case of guarantee payments, the Secretary of State must round the sum up to the nearest 10 pence, in the case of the minimum basic award, the compensatory award, and compensation for exclusion or expulsion from a trade union, the Secretary of State must round up to the nearest £100. In respect of the calculation of a week's pay and the limit of an employee's claim in the situation of the employer's insolvency, the Secretary of State must round up to the nearest £10.[11] As a result of these amendments, s 208 of ERA 1996, requiring an annual review of limits, has now been repealed.[12]

1	ERA 1996, s 208.
2	ERA 1999, s 34.
3	ERA 1996, s 31(1).
4	Ibid, s 120(1); TULR(C)A 1992, s 156(1).
5	Ibid, s 124(1).
6	Ibid, s 186(1)(a) and (b).
7	Ibid, s 227(1).
8	TULR(C)A 1992, s 176(6).
9	ERA 1999, s 34(2).
10	Ibid.
11	Ibid, s 34(3).
12	Ibid, s 36(2).

Compensatory award

6.3.3 The compensatory award in unfair dismissal is to compensate an employee for the employee's actual loss as a consequence of being unfairly dismissed. A tribunal has the discretion to award 'such amount as they consider just and equitable in all the circumstances, having regard to the loss sustained by the complainant in consequence of the dismissal in so far as the loss is attributable to action taken by the employer'.[1] Whilst the tribunals have a great deal of discretion, the compensatory award is not an award of punitive damages and Sir John Donaldson in *Norton Tool Co Ltd v Tewson*[2] said that tribunals should exercise their discretion 'judicially and upon the basis of principle'. As such, the compensatory award is normally based on certain heads of compensation – immediate loss of earnings, future loss of earnings, expenses incurred as a result of the dismissal, loss of statutory employment protection rights and loss of pension rights.[3] Until the passing of ERA 1999, the maximum compensatory award a tribunal could make was £12,000.[4] Whilst many awards were less than this figure, the limit meant that in some cases an employee was not fully compensated for the loss sustained. Originally, the Government proposed in *Fairness at Work* that there should be no limit on the compensatory award.[5] However, during the consultation on the White Paper, concerns were expressed about ill-founded claims, burdens on businesses and employment prospects. Taking these concerns into account, ERA 1999 raises the limit on the compensatory award from £12,000 to £50,000.[6] This is subject to index-linking discussed at **6.3.2** above. The effect of the change has yet to be assessed but it may lead to more litigation in that the dramatic increase in the limit of the award may disincline employers from entering compromise agreements[7] in that an employer may feel safer going to a tribunal rather than trying to calculate what may be awarded and encase this in a compromise agreement. In reality, given the heads of compensation, the increase should make little difference and will affect only higher-paid employees who do not find work for some time. In certain cases, there is no limit on the compensatory award. This is where the dismissal is for reasons connected with health and safety matters[8] and making a protected disclosure under the Public Interest Disclosure Act 1998 (PIDA 1998).[9] To some extent, this will counter the abolition of the special award discussed at **6.3.1** above.

---

1 ERA 1996, s 123(1).
2 [1972] ICR 501.
3 *Tidman v Aveling Marshall Ltd* [1977] IRLR 218.
4 Increased by the Employment Rights (Increase of Limits) Order 1998, SI 1998/924.
5 *Fairness at Work*, para 3.5.
6 ERA 1999, s 34(4) amending s 124(1) of ERA 1996.
7 Under s 203(2)(f) of ERA 1996.
8 Ibid, s 100.
9 Ibid, ss 103A and 105(6A) inserted by ss 5 and 6 of PIDA 1998.

Guarantee payments

6.3.4 Under the original provisions contained in ss 28–35 of ERA 1996, guarantee payments are made to employees for days when they are laid off. By s 31(2)–(4) they are paid for five days in any three-month period. Originally, the Secretary of State was required to review the time periods and limits once a year.[1] Given the index-linking of such payments discussed at **6.3.2** above, ERA 1999 amends ERA 1996 so that there is no requirement to review the amount of the payment and enabling the Secretary of State to vary the time periods specified in s 31(2)–(4) subject to the negative resolution procedure.[2]

---

1 ERA 1996, s 208.
2 Section 35 of ERA 1999 amending s 31(7) of ERA 1996.

6.4 NATIONAL SECURITY

6.4.1 The original s 193 of ERA 1996 provided that its provisions did not apply to any Crown employment in respect of which there was a certificate in force issued by the Minister of the Crown certifying that the employment was required to be exempted from the legislation on the grounds of national security. Similar provisions also existed in SDA 1975, RRA 1976 and the Disability Discrimination Act 1995 (DDA 1995). Whilst allowing Crown employees to pursue employment protection rights in employment tribunals, s 193 and the corresponding provisions in other legislation meant that essentially these rights could be taken away by the issue of a certificate. Section 41 of ERA 1999 brings into force Sch 8 to the Act. This and other provisions relating to national security discussed below were brought in at a late stage by the Government and were brought in as a result of the 1997–98 report of the Intelligence and Security Committee which recommended that the procedure should be altered in matters of national security so as to give employees rights which hitherto they had not had.[1] The amendments introduced by ERA 1999 exclude certain rights completely. For example the right to be accompanied at disciplinary and grievance hearings, and the right not to suffer a detriment or be dismissed for seeking to exercise that right does not extend to employment for the purposes of the Security Services, the Secret Intelligence Service or the Government Communications Headquarters by virtue of s 15 of ERA 1999. Further, the right not to suffer a detriment for making a protected disclosure under PIDA 1998 does not apply in relation to employment in those areas.[2] On the other hand, all other rights do apply, but there are limitations. If the complaint is one of suffering a detriment due to trade union membership[3] or unfair dismissal,[4] a tribunal must dismiss the complaint if it is shown that the action complained of was taken for the purpose of safeguarding national security.[5] It is not necessary to show that the action had that effect nor that the action was reasonable to take for the purposes of safeguarding national security. Furthermore, although on the face of ERA 1999, it would appear that employees in this area will have the right generally to go to an employment tribunal, to some extent this can be negated by other amendments made by the Act. In particular, the Minister, if he or she considers it expedient in the interests of national security, can direct a tribunal to sit in private, exclude the applicant and the applicant's representative from all or part of the proceedings, conceal the identity of a witness and keep all or part of the reasons for its decision secret.[6] The tribunal will also have the power to take any of these steps where it considers it expedient to do so in the interests of national security.[7] Where the applicant or the applicant's representative has been excluded, the Attorney General or Lord Advocate may appoint a person to represent the applicant.[8] The provisions were criticised in the House of Lords.[9] They allow the Minister to control the procedure of the tribunal and effectively can deprive the applicant of his or her right of complaint if the applicant and/or representative are excluded from all of the proceedings. The appointment of a representative to attend the hearing in the applicant's place could hardly be said to be a satisfactory compromise. As a result of these criticisms, a late amendment was made. This amendment inserts subs (7)(c) into the new s 10 of ETA 1996 (tribunal procedure regulations). The new subsection allows for regulations to permit an excluded person to make a statement to the tribunal before the commencement of the proceedings or part of the proceedings from which that person is excluded. Whilst the amendment is to be welcomed, it does not cover the issue of the review of the Minister's use of directional power. The only challenge to the Minister's direction is by judicial review. Whilst this may seem appropriate, it is an expensive remedy and it is hoped that the Government's assurances that the Minister's power would be used very sparingly prove true in practice, otherwise the Government will be taking away with one hand what it has given with the other.

---

1   HL Deb, vol 604, col 578, 15 July 1999 (Lord Razzall).
2   ERA 1999, Sch 8, para 1 amending s 193 of ERA 1996.
3   Under s 146 of TULR(C)A 1992.
4   Under s 111 of ERA 1996.
5   Section 10(1), ETA 1996 amended by Sch 8, para 3 to ERA 1999.

6   Ibid, s 10(5), as amended.
7   Ibid, s 10(6), as amended.
8   Ibid, s 10(7), as amended.
9   HL Deb, vol 604, vols 578–582, 15 July 1999 (Lord Razzall and Lord Archer).

6.4.2   Schedule 8 introduces further measures to protect national security. It provides for employment tribunal procedure regulations to enable a tribunal to sit in private for the purposes of hearing evidence which, in the opinion of the tribunal, is likely to consist of: information which could not be disclosed without contravention of an enactment, information communicated to the person in confidence or acquired in consequence of confidence reposed in that person by another and information the disclosure of which would, for reasons other than its effect on negotiations on collective bargaining issues, cause substantial injury to any of his or her undertakings or an undertaking in which he or she works.[1] Reference to 'undertaking' means, in relation to Crown employment, the national interest and, in relation to House of Lords or House of Commons staff, the national interest or the interest of the relevant House.[2] In cases where the Minister has directed the tribunal or the tribunal itself has determined to take steps to conceal the identity of a witness or to keep secret all or part of the reasons for its decision,[3] it is an offence to publish anything likely to lead to the identification of the witness or the reasons for the decision which were to be secret.[4] There is a defence if the person charged can prove that at the time of the alleged offence that person was not aware and neither suspected nor had reason to suspect that the publication was prohibited.[5] If the offence is committed by a body corporate with the consent or connivance of or is attributable to the neglect of a director, manager, secretary or similar officer, or a person purporting to act in such capacity, the person as well as the body corporate is guilty of an offence.[6] Publication includes reference to inclusion in a programme included in a programme service within the meaning of the Broadcasting Act 1990.[7]

1   ETA 1996, s 10A(1), as amended.
2   Ibid, s 10A(2).
3   Ibid, under s 10(5) or (6) above.
4   Ibid, s 10B(2). A person found guilty is liable on summary conviction to a fine not exceeding level 5 on the standard scale (s 10B(3)).
5   Ibid, s 10B(4).
6   Ibid, s 10B(5).
7   Ibid, s 10B(6).

6.5   EMPLOYMENT OUTSIDE GREAT BRITAIN

6.5.1   Section 196 of ERA 1996 limits the operation of the Act to employees who ordinarily work in Great Britain. Section 32 of ERA 1999 repeals this s 196. Whilst there still must be a proper connection with Great Britain for domestic law to apply, the repeal of s 196 means that domestic law will extend to those employees who are temporarily working here and will facilitate the implementation of the Posted Workers Directive.[1] The repeal will also mean that employees who have a base in Great Britain but by their contract are deemed to be based elsewhere even though in reality their work is in Great Britain (for example the situation in *Carver v Saudi Arabian Airlines*)[2] will also be able to claim the protection of domestic legislation. Section 32 also makes a parallel change to s 285(1) of TULR(C)A 1992 removing the territorial restriction in respect of consultation on mass redundancies.

---

1   Council Directive 96/71/EC.
2   [1999] IRLR 370.

6.6   TRANSFERS OF UNDERTAKINGS

6.6.1   The Government in *Fairness at Work*[1] stated that it was the intention to revise the Transfer of Undertakings (Protection of Employment) Regulations 1981,[2] which were brought in to implement the Acquired Rights Directive.[3] Since the publication of *Fairness at Work*, a new, revised Business Transfers Directive has been agreed.[4] The Government is, at present, consulting on new regulations but it has become apparent that some changes cannot be made under the existing powers in s 2(2) of the European Communities Act 1972 in particular by giving rights to individuals where those rights are not given in the Directive. Three major areas are affected by this restriction: the application of the regulations to contracting-out situations; their application to transfers involving public sector bodies; and their application to the transfer of purely administrative functions between public administrative bodies. As such, s 38 of ERA 1999 removes the technical obstacles so that the Government can put forward proposals as a result of its consultation.

---

1   *Fairness at Work*, para 4.32.
2   SI 1981/1794.
3   Council Directive 77/187/EEC.
4   Council Directive 98/50/EC.

6.7   MINIMUM WAGE INFORMATION

6.7.1   Section 39 is a provision to make the enforcement of the minimum wage more effective. Whilst the Inland Revenue has the overall responsibility for the enforcement of the minimum wage, until s 39 was enacted, if Inland Revenue officers obtained information that someone was paying less than the minimum wage while carrying out their tax and National Insurance duties, they could not pass that information on to the national minimum wage officers. Section 39 allows national minimum wage officers access to the Inland Revenue's tax and National Insurance contributions information.

6.8 DISMISSAL OF SCHOOL STAFF

6.8.1 Section 40 amends Schs 16 and 17 to the School Standards and Framework Act 1998 and is a technical amendment to ensure that the provisions governing the dismissal of staff on fixed-term contracts under those Schedules take account of the reduction in the qualifying period for unfair dismissal to one year. Previously, school governing bodies had to hear representations of appeals before terminating a contract of fixed term where the member of staff had been employed for two years or more. Section 40 amends this to one year or more.

APPENDIX

Employment Relations Act 1999

(1999 c 26)

ARRANGEMENT OF SECTIONS

Trade unions

Section		Page
1	Collective bargaining: recognition	116
2	Detriment related to trade union membership	117
3	Blacklists	117
4	Ballots and notices	118
5	Training	118
6	Unfair dismissal connected with recognition: interim relief	120

Leave for family and domestic reasons

7	Maternity and parental leave	120
8	Time off for domestic incidents	120
9	Consequential amendments	120

Disciplinary and grievance hearings

10	Right to be accompanied	120
11	Complaint to employment tribunal	121
12	Detriment and dismissal	122
13	Interpretation	122
14	Contracting out and conciliation	123
15	National security employees	124

Other rights of individuals

16	Unfair dismissal of striking workers	124
17	Collective agreements: detriment and dismissal	124
18	Agreement to exclude dismissal rights	124
19	Part-time work: discrimination	125
20	Part-time work: code of practice	126
21	Code of practice: supplemental	127
22	National minimum wage: communities	127
23	Power to confer rights on individuals	128

CAC, ACAS, Commissioners and Certification Officer

24	CAC: members	129
25	CAC: proceedings	129
26	ACAS: general duty	130
27	ACAS: reports	130
28	Abolition of Commissioners	130
29	The Certification Officer	131

Miscellaneous

30   Partnerships at work   131
31   Employment agencies   131
32   Employment rights: employment outside Great Britain   131
33   Unfair dismissal: special and additional awards   132
34   Indexation of amounts, etc   132
35   Guarantee payments   133
36   Sections 33 to 35: consequential   133
37   Compensatory award etc: removal of limit in certain cases   134
38   Transfer of undertakings   134
39   Minimum wage: information   134
40   Dismissal of school staff   134
41   National security   135

General

42   Orders and regulations   135
43   Finance   135
44   Repeals   135
45   Commencement   135
46   Extent   135
47   Citation   136

SCHEDULES:

Schedule 1—Collective Bargaining: Recognition   137
Schedule 2—Union Membership: Detriment   201
Schedule 3—Ballots and notices   203
Schedule 4—Leave for Family Reasons Etc   208
           Part I   —Maternity Leave and Parental Leave   208
           Part II —Time off for Dependants   214
           Part III—Consequential Amendments   216
Schedule 5—Unfair Dismissal of Striking Workers   220
Schedule 6—The Certification Officer   222
Schedule 7—Employment Agencies   235
Schedule 8—National Security   238
Schedule 9—Repeals   242

An Act to amend the law relating to employment, to trade unions and to employment agencies and businesses.   [27th July 1991]

Trade unions

1   Collective bargaining: recognition

(1) The Trade Union and Labour Relations (Consolidation) Act 1992 shall be amended as follows.

(2) After Chapter V of Part I (rights of trade union members) there shall be inserted—

'CHAPTER VA

COLLECTIVE BARGAINING: RECOGNITION

70A   Recognition of trade unions

Schedule A1 shall have effect.'

(3) Immediately before Schedule 1 there shall be inserted the Schedule set out in Schedule 1 to this Act.

2   Detriment related to trade union membership

Schedule 2 shall have effect.

3   Blacklists

(1) The Secretary of State may make regulations prohibiting the compilation of lists which—

  (a)   contain details of members of trade unions or persons who have taken part in the activities of trade unions, and

  (b)   are compiled with a view to being used by employers or employment agencies for the purposes of discrimination in relation to recruitment or in relation to the treatment of workers.

(2) The Secretary of State may make regulations prohibiting—

  (a)   the use of lists to which subsection (1) applies;

  (b)   the sale or supply of lists to which subsection (1) applies.

(3) Regulations under this section may, in particular—

  (a)   confer jurisdiction (including exclusive jurisdiction) on employment tribunals and on the Employment Appeal Tribunal;

  (b)   include provision for or about the grant and enforcement of specified remedies by courts and tribunals;

  (c)   include provision for the making of awards of compensation calculated in accordance with the regulations;

  (d)   include provision permitting proceedings to be brought by trade unions on behalf of members in specified circumstances;

  (e)   include provision about cases where an employee is dismissed by his employer and the reason or principal reason for the dismissal, or why the employee was selected for dismissal, relates to a list to which subsection (1) applies;

  (f)   create criminal offences;

  (g)   in specified cases or circumstances, extend liability for a criminal offence created under paragraph (f) to a person who aids the commission of the offence or to a person who is an agent, principal, employee, employer or officer of a person who commits the offence;

  (h)   provide for specified obligations or offences not to apply in specified circumstances;

  (i)   include supplemental, incidental, consequential and transitional provision, including provision amending an enactment;

  (j)   make different provision for different cases or circumstances.

(4) Regulations under this section creating an offence may not provide for it to be punishable—

  (a)   by imprisonment,

(b) by a fine in excess of level 5 on the standard scale in the case of an offence triable only summarily, or

(c) by a fine in excess of the statutory maximum in the case of summary conviction for an offence triable either way.

(5) In this section—

'list' includes any index or other set of items whether recorded electronically or by any other means, and

'worker' has the meaning given by section 13.

(6) Subject to subsection (5), expressions used in this section and in the Trade Union and Labour Relations (Consolidation) Act 1992 have the same meaning in this section as in that Act.

4 Ballots and notices

Schedule 3 shall have effect.

5 Training

In Chapter VA of Part I of the Trade Union and Labour Relations (Consolidation) Act 1992 (collective bargaining: recognition) as inserted by section 1 above, there shall be inserted after section 70A—

'70B Training

(1) This section applies where—

(a) a trade union is recognised, in accordance with Schedule A1, as entitled to conduct collective bargaining on behalf of a bargaining unit (within the meaning of Part I of that Schedule), and

(b) a method for the conduct of collective bargaining is specified by the Central Arbitration Committee under paragraph 31 (3) of that Schedule (and is not the subject of an agreement under paragraph 31 (5) (a) or (b)).

(2) The employer must from time to time invite the trade union to send representatives to a meeting for the purpose of—

(a) consulting about the employer's policy on training for workers within the bargaining unit,

(b) consulting about his plans for training for those workers during the period of six months starting with the day of the meeting, and

(c) reporting about training provided for those workers since the previous meeting.

(3) The date set for a meeting under subsection (2) must not be later than—

(a) in the case of a first meeting, the end of the period of six months starting with the day on which this section first applies in relation to a bargaining unit, and

(b) in the case of each subsequent meeting, the end of the period of six months starting with the day of the previous meeting.

(4) The employer shall, before the period of two weeks ending with the date of a meeting, provide to the trade union any information—

(a) without which the union's representatives would be to a material extent impeded in participating in the meeting, and

(b) which it would be in accordance with good industrial relations practice to disclose for the purposes of the meeting.

(5) Section 182(1) shall apply in relation to the provision of information under subsection (4) as it applies in relation to the disclosure of information under section 181.

(6) The employer shall take account of any written representations about matters raised at a meeting which he receives from the trade union within the period of four weeks starting with the date of the meeting.

(7) Where more than one trade union is recognised as entitled to conduct collective bargaining on behalf of a bargaining unit, a reference in this section to "the trade union" is a reference to each trade union.

(8) Where at a meeting under this section (Meeting 1) an employer indicates his intention to convene a subsequent meeting (Meeting 2) before the expiry of the period of six months beginning with the date of Meeting 1, for the reference to a period of six months in subsection (2)(b) there shall be substituted a reference to the expected period between Meeting 1 and Meeting 2.

(9) The Secretary of State may by order made by statutory instrument amend any of subsections (2) to (6).

(10) No order shall be made under subsection (9) unless a draft has been laid before, and approved by resolution of, each House of Parliament.

70C   Section 70B: complaint to employment tribunal

(1) A trade union may present a complaint to an employment tribunal that an employer has failed to comply with his obligations under section 70B in relation to a bargaining unit.

(2) An employment tribunal shall not consider a complaint under this section unless it is presented—

(a) before the end of the period of three months beginning with the date of the alleged failure, or

(b) within such further period as the tribunal considers reasonable in a case where it is satisfied that it was not reasonably practicable for the complaint to be presented before the end of that period of three months.

(3) Where an employment tribunal finds a complaint under this section well-founded it—

(a) shall make a declaration to that effect, and

(b) may make an award of compensation to be paid by the employer to each person who was, at the time when the failure occurred, a member of the bargaining unit.

(4) The amount of the award shall not, in relation to each person, exceed two weeks' pay.

(5) For the purpose of subsection (4) a week's pay—

    (a) shall be calculated in accordance with Chapter II of Part XIV of the Employment Rights Act 1996 (taking the date of the employer's failure as the calculation date), and

    (b) shall be subject to the limit in section 227(1) of that Act.

(6) Proceedings for enforcement of an award of compensation under this section—

    (a) may, in relation to each person to whom compensation is payable, be commenced by that person, and

    (b) may not be commenced by a trade union.'

6 Unfair dismissal connected with recognition: interim relief

In sections 128(1)(b) and 129(1) of the Employment Rights Act 1996 (interim relief) after '103' there shall be inserted 'or in paragraph 161(2) of Schedule A1 to the Trade Union and Labour Relations (Consolidation) Act 1992'.

Leave for family and domestic reasons

7 Maternity and parental leave

The provisions set out in Part I of Schedule 4 shall be substituted for Part VIII of the Employment Rights Act 1996.

8 Time off for domestic incidents

The provisions set out in Part II of Schedule 4 shall be inserted after section 57 of that Act.

9 Consequential amendments

Part III of Schedule 4 (which makes amendments consequential on sections 7 and 8) shall have effect.

Disciplinary and grievance hearings

10 Right to be accompanied

(1) This section applies where a worker—

    (a) is required or invited by his employer to attend a disciplinary or grievance hearing, and

    (b) reasonably requests to be accompanied at the hearing.

(2) Where this section applies the employer must permit the worker to be accompanied at the hearing by a single companion who—

    (a) is chosen by the worker and is within subsection (3),

    (b) is to be permitted to address the hearing (but not to answer questions on behalf of the worker), and

    (c) is to be permitted to confer with the worker during the hearing.

(3) A person is within this subsection if he is—

- (a) employed by a trade union of which he is an official within the meaning of sections 1 and 119 of the Trade Union and Labour Relations (Consolidation) Act 1992,
- (b) an official of a trade union (within that meaning) whom the union has reasonably certified in writing as having experience of, or as having received training in, acting as a worker's companion at disciplinary or grievance hearings, or
- (c) another of the employer's workers.

(4) If—

- (a) a worker has a right under this section to be accompanied at a hearing,
- (b) his chosen companion will not be available at the time proposed for the hearing by the employer, and
- (c) the worker proposes an alternative time which satisfies subsection (5),

the employer must postpone the hearing to the time proposed by the worker.

(5) An alternative time must—

- (a) be reasonable, and
- (b) fall before the end of the period of five working days beginning with the first working day after the day proposed by the employer.

(6) An employer shall permit a worker to take time off during working hours for the purpose of accompanying another of the employer's workers in accordance with a request under subsection (1)(b).

(7) Sections 168(3) and (4), 169 and 171 to 173 of the Trade Union and Labour Relations (Consolidation) Act 1992 (time off for carrying out trade union duties) shall apply in relation to subsection (6) above as they apply in relation to section 168(1) of that Act.

11 Complaint to employment tribunal

(1) A worker may present a complaint to an employment tribunal that his employer has failed, or threatened to fail, to comply with section 10(2) or (4).

(2) A tribunal shall not consider a complaint under this section in relation to a failure or threat unless the complaint is presented—

- (a) before the end of the period of three months beginning with the date of the failure or threat, or
- (b) within such further period as the tribunal considers reasonable in a case where it is satisfied that it was not reasonably practicable for the complaint to be presented before the end of that period of three months.

(3) Where a tribunal finds that a complaint under this section is well-founded it shall order the employer to pay compensation to the worker of an amount not exceeding two weeks' pay.

(4) Chapter II of Part XIV of the Employment Rights Act 1996 (calculation of a week's pay) shall apply for the purposes of subsection (3); and in applying that Chapter the calculation date shall be taken to be—

(a) in the case of a claim which is made in the course of a claim for unfair dismissal, the date on which the employer's notice of dismissal was given or, if there was no notice, the effective date of termination, and

(b) in any other case, the date on which the relevant hearing took place (or was to have taken place).

(5) The limit in section 227(1) of the Employment Rights Act 1996 (maximum amount of week's pay) shall apply for the purposes of subsection (3) above.

(6) No award shall be made under subsection (3) in respect of a claim which is made in the course of a claim for unfair dismissal if the tribunal makes a supplementary award under section 127A(2) of the Employment Rights Act 1996 (internal appeal procedures).

12 Detriment and dismissal

(1) A worker has the right not to be subjected to any detriment by any act, or any deliberate failure to act, by his employer done on the ground that he—

(a) exercised or sought to exercise the right under section 10(2) or (4), or

(b) accompanied or sought to accompany another worker (whether of the same employer or not) pursuant to a request under that section.

(2) Section 48 of the Employment Rights Act 1996 shall apply in relation to contraventions of subsection (1) above as it applies in relation to contraventions of certain sections of that Act.

(3) A worker who is dismissed shall be regarded for the purposes of Part X of the Employment Rights Act 1996 as unfairly dismissed if the reason (or, if more than one, the principal reason) for the dismissal is that he—

(a) exercised or sought to exercise the right under section 10(2) or (4), or

(b) accompanied or sought to accompany another worker (whether of the same employer or not) pursuant to a request under that section.

(4) Sections 108 and 109 of that Act (qualifying period of employment and upper age limit) shall not apply in relation to subsection (3) above.

(5) Sections 128 to 132 of that Act (interim relief) shall apply in relation to dismissal for the reason specified in subsection (3)(a) or (b) above as they apply in relation to dismissal for a reason specified in section 128(1)(b) of that Act.

(6) In the application of Chapter II of Part X of that Act in relation to subsection (3) above, a reference to an employee shall be taken as a reference to a worker.

13 Interpretation

(1) In sections 10 to 12 and this section 'worker' means an individual who is—

(a) a worker within the meaning of section 230(3) of the Employment Rights Act 1996,

(b) an agency worker,

(c) a home worker,

(d) a person in Crown employment within the meaning of section 191 of that Act, other than a member of the naval, military, air or reserve forces of the Crown, or

    (e)   employed as a relevant member of the House of Lords staff or the House of Commons staff within the meaning of section 194(6) or 195(5) of that Act.

(2) In subsection (1) 'agency workers' means an individual who—

    (a)   is supplied by a person ('the agent') to do work for another ('the principal') by arrangement between the agent and the principal,

    (b)   is not a party to a worker's contract, within the meaning of section 230(3) of that Act, relating to that work, and

    (c)   is not a party to a contract relating to that work under which he undertakes to do the work for another party to the contract whose status is, by virtue of the contract, that of a client or customer of any professional or business undertaking carried on by the individual;

and, for the purposes of sections 10 to 12, both the agent and the principal are employers of an agency worker.

(3) In subsection (1) 'home worker' means an individual who—

    (a)   contracts with a person, for the purposes of the person's business, for the execution of work to be done in a place not under the person's control or management, and

    (b)   is not a party to a contract relating to that work under which the work is to be executed for another party to the contract whose status is, by virtue of the contract, that of a client or customer of any professional or business undertaking carried on by the individual;

and, for the purposes of sections 10 to 12, the person mentioned in paragraph (a) is the home worker's employer.

(4) For the purposes of section 10 a disciplinary hearing is a hearing which could result in—

    (a)   the administration of a formal warning to a worker by his employer,

    (b)   the taking of some other action in respect of a worker by his employer, or

    (c)   the confirmation of a warning issued or some other action taken.

(5) For the purposes of section 10 a grievance hearing is a hearing which concerns the performance of a duty by an employer in relation to a worker.

(6) For the purposes of section 10(5)(b) in its application to a part of Great Britain a working day is a day other than—

    (a)   a Saturday or a Sunday,

    (b)   Christmas Day or Good Friday, or

    (c)   a day which is a bank holiday under the Banking and Financial Dealings Act 1971 in that part of Great Britain.

14   Contracting out and conciliation

Sections 10 to 13 of this Act shall be treated as provisions of Part V of the Employment Rights Act 1996 for the purposes of—

    (a)   section 203(1), (2)(e) and (f), (3) and (4) of that Act (restrictions on contracting out), and

    (b)   section 18(1)(d) of the Employment Tribunals Act 1996 (conciliation).

15 National security employees

Sections 10 to 13 of this Act shall not apply in relation to a person employed for the purposes of—

(a) the Security Service,
(b) the Secret Intelligence Service, or
(c) the Government Communications Headquarters.

Other rights of individuals

16 Unfair dismissal of striking workers

Schedule 5 shall have effect.

17 Collective agreements: detriment and dismissal

(1) The Secretary of State may make regulations about cases where a worker—

(a) is subjected to detriment by his employer, or
(b) is dismissed,

on the grounds that he refuses to enter into a contract which includes terms which differ from the terms of a collective agreement which applies to him.

(2) The regulations may—

(a) make provision which applies only in specified classes of case;
(b) make different provision for different circumstances;
(c) include supplementary, incidental and transitional provision.

(3) In this section—

'collective agreement' has the meaning given by section 178(1) of the Trade Union and Labour Relations (Consolidation) Act 1992; and
'employer' and 'worker' have the same meaning as in section 296 of that Act.

(4) The payment of higher wages or higher rates of pay or overtime or the payment of any signing on or other bonuses or the provision of other benefits having a monetary value to other workers employed by the same employer shall not constitute a detriment to any worker not receiving the same or similar payments or benefits within the meaning of subsection (1)(a) of this section so long as—

(a) there is no inhibition in the contract of employment of the worker receiving the same from being the member of any trade union, and
(b) the said payments of higher wages or rates of pay or overtime or bonuses or the provision of other benefits are in accordance with the terms of a contract of employment and reasonably relate to services provided by the worker under that contract.

18 Agreement to exclude dismissal rights

(1) In section 197 of the Employment Rights Act 1996 (fixed-term contracts) subsections (1) and (2) (agreement to exclude unfair dismissal provisions) shall be omitted; and subsections (2) to (5) below shall have effect in consequence.

(2) In sections 44(4), 46(2), 47(2), 47A(2) and 47B(2) of that Act—

    (a) the words from the beginning to 'the dismissal,' shall be omitted, and

    (b) for 'that Part' there shall be substituted 'Part X'.

(3) In section 45A(4) of that Act the words from ', unless' to the end shall be omitted.

(4) In section 23 of the National Minimum Wage Act 1998, for subsection (4) there shall be substituted—

    '(4) This section does not apply where the detriment in question amounts to dismissal within the meaning of—

        (a) Part X of the Employment Rights Act 1996 (unfair dismissal), or

        (b) Part XI of the Employment Rights (Northern Ireland) Order 1996 (corresponding provision for Northern Ireland),

except where in relation to Northern Ireland the person in question is dismissed in circumstances in which, by virtue of Article 240 of that Order (fixed term contracts), Part XI does not apply to the dismissal.'

(5) In paragraph 1 of Schedule 3 to the Tax Credits Act 1999, for subparagraph (3) there shall be substituted—

    '(3) This paragraph does not apply where the detriment in question amounts to dismissal within the meaning of—

        (a) Part X of the Employment Rights Act 1996 (unfair dismissal), or

        (b) Part XI of the Employment Rights (Northern Ireland) Order 1996 (corresponding provision for Northern Ireland),

except where in relation to Northern Ireland the employee is dismissed in circumstances in which, by virtue of Article 240 of that Order (fixed term contracts), Part XI does not apply to the dismissal.'

(6) Section 197(1) of the Employment Rights Act 1996 does not prevent Part X of that Act from applying to a dismissal which is regarded as unfair by virtue of section 99 or 104 of that Act (pregnancy and childbirth, and assertion of statutory right).

19 Part-time work: discrimination

(1) The Secretary of State shall make regulations for the purpose of securing that persons in part-time employment are treated, for such purposes and to such extent as the regulations may specify, no less favourably than persons in full-time employment.

(2) The regulations may—

    (a) specify classes of person who are to be taken to be, or not to be, in part-time employment;

    (b) specify classes of person who are to be taken to be, or not to be, in full-time employment;

    (c) specify circumstances in which persons in part-time employment are to be taken to be, or not to be, treated less favourably than persons in full-time employment;

    (d) make provision which has effect in relation to persons in part-time employment generally or provision which has effect only in relation to specified classes of persons in part-time employment.

(3) The regulations may—

(a) confer jurisdiction (including exclusive jurisdiction) on employment tribunals and on the Employment Appeal Tribunal;

(b) create criminal offences in relation to specified acts or omissions by an employer, by an organisation of employers, by an organisation of workers or by an organisation existing for the purposes of a profession or trade carried on by the organisation's members;

(c) in specified cases or circumstances, extend liability for a criminal offence created under paragraph (b) to a person who aids the commission of the offence or to a person who is an agent, principal, employee, employer or officer of a person who commits the offence;

(d) provide for specified obligations or offences not to apply in specified circumstances;

(e) make provision about notices or information to be given, evidence to be produced and other procedures to be followed;

(f) amend, apply with or without modifications, or make provision similar to any provision of the Employment Rights Act 1996 (including, in particular, Parts V, X and XIII) or the Trade Union and Labour Relations (Consolidation) Act 1992;

(g) provide for the provisions of specified agreements to have effect in place of provisions of the regulations to such extent and in such circumstances as may be specified;

(h) include supplemental, incidental, consequential and transitional provision, including provision amending an enactment;

(i) make different provision for different cases or circumstances.

(4) Without prejudice to the generality of this section the regulations may make any provision which appears to the Secretary of State to be necessary or expedient—

(a) for the purpose of implementing Council Directive 97/81/EC on the framework agreement on part-time work in its application to terms and conditions of employment;

(b) for the purpose of dealing with any matter arising out of or related to the United Kingdom's obligations under that Directive;

(c) for the purpose of any matter dealt with by the framework agreement or for the purpose of applying the provisions of the framework agreement to any matter relating to part-time workers.

(5) Regulations under this section which create an offence—

(a) shall provide for it to be triable summarily only, and

(b) may not provide for it to be punishable by imprisonment or by a fine in excess of level 5 on the standard scale.

20 Part-time work: code of practice

(1) The Secretary of State may issue codes of practice containing guidance for the purpose of—

(a) eliminating discrimination in the field of employment against part-time workers;

(b) facilitating the development of opportunities for part-time work;

    (c) facilitating the flexible organisation of working time taking into account the needs of workers and employers;

    (d) any matter dealt with in the framework agreement on part-time work annexed to Council Directive 97/81/EC.

(2) The Secretary of State may revise a code and issue the whole or part of the revised code.

(3) A person's failure to observe a provision of a code does not make him liable to any proceedings.

(4) A code—

    (a) is admissible in evidence in proceedings before an employment tribunal, and

    (b) shall be taken into account by an employment tribunal in any case in which it appears to the tribunal to be relevant.

21 Code of practice: supplemental

(1) Before issuing or revising a code of practice under section 20 the Secretary of State shall consult such persons as he considers appropriate.

(2) Before issuing a code the Secretary of State shall—

    (a) publish a draft code,

    (b) consider any representations made to him about the draft,

    (c) if he thinks it appropriate, modify the draft in the light of any representations made to him.

(3) If, having followed the procedure under subsection (2), the Secretary of State decides to issue a code, he shall lay a draft code before each House of Parliament.

(4) If the draft code is approved by resolution of each House of Parliament, the Secretary of State shall issue the code in the form of the draft.

(5) In this section and section 20(3) and (4)—

    (a) a reference to a code includes a reference to a revised code,

    (b) a reference to a draft code includes a reference to a draft revision, and

    (c) a reference to issuing a code includes a reference to issuing part of a revised code.

22 National minimum wage: communities

The following shall be inserted after section 44 of the National Minimum Wage Act 1998 (exclusions: voluntary workers)—

'44A Religious and other communities: resident workers

(1) A residential member of a community to which this section applies does not qualify for the national minimum wage in respect of employment by the community.

(2) Subject to subsection (3), this section applies to a community if—

    (a) it is a charity or is established by a charity,

    (b) a purpose of the community is to practise or advance a belief of a religious or similar nature, and

(c) all or some of its members live together for that purpose.

(3) This section does not apply to a community which—

(a) is an independent school, or
(b) provides a course of further or higher education.

(4) The residential members of a community are those who live together as mentioned in subsection (2)(c).

(5) In this section—

(a) "charity" has the same meaning as in section 44, and
(b) "independent school" has the same meaning as in section 463 of the Education Act 1996 (in England and Wales), section 135 of the Education (Scotland) Act 1980 (in Scotland) and Article 2 of the Education and Libraries (Northern Ireland) Order 1986 (in Northern Ireland).

(6) In this section "course of further or higher education" means—

(a) in England and Wales, a course of a description referred to in Schedule 6 to the Education Reform Act 1988 or Schedule 2 to the Further and Higher Education Act 1992;
(b) in Scotland, a course or programme of a description mentioned in or falling within section 6(1) or 38 of the Further and Higher Education (Scotland) Act 1992;
(c) in Northern Ireland, a course of a description referred to in Schedule 1 to the Further Education (Northern Ireland) Order 1997 or a course providing further education within the meaning of Article 3 of that Order.'

23 Power to confer rights on individuals

(1) This section applies to any right conferred on an individual against an employer (however defined) under or by virtue of any of the following—

(a) the Trade Union and Labour Relations (Consolidation) Act 1992;
(b) the Employment Rights Act 1996;
(c) this Act;
(d) any instrument made under section 2(2) of the European Communities Act 1972.

(2) The Secretary of State may by order make provision which has the effect of conferring any such right on individuals who are of a specified description.

(3) The reference in subsection (2) to individuals includes a reference to individuals expressly excluded from exercising the right.

(4) An order under this section may—

(a) provide that individuals are to be treated as parties to workers' contracts or contracts of employment;
(b) make provision as to who are to be regarded as the employers of individuals;
(c) make provision which has the effect of modifying the operation of any right as conferred on individuals by the order;

(d) include such consequential, incidental or supplementary provisions as the Secretary of State thinks fit.

(5) An order under this section may make provision in such way as the Secretary of State thinks fit, whether by amending Acts or instruments or otherwise.

(6) Section 209(7) of the Employment Rights Act 1996 (which is superseded by this section) shall be omitted.

(7) Any order made or having effect as if made under section 209(7), so far as effective immediately before the commencement of this section, shall have effect as if made under this section.

CAC, ACAS, Commissioners and Certification Officer

24 CAC: members

In section 260 of the Trade Union and Labour Relations (Consolidation) Act 1992 (members of the Committee) these subsections shall be substituted for subsections (1) to (3)—

'(1) The Central Arbitration Committee shall consist of members appointed by the Secretary of State.

(2) The Secretary of State shall appoint a member as chairman, and may appoint a member as deputy chairman or members as deputy chairmen.

(3) The Secretary of State may appoint as members only persons experienced in industrial relations, and they shall include some persons whose experience is as representatives of employers and some whose experience is as representatives of workers.
(3A) Before making an appointment under subsection (1) or (2) the Secretary of State shall consult ACAS and may consult other persons.'

25 CAC: proceedings

(1) The Trade Union and Labour Relations (Consolidation) Act 1992 shall be amended as follows.

(2) In section 263 (proceedings of the Committee) this subsection shall be inserted after subsection (6)—

'(7) In relation to the discharge of the Committee's functions under Schedule A1—

(a) section 263A and subsection (6) above shall apply, and
(b) subsections (1) to (5) above shall not apply.'

(3) This section shall be inserted after section 263—

'263A Proceedings of the Committee under Schedule A1

(1) For the purpose of discharging its functions under Schedule A1 in any particular case, the Central Arbitration Committee shall consist of a panel established under this section.

(2) The chairman of the Committee shall establish a panel or panels, and a panel shall consist of these three persons appointed by him—

    (a) the chairman or a deputy chairman of the Committee, who shall be chairman of the panel;

    (b) a member of the Committee whose experience is as a representative of employers;

    (c) a member of the Committee whose experience is as a representative of workers.

(3) The chairman of the Committee shall decide which panel is to deal with a particular case.

(4) A panel may at the discretion of its chairman sit in private where it appears expedient to do so.

(5) If—

    (a) a panel cannot reach a unanimous decision on a question arising before it, and

    (b) a majority of the panel have the same opinion,

the question shall be decided according to that opinion.

(6) If—

    (a) a panel cannot reach a unanimous decision on a question arising before it, and

    (b) a majority of the panel do not have the same opinion,

the chairman of the panel shall decide the question acting with the full powers of an umpire or, in Scotland, an oversman.

(7) Subject to the above provisions, a panel shall determine its own procedure.'

(4) In section 264 (awards of the Committee)—

    (a) in subsection (1) after 'award' there shall be inserted ', or in any decision or declaration of the Committee under Schedule A1,';

    (b) in subsection (2) after 'of the Committee,' there shall be inserted 'or of a decision or declaration of the Committee under Schedule A1,'.

26 ACAS: general duty

In section 209 of the Trade Union and Labour Relations (Consolidation) Act 1992 (ACAS' general duty) the words from ', in particular' to the end shall be omitted.

27 ACAS: reports

(1) In section 253(1) of the Trade Union and Labour Relations (Consolidation) Act 1992 (ACAS: annual report) for 'calendar year' there shall be substituted 'financial year'.

(2) In section 265(1) of that Act (ACAS: report about CAC) for 'calendar year' there shall be substituted 'financial year'.

28 Abolition of Commissioners

(1) These offices shall cease to exist—

    (a) the office of Commissioner for the Rights of Trade Union Members;

(b) the office of Commissioner for Protection Against Unlawful Industrial Action.

(2) In the Trade Union and Labour Relations (Consolidation) Act 1992 these provisions shall cease to have effect—

(a) Chapter VIII of Part I (provision by Commissioner for the Rights of Trade Union Members of assistance in relation to certain proceedings);

(b) sections 235B and 235C (provision of assistance by Commissioner for Protection Against Unlawful Industrial Action of assistance in relation to certain proceedings);

(c) section 266 (and the heading immediately preceding it) and sections 267 to 271 (Commissioners' appointment, remuneration, staff, reports, accounts, etc).

(3) In section 32A of that Act (statement to members of union following annual return) in the third paragraph of subsection (6)(a) (application for assistance from Commissioner for the Rights of Trade Union Members) for the words from 'may' to 'case,' there shall be substituted 'should'.

29 The Certification Officer

Schedule 6 shall have effect.

Miscellaneous

30 Partnerships at work

(1) The Secretary of State may spend money or provide money to other persons for the purpose of encouraging and helping employers (or their representatives) and employees (or their representatives) to improve the way they work together.

(2) Money may be provided in such way as the Secretary of State thinks fit (whether as grants or otherwise) and on such terms as he thinks fit (whether as to repayment or otherwise).

31 Employment agencies

Schedule 7 shall have effect.

32 Employment rights: employment outside Great Britain

(1) In section 285(1) of the Trade Union and Labour Relations (Consolidation) Act 1992 (employment outside Great Britain) for 'Chapter II (procedure for handling redundancies)' there shall be substituted 'sections 193 and 194 (duty to notify Secretary of State of certain redundancies)'.

(2) After section 287(3) of that Act (offshore employment) there shall be inserted—

'(3A) An Order in Council under this section shall be subject to annulment in pursuance of a resolution of either House of Parliament.'.

(3) Section 196 of the Employment Rights Act 1996 (employment outside Great Britain) shall cease to have effect; and in section 5(1) for 'sections 196 and' there shall be substituted 'section'.

(4) After section 199(6) of that Act (mariners) there shall be inserted—

'(7) The provisions mentioned in subsection (8) apply to employment on board a ship registered in the register maintained under section 8 of the Merchant Shipping Act 1995 if and only if—

    (a) the ship's entry in the register specifies a port in Great Britain as the port to which the vessel is to be treated as belonging,

    (b) under his contract of employment the person employed does not work wholly outside Great Britain, and

    (c) the person employed is ordinarily resident in Great Britain.

(8) The provisions are—

    (a) sections 8 to 10,

    (b) Parts II, III and V,

    (c) Part VI, apart from sections 58 to 60,

    (d) Parts VII and VIII,

    (e) sections 92 and 93, and

    (f) Part X.

33   Unfair dismissal: special and additional awards

(1) The following provisions (which require, or relate to, the making of special awards by employment tribunals in unfair dismissal cases) shall cease to have effect—

    (a) sections 117(4)(b), 118(2) and (3) and 125 of the Employment Rights Act 1996 (and the word 'or' before section 117(4)(b));

    (b) sections 157 and 158 of the Trade Union and Labour Relations (Consolidation) Act 1992.

(2) In section 117(3)(b) of the Employment Rights Act 1996 (amount of additional award) for 'the appropriate amount' there shall be substituted 'an amount not less than twenty-six nor more than fifty-two weeks' pay'; and subsections (5) and (6) of section 117 shall cease to have effect.

(3) In section 14 of the Employment Rights (Dispute Resolution) Act 1998—

    (a) subsection (1) shall cease to have effect, and

    (b) in subsection (2) for 'that Act' substitute 'the Employment Rights Act 1996'.

34   Indexation of amounts, etc

(1) This section applies to the sums specified in the following provisions—

    (a) section 31(1) of the Employment Rights Act 1996 (guarantee payments: limits);

    (b) section 120(1) of that Act (unfair dismissal: minimum amount of basic award);

    (c) section 124(1) of that Act (unfair dismissal: limit of compensatory award);

    (d) section 186(1)(a) and (b) of that Act (employee's rights on insolvency of employer: maximum amount payable);

    (e) section 227(1) of that Act (maximum amount of a week's pay for purposes of certain calculations);

    (f) section 156(1) of the Trade Union and Labour Relations (Consolidation) Act 1992 (unfair dismissal: minimum basic award);

    (g) section 176(6) of that Act (right to membership of trade union: remedies).

(2) If the retail prices index for September of a year is higher or lower than the index for the previous September, the Secretary of State shall as soon as practicable make an order in relation to each sum mentioned in subsection (1)—

    (a) increasing each sum, if the new index is higher, or

    (b) decreasing each sum, if the new index is lower,

by the same percentage as the amount of the increase or decrease of the index.

(3) In making the calculation required by subsection (2) the Secretary of State shall—

    (a) in the case of the sum mentioned in subsection (1)(a), round the result up to the nearest 10 pence,

    (b) in the case of the sums mentioned in subsection (1)(b), (c), (f) and (g), round the result up to the nearest £100, and

    (c) in the case of the sums mentioned in subsection (1)(d) and (e), round the result up to the nearest £10.

(4) For the sum specified in section 124(1) of the Employment Rights Act 1996 (unfair dismissal: limit of compensatory award) there shall be substituted the sum of £50,000 (subject to subsection (2) above).

(5) In this section 'the retail prices index' means—

    (a) the general index of retail prices (for all items) published by the Office for National Statistics, or

    (b) where that index is not published for a month, any substituted index or figures published by that Office.

(6) An order under this section—

    (a) shall be made by statutory instrument,

    (b) may include transitional provision, and

    (c) shall be laid before Parliament after being made.

35 Guarantee payments

For section 31(7) of the Employment Rights Act 1996 (guarantee payments: limits) there shall be substituted—

    '(7) The Secretary of State may by order vary—

        (a) the length of the period specified in subsection (2);

        (b) a limit specified in subsection (3) or (4).'

36 Sections 33 to 35: consequential

(1) The following provisions (which confer power to increase sums) shall cease to have effect—

    (a) sections 120(2), 124(2), 186(2) and 227(2) to (4) of the Employment Rights Act 1996;

    (b) sections 159 and 176(7) and (8) of the Trade Union and Labour Relations (Consolidation) Act 1992.

(2) Section 208 of the Employment Rights Act 1996 (review of limits) shall cease to have effect.

(3) An increase effected, before section 34 comes into force, by virtue of a provision repealed by this section shall continue to have effect notwithstanding this section (but subject to section 34(2) and (4)).

37 Compensatory award etc: removal of limit in certain cases

(1) After section 124(1) of the Employment Rights Act 1996 (limit of compensatory award etc) there shall be inserted—

'(1A) Subsection (1) shall not apply to compensation awarded, or a compensatory award made, to a person in a case where he is regarded as unfairly dismissed by virtue of section 100, 103A, 105(3) or 105(6A).'

(2) Section 127B of that Act (power to specify method of calculation of compensation where dismissal a result of protected disclosure) shall cease to have effect.

38 Transfer of undertakings

(1) This section applies where regulations under section 2(2) of the European Communities Act 1972 (general implementation of Treaties) make provision for the purpose of implementing, or for a purpose concerning, a Community obligation of the United Kingdom which relates to the treatment of employees on the transfer of an undertaking or business or part of an undertaking or business.

(2) The Secretary of State may by regulations make the same or similar provision in relation to the treatment of employees in circumstances other than those to which the Community obligation applies (including circumstances in which there is no transfer, or no transfer to which the Community obligation applies).

(3) Regulations under this section shall be subject to annulment in pursuance of a resolution of either House of Parliament.

39 Minimum wage: information

(1) Information obtained by a revenue official in the course of carrying out a function of the Commissioners of Inland Revenue may be—

(a) supplied by the Commissioners of Inland Revenue to the Secretary of State for any purpose relating to the National Minimum Wage Act 1998;
(b) supplied by the Secretary of State with the authority of the Commissioners of Inland Revenue to any person acting under section 13(1)(b) of that Act;
(c) supplied by the Secretary of State with the authority of the Commissioners of Inland Revenue to an officer acting for the purposes of any of the agricultural wages legislation.

(2) In this section—

'revenue official' means an officer of the Commissioners of Inland Revenue appointed under section 4 of the Inland Revenue Regulation Act 1890 (appointment of collectors, officers and other persons), and
'the agricultural wages legislation' has the same meaning as in section 16 of the National Minimum Wage Act 1998 (agricultural wages officers).

40 Dismissal of school staff

(1) In paragraph 27(3)(b) of Schedule 16 to the School Standards and Framework Act 1998 (dismissal of staff: representations and appeal) for 'for a period of two years or

more (within the meaning of the Employment Rights Act 1996)' there shall be substituted ', within the meaning of the Employment Rights Act 1996, for a period at least as long as the period for the time being specified in section 108(1) of that Act (unfair dismissal: qualifying period).

(2) In paragraph 24(4)(b) of Schedule 17 to the School Standards and Framework Act 1998 (dismissal of staff: representations and appeal) for 'for a period of two years or more (within the meaning of the Employment Rights Act 1996)' there shall be substituted ', within the meaning of the Employment Rights Act 1996, for a period a least as long as the period for the time being specified in section 108(1) of that Act (unfair dismissal: qualifying period)'.

41   National security

Schedule 8 shall have effect.

General

42   Orders and regulations

(1) Any power to make an order or regulations under this Act shall be exercised by statutory instrument.

(2) No order or regulations shall be made under section 3, 17, 19 or 23 unless a draft has been laid before, and approved by resolution of, each House of Parliament.

43   Finance

There shall be paid out of money provided by Parliament—

(a)   any increase attributable to this Act in the sums so payable under any other enactment;
(b)   any other expenditure of the Secretary of State under this Act.

44   Repeals

The provisions mentioned in Schedule 9 are repealed (or revoked) to the extent specified in column 3.

45   Commencement

(1) The preceding provisions of this Act shall come into force in accordance with provision made by the Secretary of State by order made by statutory instrument.

(2) An order under this section—

(a)   may make different provision for different purposes;
(b)   may include supplementary, incidental, saving or transitional provisions.

46   Extent

(1) Any amendment or repeal in this Act has the same extent as the provision amended or repealed.

(2) An Order in Council under paragraph 1(1)(b) of Schedule 1 to the Northern Ireland Act 1974 (legislation for Northern Ireland in the interim period) which contains a statement that it is made only for purposes corresponding to any of the purposes of this Act—

    (a) shall not be subject to paragraph 1(4) and (5) of that Schedule (affirmative resolution of both Houses of Parliament), but

    (b) shall be subject to annulment in pursuance of a resolution of either House of Parliament.

(3) Apart from sections 39 and 45 and subject to subsection (1), the preceding sections of this Act shall not extend to Northern Ireland.

47 Citation

This Act may be cited as the Employment Relations Act 1999.

SCHEDULES

Section 1

SCHEDULE 1

COLLECTIVE BARGAINING: RECOGNITION

The Schedule to be inserted immediately before Schedule 1 to the Trade Union and Labour Relations (Consolidation) Act 1992 is as follows—

'SCHEDULE A1

COLLECTIVE BARGAINING: RECOGNITION

PART I

RECOGNITION

Introduction

1. A trade union (or trade unions) seeking recognition to be entitled to conduct collective bargaining on behalf of a group or groups of workers may make a request in accordance with this Part of this Schedule.

2.—(1) This paragraph applies for the purposes of this Part of this Schedule.

(2) References to the bargaining unit are to the group of workers concerned (or the groups taken together).

(3) References to the proposed bargaining unit are to the bargaining unit proposed in the request for recognition.

(4) References to the employer are to the employer of the workers constituting the bargaining unit concerned.

(5) References to the parties are to the union (or unions) and the employer.

3.—(1) This paragraph applies for the purposes of this Part of this Schedule.

(2) The meaning of collective bargaining given by section 178(1) shall not apply.

(3) References to collective bargaining are to negotiations relating to pay, hours and holidays; but this has effect subject to sub-paragraph (4).

(4) If the parties agree matters as the subject of collective bargaining, references to collective bargaining are to negotiations relating to the agreed matters; and this is the case whether the agreement is made before or after the time when the CAC issues a declaration, or the parties agree, that the union is (or unions are) entitled to conduct collective bargaining on behalf of a bargaining unit.

(5) Sub-paragraph (4) does not apply in construing paragraph 31(3).

(6) Sub-paragraphs (2) to (5) do not apply in construing paragraph 35 or 44.

Request for recognition

4.—(1) The union or unions seeking recognition must make a request for recognition to the employer.

(2) Paragraphs 5 to 9 apply to the request.

5. The request is not valid unless it is received by the employer.

6. The request is not valid unless the union (or each of the unions) has a certificate under section 6 that it is independent.

7.—(1) The request is not valid unless the employer, taken with any associated employer or employers, employs—

(a) at least 21 workers on the day the employer receives the request, or

(b) an average of at least 21 workers in the 13 weeks ending with that day.

(2) To find the average under sub-paragraph (1)(b)—

(a) take the number of workers employed in each of the 13 weeks (including workers not employed for the whole of the week);

(b) aggregate the 13 numbers;

(c) divide the aggregate by 13.

(3) For the purposes of sub-paragraph (1)(a) any worker employed by an associated company incorporated outside Great Britain must be ignored unless the day the request was made fell within a period during which he ordinarily worked in Great Britain.

(4) For the purposes of sub-paragraph (1)(b) any worker employed by an associated company incorporated outside Great Britain must be ignored in relation to a week unless the whole or any part of that week fell within a period during which he ordinarily worked in Great Britain.

(5) For the purposes of sub-paragraphs (3) and (4) a worker who is employed on board a ship registered in the register maintained under section 8 of the Merchant Shipping Act 1995 shall be treated as ordinarily working in Great Britain unless—

(a) the ship's entry in the register specifies a port outside Great Britain as the port to which the vessel is to be treated as belonging,

(b) the employment is wholly outside Great Britain, or

(c) the worker is not ordinarily resident in Great Britain.

(6) The Secretary of State may by order—

(a) provide that sub-paragraphs (1) to (5) are not to apply, or are not to apply in specified circumstances, or

(b) vary the number of workers for the time being specified in subparagraph (1);

and different provision may be made for different circumstances.

(7) An order under sub-paragraph (6)—

(a) shall be made by statutory instrument, and

(b) may include supplementary, incidental, saving or transitional provisions.

(8) No such order shall be made unless a draft of it has been laid before Parliament and approved by a resolution of each House of Parliament.

8. The request is not valid unless it—

    (a) is in writing,

    (b) identifies the union or unions and the bargaining unit, and

    (c) states that it is made under this Schedule.

9. The Secretary of State may by order made by statutory instrument prescribe the form of requests and the procedure for making them; and if he does so the request is not valid unless it complies with the order.

Parties agree

10.—(1) If before the end of the first period the parties agree a bargaining unit and that the union is (or unions are) to be recognised as entitled to conduct collective bargaining on behalf of the unit, no further steps are to be taken under this Part of this Schedule.

(2) If before the end of the first period the employer informs the union (or unions) that the employer does not accept the request but is willing to negotiate, sub-paragraph (3) applies.

(3) The parties may conduct negotiations with a view to agreeing a bargaining unit and that the union is (or unions are) to be recognised as entitled to conduct collective bargaining on behalf of the unit.

(4) If such an agreement is made before the end of the second period no further steps are to be taken under this Part of this Schedule.

(5) The employer and the union (or unions) may request ACAS to assist in conducting the negotiations.

(6) The first period is the period of 10 working days starting with the day after that on which the employer receives the request for recognition.

(7) The second period is—

    (a) the period of 20 working days starting with the day after that on which the first period ends, or

    (b) such longer period (so starting) as the parties may from time to time agree.

Employer rejects request

11.—(1) This paragraph applies if—

    (a) before the end of the first period the employer fails to respond to the request, or

    (b) before the end of the first period the employer informs the union (or unions) that the employer does not accept the request (without indicating a willingness to negotiate).

(2) The union (or unions) may apply to the CAC to decide both these questions—

    (a) whether the proposed bargaining unit is appropriate or some other bargaining unit is appropriate;

(b) whether the union has (or unions have) the support of a majority of the workers constituting the appropriate bargaining unit.

Negotiations fail

12.—(1) Sub-paragraph (2) applies if—

(a) the employer informs the union (or unions) under paragraph 10(2), and
(b) no agreement is made before the end of the second period.

(2) The union (or unions) may apply to the CAC to decide both these questions—

(a) whether the proposed bargaining unit is appropriate or some other bargaining unit is appropriate;
(b) whether the union has (or unions have) the support of a majority of the workers constituting the appropriate bargaining unit.

(3) Sub-paragraph (4) applies if—

(a) the employer informs the union (or unions) under paragraph 10(2), and
(b) before the end of the second period the parties agree a bargaining unit but not that the union is (or unions are) to be recognised as entitled to conduct collective bargaining on behalf of the unit.

(4) The union (or unions) may apply to the CAC to decide the question whether the union has (or unions have) the support of a majority of the workers constituting the bargaining unit.

(5) But no application may be made under this paragraph if within the period of 10 working days starting with the day after that on which the employer informs the union (or unions) under paragraph 10(2) the employer proposes that ACAS be requested to assist in conducting the negotiations and—

(a) the union rejects (or unions reject) the proposal, or
(b) the union fails (or unions fail) to accept the proposal within the period of 10 working days starting with the day after that on which the employer makes the proposal.

Acceptance of applications

13. The CAC must give notice to the parties of receipt of an application under paragraph 11 or 12.

14.—(1) This paragraph applies if—

(a) two or more relevant applications are made,
(b) at least one worker falling within one of the relevant bargaining units also falls within the other relevant bargaining unit (or units), and
(c) the CAC has not accepted any of the applications.

(2) A relevant application is an application under paragraph 11 or 12.

(3) In relation to a relevant application, the relevant bargaining unit is—

(a) the proposed bargaining unit, where the application is under paragraph 11(2) or 12(2);

(b) the agreed bargaining unit, where the application is under paragraph 12(4).

(4) Within the acceptance period the CAC must decide, with regard to each relevant application, whether the 10 per cent test is satisfied.

(5) The 10 per cent test is satisfied if members of the union (or unions) constitute at least 10 per cent of the workers constituting the relevant bargaining unit.

(6) The acceptance period is—

(a) the period of 10 working days starting with the day after that on which the CAC receives the last relevant application, or

(b) such longer period (so starting) as the CAC may specify to the parties by notice containing reasons for the extension.

(7) If the CAC decides that—

(a) the 10 per cent test is satisfied with regard to more than one of the relevant applications, or

(b) the 10 per cent test is satisfied with regard to none of the relevant applications,

the CAC must not accept any of the relevant applications.

(8) If the CAC decides that the 10 per cent test is satisfied with regard to one only of the relevant applications the CAC—

(a) must proceed under paragraph 15 with regard to that application, and

(b) must not accept any of the other relevant applications.

(9) The CAC must give notice of its decision to the parties.

(10) If by virtue of this paragraph the CAC does not accept an application, no further steps are to be taken under this Part of this Schedule in relation to that application.

15.—(1) This paragraph applies to these applications—

(a) any application with regard to which no decision has to be made under paragraph 14;

(b) any application with regard to which the CAC must proceed under this paragraph by virtue of paragraph 14.

(2) Within the acceptance period the CAC must decide whether—

(a) the request for recognition to which the application relates is valid within the terms of paragraphs 5 to 9, and

(b) the application is made in accordance with paragraph 11 or 12 and admissible within the terms of paragraphs 33 to 42.

(3) In deciding those questions the CAC must consider any evidence which it has been given by the employer or the union (or unions).

(4) If the CAC decides that the request is not valid or the application is not made in accordance with paragraph 11 or 12 or is not admissible—

(a) the CAC must give notice of its decision to the parties,

(b)   the CAC must not accept the application, and

(c)   no further steps are to be taken under this Part of this Schedule.

(5) If the CAC decides that the request is valid and the application is made in accordance with paragraph 11 or 12 and is admissible it must—

(a)   accept the application, and

(b)   give notice of the acceptance to the parties.

(6) The acceptance period is—

(a)   the period of 10 working days starting with the day after that on which the CAC receives the application, or

(b)   such longer period (so starting) as the CAC may specify to the parties by notice containing reasons for the extension.

Withdrawal of application

16.—(1) If an application under paragraph 11 or 12 is accepted by the CAC, the union (or unions) may not withdraw the application—

(a)   after the CAC issues a declaration under paragraph 22(2), or

(b)   after the union (or the last of the unions) receives notice under paragraph 22(3) or 23(2).

(2) If an application is withdrawn by the union (or unions)—

(a)   the CAC must give notice of the withdrawal to the employer, and

(b)   no further steps are to be taken under this Part of this Schedule.

Notice to cease consideration of application

17.—(1) This paragraph applies if the CAC has received an application under paragraph 11 or 12 and—

(a)   it has not decided whether the application is admissible, or

(b)   it has decided that the application is admissible.

(2) No further steps are to be taken under this Part of this Schedule if, before the final event occurs, the parties give notice to the CAC that they want no further steps to be taken.

(3) The final event occurs when the first of the following occurs—

(a)   the CAC issues a declaration under paragraph 22(2) in consequence of the application;

(b)   the last day of the notification period ends;

and the notification period is that defined by paragraph 24(5) and arising from the application.

Appropriate bargaining unit

18.—(1) If the CAC accepts an application under paragraph 11(2) or 12(2) it must try to help the parties to reach within the appropriate period an agreement as to what the appropriate bargaining unit is.

(2) The appropriate period is—

    (a) the period of 20 working days starting with the day after that on which the CAC gives notice of acceptance of the application, or

    (b) such longer period (so starting) as the CAC may specify to the parties by notice containing reasons for the extension.

19.—(1) This paragraph applies if—

    (a) the CAC accepts an application under paragraph 11(2) or 12(2), and

    (b) the parties have not agreed an appropriate bargaining unit at the end of the appropriate period.

(2) The CAC must decide the appropriate bargaining unit within—

    (a) the period of 10 working days starting with the day after that on which the appropriate period ends, or

    (b) such longer period (so starting) as the CAC may specify to the parties by notice containing reasons for the extension.

(3) In deciding the appropriate bargaining unit the CAC must take these matters into account—

    (a) the need for the unit to be compatible with effective management;

    (b) the matters listed in sub-paragraph (4), so far as they do not conflict with that need.

(4) The matters are—

    (a) the views of the employer and of the union (or unions);

    (b) existing national and local bargaining arrangements;

    (c) the desirability of avoiding small fragmented bargaining units within an undertaking;

    (d) the characteristics of workers falling within the proposed bargaining unit and of any other employees of the employer whom the CAC considers relevant;

    (e) the location of workers.

(5) The CAC must give notice of its decision to the parties.

Union recognition

20.—(1) This paragraph applies if—

    (a) the CAC accepts an application under paragraph 11(2) or 12(2),

    (b) the parties have agreed an appropriate bargaining unit at the end of the appropriate period, or the CAC has decided an appropriate bargaining unit, and

    (c) that bargaining unit differs from the proposed bargaining unit.

(2) Within the decision period the CAC must decide whether the application is invalid within the terms of paragraphs 43 to 50.

(3) In deciding whether the application is invalid, the CAC must consider any evidence which it has been given by the employer or the union (or unions).

(4) If the CAC decides that the application is invalid—

    (a) the CAC must give notice of its decision to the parties,

    (b) the CAC must not proceed with the application, and

    (c) no further steps are to be taken under this Part of this Schedule.

(5) If the CAC decides that the application is not invalid it must—

(a) proceed with the application, and

(b) give notice to the parties that it is so proceeding.

(6) The decision period is—

    (a) the period of 10 working days starting with the day after that on which the parties agree an appropriate bargaining unit or the CAC decides an appropriate bargaining unit, or

    (b) such longer period (so starting) as the CAC may specify to the parties by notice containing reasons for the extension.

21.—(1) This paragraph applies if—

    (a) the CAC accepts an application under paragraph 11(2) or 12(2),

    (b) the parties have agreed an appropriate bargaining unit at the end of the appropriate period, or the CAC has decided an appropriate bargaining unit, and

    (c) that bargaining unit is the same as the proposed bargaining unit.

(2) This paragraph also applies if the CAC accepts an application under paragraph 12(4).

(3) The CAC must proceed with the application.

22.—(1) This paragraph applies if—

    (a) the CAC proceeds with an application in accordance with paragraph 20 or 21, and

    (b) the CAC is satisfied that a majority of the workers constituting the bargaining unit are members of the union (or unions).

(2) The CAC must issue a declaration that the union is (or unions are) recognised as entitled to conduct collective bargaining on behalf of the workers constituting the bargaining unit.

(3) But if any of the three qualifying conditions is fulfilled, instead of issuing a declaration under sub-paragraph (2) the CAC must give notice to the parties that it intends to arrange for the holding of a secret ballot in which the workers constituting the bargaining unit are asked whether they want the union (or unions) to conduct collective bargaining on their behalf.

(4) These are the three qualifying conditions—

    (a) the CAC is satisfied that a ballot should be held in the interests of good industrial relations;

    (b) a significant number of the union members within the bargaining unit inform the CAC that they do not want the union (or unions) to conduct collective bargaining on their behalf;

    (c) membership evidence is produced which leads the CAC to conclude that there are doubts whether a significant number of the union members within the bargaining unit want the union (or unions) to conduct collective bargaining on their behalf.

(5) For the purposes of sub-paragraph (4)(c) membership evidence is—

    (a) evidence about the circumstances in which union members became members;

    (b)   evidence about the length of time for which union members have been members, in a case where the CAC is satisfied that such evidence should be taken into account.

23.—(1) This paragraph applies if—

    (a)   the CAC proceeds with an application in accordance with paragraph 20 or 21, and

    (b)   the CAC is not satisfied that a majority of the workers constituting the bargaining unit are members of the union (or unions).

(2) The CAC must give notice to the parties that it intends to arrange for the holding of a secret ballot in which the workers constituting the bargaining unit are asked whether they want the union (or unions) to conduct collective bargaining on their behalf.

24.—(1) This paragraph applies if the CAC gives notice under paragraph 22(3) or 23(2).

(2) Within the notification period—

    (a)   the union (or unions), or

    (b)   the union (or unions) and the employer,

may notify the CAC that the party making the notification does not (or the parties making the notification do not) want the CAC to arrange for the holding of the ballot.

(3) If the CAC is so notified—

    (a)   it must not arrange for the holding of the ballot,

    (b)   it must inform the parties that it will not arrange for the holding of the ballot, and why, and

    (c)   no further steps are to be taken under this Part of this Schedule.

(4) If the CAC is not so notified it must arrange for the holding of the ballot.

(5) The notification period is the period of 10 working days starting—

    (a)   for the purposes of sub-paragraph (2)(a), with the day on which the union (or last of the unions) receives the CAC's notice under paragraph 22(3) or 23(2), or

    (b)   for the purposes of sub-paragraph (2)(b), with that day or (if later) the day on which the employer receives the CAC's notice under paragraph 22(3) or 23(2)

25.—(1) This paragraph applies if the CAC arranges under paragraph 24 for the holding of a ballot.

(2) The ballot must be conducted by a qualified independent person appointed by the CAC.

(3) The ballot must be conducted within—

    (a)   the period of 20 working days starting with the day after that on which the qualified independent person is appointed, or

    (b)   such longer period (so starting) as the CAC may decide.

(4) The ballot must be conducted—

(a) at a workplace or workplaces decided by the CAC,

(b) by post, or

(c) by a combination of the methods described in sub-paragraphs (a) and (b),

depending on the CAC's preference.

(5) In deciding how the ballot is to be conducted the CAC must take into account—

(a) the likelihood of the ballot being affected by unfairness or malpractice if it were conducted at a workplace or workplaces;

(b) costs and practicality;

(c) such other matters as the CAC considers appropriate.

(6) The CAC may not decide that the ballot is to be conducted as mentioned in sub-paragraph (4)(c) unless there are special factors making such a decision appropriate; and special factors include—

(a) factors arising from the location of workers or the nature of their employment;

(b) factors put to the CAC by the employer or the union (or unions).

(7) A person is a qualified independent person if—

(a) he satisfies such conditions as may be specified for the purposes of this paragraph by order of the Secretary of State or is himself so specified, and

(b) there are no grounds for believing either that he will carry out any functions conferred on him in relation to the ballot otherwise than competently or that his independence in relation to the ballot might reasonably be called into question.

(8) An order under sub-paragraph (7)(a) shall be made by statutory instrument subject to annulment in pursuance of a resolution of either House of Parliament.

(9) As soon as is reasonably practicable after the CAC is required under paragraph 24 to arrange for the holding of a ballot it must inform the parties—

(a) that it is so required;

(b) of the name of the person appointed to conduct the ballot and the date of his appointment;

(c) of the period within which the ballot must be conducted;

(d) whether the ballot is to be conducted by post or at a workplace or workplaces;

(e) of the workplace or workplaces concerned (if the ballot is to be conducted at a workplace or workplaces).

26.—(1) An employer who is informed by the CAC under paragraph 25(9) must comply with the following three duties.

(2) The first duty is to co-operate generally, in connection with the ballot, with the union (or unions) and the person appointed to conduct the ballot; and the second and third duties are not to prejudice the generality of this.

(3) The second duty is to give to the union (or unions) such access to the workers constituting the bargaining unit as is reasonable to enable the union (or unions) to

inform the workers of the object of the ballot and to seek their support and their opinions on the issues involved.

(4) The third duty is to do the following (so far as it is reasonable to expect the employer to do so)—

    (a) to give to the CAC, within the period of 10 working days starting with the day after that on which the employer is informed under paragraph 25(9), the names and home addresses of the workers constituting the bargaining unit;

    (b) to give to the CAC, as soon as is reasonably practicable, the name and home address of any worker who joins the unit after the employer has complied with paragraph (a);

    (c) to inform the CAC, as soon as is reasonably practicable, of any worker whose name has been given to the CAC under paragraph (a) or (b) but who ceases to be within the unit.

(5) As soon as is reasonably practicable after the CAC receives any information under sub-paragraph (4) it must pass it on to the person appointed to conduct the ballot.

(6) If asked to do so by the union (or unions) the person appointed to conduct the ballot must send to any worker—

    (a) whose name and home address have been given under sub-paragraph (5), and

    (b) who is still within the unit (so far as the person so appointed is aware),

any information supplied by the union (or unions) to the person so appointed.

(7) The duty under sub-paragraph (6) does not apply unless the union bears (or unions bear) the cost of sending the information.

(8) Each of the following powers shall be taken to include power to issue Codes of Practice about reasonable access for the purposes of sub-paragraph (3)—

    (a) the power of ACAS under section 199(1);

    (b) the power of the Secretary of State under section 203(1)(a).

27.—(1) If the CAC is satisfied that the employer has failed to fulfil any of the three duties imposed by paragraph 26, and the ballot has not been held, the CAC may order the employer—

    (a) to take such steps to remedy the failure as the CAC considers reasonable and specifies in the order, and

    (b) to do so within such period as the CAC considers reasonable and specifies in the order.

(2) If the CAC is satisfied that the employer has failed to comply with an order under sub-paragraph (1), and the ballot has not been held, the CAC may issue a declaration that the union is (or unions are) recognised as entitled to conduct collective bargaining on behalf of the bargaining unit.

(3) If the CAC issues a declaration under sub-paragraph (2) it shall take steps to cancel the holding of the ballot; and if the ballot is held it shall have no effect.

28.—(1) This paragraph applies if the holding of a ballot has been arranged under paragraph 24 whether or not it has been cancelled.

(2) The gross costs of the ballot shall be borne—

    (a)   as to half, by the employer, and

    (b)   as to half, by the union (or unions).

(3) If there is more than one union they shall bear their half of the gross costs—

    (a)   in such proportions as they jointly indicate to the person appointed to conduct the ballot, or

    (b)   in the absence of such an indication, in equal shares.

(4) The person appointed to conduct the ballot may send to the employer and the union (or each of the unions) a demand stating—

    (a)   the gross costs of the ballot, and

    (b)   the amount of the gross costs to be borne by the recipient.

(5) In such a case the recipient must pay the amount stated to the person sending the demand, and must do so within the period of 15 working days starting with the day after that on which the demand is received.

(6) In England and Wales, if the amount stated is not paid in accordance with sub-paragraph (5) it shall, if a county court so orders, be recoverable by execution issued from that court or otherwise as if it were payable under an order of that court.

(7) References to the costs of the ballot are to—

    (a)   the costs wholly, exclusively and necessarily incurred in connection with the ballot by the person appointed to conduct it,

    (b)   such reasonable amount as the person appointed to conduct the ballot charges for his services, and

    (c)   such other costs as the employer and the union (or unions) agree.

29.—(1) As soon as is reasonably practicable after the CAC is informed of the result of a ballot by the person conducting it, the CAC must act under this paragraph.

(2) The CAC must inform the employer and the union (or unions) of the result of the ballot.

(3) If the result is that the union is (or unions are) supported by—

    (a)   a majority of the workers voting, and

    (b)   at least 40 per cent of the workers constituting the bargaining unit,

the CAC must issue a declaration that the union is (or unions are) recognised as entitled to conduct collective bargaining on behalf of the bargaining unit.

(4) If the result is otherwise the CAC must issue a declaration that the union is (or unions are) not entitled to be so recognised.

(5) The Secretary of State may by order amend sub-paragraph (3) so as to specify a different degree of support; and different provision may be made for different circumstances.

(6) An order under sub-paragraph (5) shall be made by statutory instrument.

(7) No such order shall be made unless a draft of it has been laid before Parliament and approved by a resolution of each House of Parliament.

Consequences of recognition

30.—(1) This paragraph applies if the CAC issues a declaration under this Part of this Schedule that the union is (or unions are) recognised as entitled to conduct collective bargaining on behalf of a bargaining unit.

(2) The parties may in the negotiation period conduct negotiations with a view to agreeing a method by which they will conduct collective bargaining.

(3) If no agreement is made in the negotiation period the employer or the union (or unions) may apply to the CAC for assistance.

(4) The negotiation period is—

   (a) the period of 30 working days starting with the start day, or
   (b) such longer period (so starting) as the parties may from time to time agree.

(5) The start day is the day after that on which the parties are notified of the declaration.

31.—(1) This paragraph applies if an application for assistance is made to the CAC under paragraph 30.

(2) The CAC must try to help the parties to reach in the agreement period an agreement on a method by which they will conduct collective bargaining.

(3) If at the end of the agreement period the parties have not made such an agreement the CAC must specify to the parties the method by which they are to conduct collective bargaining.

(4) Any method specified under sub-paragraph (3) is to have effect as if it were contained in a legally enforceable contract made by the parties.

(5) But if the parties agree in writing—

   (a) that sub-paragraph (4) shall not apply, or shall not apply to particular parts of the method specified by the CAC, or
   (b) to vary or replace the method specified by the CAC,

the written agreement shall have effect as a legally enforceable contract made by the parties.

(6) Specific performance shall be the only remedy available for breach of anything which is a legally enforceable contract by virtue of this paragraph.

(7) If at any time before a specification is made under sub-paragraph (3) the parties jointly apply to the CAC requesting it to stop taking steps under this paragraph, the CAC must comply with the request.

(8) The agreement period is—

   (a) the period of 20 working days starting with the day after that on which the CAC receives the application under paragraph 30, or
   (b) such longer period (so starting) as the CAC may decide with the consent of the parties.

Method not carried out

32.—(1) This paragraph applies if—

    (a) the CAC issues a declaration under this Part of this Schedule that the union is (or unions are) recognised as entitled to conduct collective bargaining on behalf of a bargaining unit,

    (b) the parties agree a method by which they will conduct collective bargaining, and

    (c) one or more of the parties fails to carry out the agreement.

(2) The parties may apply to the CAC for assistance.

(3) Paragraph 31 applies as if "paragraph 30" (in each place) read "paragraph 30 or paragraph 32".

General provisions about admissibility

33. An application under paragraph 11 or 12 is not admissible unless—

    (a) it is made in such form as the CAC specifies, and

    (b) it is supported by such documents as the CAC specifies.

34. An application under paragraph 11 or 12 is not admissible unless the union gives (or unions give) to the employer—

    (a) notice of the application, and

    (b) a copy of the application and any documents supporting it.

35.—(1) An application under paragraph 11 or 12 is not admissible if the CAC is satisfied that there is already in force a collective agreement under which a union is (or unions are) recognised as entitled to conduct collective bargaining on behalf of any workers falling within the relevant bargaining unit.

(2) But sub-paragraph (1) does not apply to an application under paragraph 11 or 12 if—

    (a) the union (or unions) recognised under the collective agreement and the union (or unions) making the application under paragraph 11 or 12 are the same, and

    (b) the matters in respect of which the union is (or unions are) entitled to conduct collective bargaining do not include pay, hours or holidays.

(3) A declaration of recognition which is the subject of a declaration under paragraph 83(2) must for the purposes of sub-paragraph (1) be treated as ceasing to have effect to the extent specified in paragraph 83(2) on the making of the declaration under paragraph 83(2).

(4) In applying sub-paragraph (1) an agreement for recognition (the agreement in question) must be ignored if—

    (a) the union does not have (or none of the unions has) a certificate under section 6 that it is independent,

    (b) at some time there was an agreement (the old agreement) between the employer and the union under which the union (whether alone or with other unions) was recognised as entitled to conduct collective bargaining on behalf of a group of workers which was the same or substantially the same as the group covered by the agreement in question, and

(c) the old agreement ceased to have effect in the period of three years ending with the date of the agreement in question.

(5) It is for the CAC to decide whether one group of workers is the same or substantially the same as another, but in deciding the CAC may take account of the views of any person it believes has an interest in the matter.

(6) The relevant bargaining unit is—

(a) the proposed bargaining unit, where the application is under paragraph 11(2) or 12(2);

(b) the agreed bargaining unit, where the application is under paragraph 12(4).

36.—(1) An application under paragraph 11 or 12 is not admissible unless the CAC decides that—

(a) members of the union (or unions) constitute at least 10 per cent of the workers constituting the relevant bargaining unit, and

(b) a majority of the workers constituting the relevant bargaining unit would be likely to favour recognition of the union (or unions) as entitled to conduct collective bargaining on behalf of the bargaining unit.

(2) The relevant bargaining unit is—

(a) the proposed bargaining unit, where the application is under paragraph 11(2) or 12(2);

(b) the agreed bargaining unit, where the application is under paragraph 12(4).

(3) The CAC must give reasons for the decision.

37.—(1) This paragraph applies to an application made by more than one union under paragraph 11 or 12.

(2) The application is not admissible unless—

(a) the unions show that they will co-operate with each other in a manner likely to secure and maintain stable and effective collective bargaining arrangements, and

(b) the unions show that, if the employer wishes, they will enter into arrangements under which collective bargaining is conducted by the unions acting together on behalf of the workers constituting the relevant bargaining unit.

(3) The relevant bargaining unit is—

(a) the proposed bargaining unit, where the application is under paragraph 11(2) or 12(2);

(b) the agreed bargaining unit, where the application is under paragraph 11(4).

38.—(1) This paragraph applies if—

   (a)   the CAC accepts a relevant application relating to a bargaining unit or proceeds under paragraph 20 with an application relating to a bargaining unit,

   (b)   the application has not been withdrawn,

   (c)   no notice has been given under paragraph 17(2),

   (d)   the CAC has not issued a declaration under paragraph 22(2), 27(2), 29(3) or 29(4) in relation to that bargaining unit, and

   (e)   no notification has been made under paragraph 24(2).

(2) Another relevant application is not admissible if—

   (a)   at least one worker falling within the relevant bargaining unit also falls within the bargaining unit referred to in sub-paragraph (1), and

   (b)   the application is made by a union (or unions) other than the union (or unions) which made the application referred to in sub-paragraph (1).

(3) A relevant application is an application under paragraph 11 or 12.

(4) The relevant bargaining unit is—

   (a)   the proposed bargaining unit, where the application is under paragraph 11(2) or 12(2);

   (b)   the agreed bargaining unit, where the application is under paragraph 12(4).

39.—(1) This paragraph applies if the CAC accepts a relevant application relating to a bargaining unit or proceeds under paragraph 20 with an application relating to a bargaining unit.

(2) Another relevant application is not admissible if—

   (a)   the application is made within the period of 3 years starting with the day after that on which the CAC gave notice of acceptance of the application mentioned in sub-paragraph (1),

   (b)   the relevant bargaining unit is the same or substantially the same as the bargaining unit mentioned in sub-paragraph (1), and

   (c)   the application is made by the union (or unions) which made the application mentioned in sub-paragraph (1).

(3) A relevant application is an application under paragraph 11 or 12.

(4) The relevant bargaining unit is—

   (a)   the proposed bargaining unit, where the application is under paragraph 11(2) or 12(2);

   (b)   the agreed bargaining unit, where the application is under paragraph 12(4).

(5) This paragraph does not apply if paragraph 40 or 41 applies.

40.—(1) This paragraph applies if the CAC issues a declaration under paragraph 29(4) that a union is (or unions are) not entitled to be recognised as entitled to conduct collective bargaining on behalf of a bargaining unit; and this is so whether the ballot concerned is held under this Part or Part III of this Schedule.

(2) An application under paragraph 11 or 12 is not admissible if—

(a) the application is made within the period of 3 years starting with the day after that on which the declaration was issued,

(b) the relevant bargaining unit is the same or substantially the same as the bargaining unit mentioned in sub-paragraph (1), and

(c) the application is made by the union (or unions) which made the application leading to the declaration.

(3) The relevant bargaining unit is—

(a) the proposed bargaining unit, where the application is under paragraph 11(2) or 12(2);

(b) the agreed bargaining unit, where the application is under paragraph 12(4).

41.—(1) This paragraph applies if the CAC issues a declaration under paragraph 121(3) that bargaining arrangements are to cease to have effect; and this is so whether the ballot concerned is held under Part IV or Part V of this Schedule.

(2) An application under paragraph 11 or 12 is not admissible if—

(a) the application is made within the period of 3 years starting with the day after that on which the declaration was issued,

(b) the relevant bargaining unit is the same or substantially the same as the bargaining unit to which the bargaining arrangements mentioned in sub-paragraph (1) relate, and

(c) the application is made by the union which was a party (or unions which were parties) to the proceedings leading to the declaration.

(3) The relevant bargaining unit is—

(a) the proposed bargaining unit, where the application is under paragraph 11(2) or 12(2);

(b) the agreed bargaining unit, where the application is under paragraph 12(4).

42.—(1) This paragraph applies for the purposes of paragraphs 39 to 41.

(2) It is for the CAC to decide whether one bargaining unit is the same or substantially the same as another, but in deciding the CAC may take account of the views of any person it believes has an interest in the matter.

General provisions about validity

43.—(1) Paragraphs 44 to 50 apply if the CAC has to decide under paragraph 20 whether an application is valid.

(2) In those paragraphs—

(a) references to the application in question are to that application, and

(b) references to the relevant bargaining unit are to the bargaining unit agreed by the parties or decided by the CAC.

44.—(1) The application in question is invalid if the CAC is satisfied that there is already in force a collective agreement under which a union is (or unions are) recognised as entitled to conduct collective bargaining on behalf of any workers falling within the relevant bargaining unit.

(2) But sub-paragraph (1) does not apply to the application in question if—

(a) the union (or unions) recognised under the collective agreement and the union (or unions) making the application in question are the same, and

(b) the matters in respect of which the union is (or unions are) entitled to conduct collective bargaining do not include pay, hours or holidays.

(3) A declaration of recognition which is the subject of a declaration under paragraph 83(2) must for the purposes of sub-paragraph (1) be treated as ceasing to have effect to the extent specified in paragraph 83(2) on the making of the declaration under paragraph 83(2).

(4) In applying sub-paragraph (1) an agreement for recognition (the agreement in question) must be ignored if—

(a) the union does not have (or none of the unions has) a certificate under section 6 that it is independent,

(b) at some time there was an agreement (the old agreement) between the employer and the union under which the union (whether alone or with other unions) was recognised as entitled to conduct collective bargaining on behalf of a group of workers which was the same or substantially the same as the group covered by the agreement in question, and

(c) the old agreement ceased to have effect in the period of three years ending with the date of the agreement in question.

(5) It is for the CAC to decide whether one group of workers is the same or substantially the same as another, but in deciding the CAC may take account of the views of any person it believes has an interest in the matter.

45. The application in question is invalid unless the CAC decides that—

(a) members of the union (or unions) constitute at least 10 per cent of the workers constituting the relevant bargaining unit, and

(b) a majority of the workers constituting the relevant bargaining unit would be likely to favour recognition of the union (or unions) as entitled to conduct collective bargaining on behalf of the bargaining unit.

46.—(1) This paragraph applies if—

(a) the CAC accepts an application under paragraph 11 or 12 relating to a bargaining unit or proceeds under paragraph 20 with an application relating to a bargaining unit,

(b) the application has not been withdrawn,

(c) no notice has been given under paragraph 17(2),

(d) the CAC has not issued a declaration under paragraph 22(2), 27(2), 29(3) or 29(4) in relation to that bargaining unit, and

(e) no notification has been made under paragraph 24(2).

(2) The application in question is invalid if—

(a) at least one worker falling within the relevant bargaining unit also falls within the bargaining unit referred to in sub-paragraph (1), and

(b) the application in question is made by a union (or unions) other than the union (or unions) which made the application referred to in sub-paragraph (1).

47.—(1) This paragraph applies if the CAC accepts an application under paragraph 11 or 12 relating to a bargaining unit or proceeds under paragraph 20 with an application relating to a bargaining unit.

(2) The application in question is invalid if—

    (a) the application is made within the period of 3 years starting with the day after that on which the CAC gave notice of acceptance of the application mentioned in sub-paragraph (1),

    (b) the relevant bargaining unit is the same or substantially the same as the bargaining unit mentioned in sub-paragraph (1), and

    (c) the application is made by the union (or unions) which made the application mentioned in sub-paragraph (1).

(3) This paragraph does not apply if paragraph 48 or 49 applies.

48.—(1) This paragraph applies if the CAC issues a declaration under paragraph 29(4) that a union is (or unions are) not entitled to be recognised as entitled to conduct collective bargaining on behalf of a bargaining unit; and this is so whether the ballot concerned is held under this Part or Part III of this Schedule.

(2) The application in question is invalid if—

    (a) the application is made within the period of 3 years starting with the date of the declaration,

    (b) the relevant bargaining unit is the same or substantially the same as the bargaining unit mentioned in sub-paragraph (1), and

    (c) the application is made by the union (or unions) which made the application leading to the declaration.

49.—(1) This paragraph applies if the CAC issues a declaration under paragraph 121(3) that bargaining arrangements are to cease to have effect; and this is so whether the ballot concerned is held under Part IV or Part V of this Schedule.

(2) The application in question is invalid if—

    (a) the application is made within the period of 3 years starting with the day after that on which the declaration was issued,

    (b) the relevant bargaining unit is the same or substantially the same as the bargaining unit to which the bargaining arrangements mentioned in sub-paragraph (1) relate, and

    (c) the application is made by the union which was a party (or unions which were parties) to the proceedings leading to the declaration.

50.—(1) This paragraph applies for the purposes of paragraphs 47 to 49.

(2) It is for the CAC to decide whether one bargaining unit is the same or substantially the same as another, but in deciding the CAC may take account of the views of any person it believes has an interest in the matter.

Competing applications

51.—(1) For the purposes of this paragraph—

    (a) the original application is the application referred to in paragraph 38(1) or 46(1), and

    (b) the competing application is the other application referred to in paragraph 38(2) or the application in question referred to in paragraph 46(2);

but an application cannot be an original application unless it was made under paragraph 11(2) or 12(2).

(2) This paragraph applies if—

    (a) the CAC decides that the competing application is not admissible by reason of paragraph 38 or is invalid by reason of paragraph 46,

    (b) at the time the decision is made the parties to the original application have not agreed the appropriate bargaining unit under paragraph 18, and the CAC has not decided the appropriate bargaining unit under paragraph 19, in relation to the application, and

    (c) the 10 per cent test (within the meaning given by paragraph 14) is satisfied with regard to the competing application.

(3) In such a case—

    (a) the CAC must cancel the original application,

    (b) the CAC must give notice to the parties to the application that it has been cancelled,

    (c) no further steps are to be taken under this Part of this Schedule in relation to the application, and

    (d) the application shall be treated as if it had never been admissible.

PART II

VOLUNTARY RECOGNITION

Agreements for recognition

52.—(1) This paragraph applies for the purposes of this Part of this Schedule.

(2) An agreement is an agreement for recognition if the following conditions are fulfilled in relation to it—

    (a) the agreement is made in the permitted period between a union (or unions) and an employer in consequence of a request made under paragraph 4 and valid within the terms of paragraphs 5 to 9;

    (b) under the agreement the union is (or unions are) recognised as entitled to conduct collective bargaining on behalf of a group or groups of workers employed by the employer;

    (c) if sub-paragraph (5) applies to the agreement, it is satisfied.

(3) The permitted period is the period which begins with the day on which the employer receives the request and ends when the first of the following occurs—

    (a) the union withdraws (or unions withdraw) the request;

    (b) the union withdraws (or unions withdraw) any application under paragraph 11 or 12 made in consequence of the request;

    (c) the CAC gives notice of a decision under paragraph 14(7) which precludes it from accepting such an application under paragraph 11 or 12;

(d) the CAC gives notice under paragraph 15(4)(a) or 20(4)(a) in relation to such an application under paragraph 11 or 12;

(e) the parties give notice to the CAC under paragraph 17(2) in relation to such an application under paragraph 11 or 12;

(f) the CAC issues a declaration under paragraph 22(2) in consequence of such an application under paragraph 11 or 12;

(g) the CAC is notified under paragraph 24(2) in relation to such an application under paragraph 11 or 12;

(h) the last day of the notification period ends (the notification period being that defined by paragraph 24(5) and arising from such an application under paragraph 11 or 12);

(i) the CAC is required under paragraph 51(3) to cancel such an application under paragraph 11 or 12.

(4) Sub-paragraph (5) applies to an agreement if—

(a) at the time it is made the CAC has received an application under paragraph 11 or 12 in consequence of the request mentioned in subparagraph (2), and

(b) the CAC has not decided whether the application is admissible or it has decided that it is admissible.

(5) This sub-paragraph is satisfied if, in relation to the application under paragraph 11 or 12, the parties give notice to the CAC under paragraph 17 before the final event (as defined in paragraph 17) occurs.

Other interpretation

53.—(1) This paragraph applies for the purposes of this Part of this Schedule.

(2) In relation to an agreement for recognition, references to the bargaining unit are to the group of workers (or the groups taken together) to which the agreement for recognition relates.

(3) In relation to an agreement for recognition, references to the parties are to the union (or unions) and the employer who are parties to the agreement.

54.—(1) This paragraph applies for the purposes of this Part of this Schedule.

(2) The meaning of collective bargaining given by section 178(1) shall not apply.

(3) Except in paragraph 63(2), in relation to an agreement for recognition references to collective bargaining are to negotiations relating to the matters in respect of which the union is (or unions are) recognised as entitled to conduct negotiations under the agreement for recognition.

(4) In paragraph 63(2) the reference to collective bargaining is to negotiations relating to pay, hours and holidays.

Determination of type of agreement

55.—(1) This paragraph applies if one or more of the parties to an agreement applies to the CAC for a decision whether or not the agreement is an agreement for recognition.

(2) The CAC must give notice of receipt of an application under sub-paragraph (1) to any parties to the agreement who are not parties to the application.

(3) The CAC must within the decision period decide whether the agreement is an agreement for recognition.

(4) If the CAC decides that the agreement is an agreement for recognition it must issue a declaration to that effect.

(5) If the CAC decides that the agreement is not an agreement for recognition it must issue a declaration to that effect.

(6) The decision period is—

    (a) the period of 10 working days starting with the day after that on which the CAC receives the application under sub-paragraph (1), or

    (b) such longer period (so starting) as the CAC may specify to the parties to the agreement by notice containing reasons for the extension.

Termination of agreement for recognition

56.—(1) The employer may not terminate an agreement for recognition before the relevant period ends.

(2) After that period ends the employer may terminate the agreement, with or without the consent of the union (or unions).

(3) The union (or unions) may terminate an agreement for recognition at any time, with or without the consent of the employer.

(4) Sub-paragraphs (1) to (3) have effect subject to the terms of the agreement or any other agreement of the parties.

(5) The relevant period is the period of three years starting with the day after the date of the agreement.

57.—(1) If an agreement for recognition is terminated, as from the termination the agreement and any provisions relating to the collective bargaining method shall cease to have effect.

(2) For this purpose provisions relating to the collective bargaining method are—

    (a) any agreement between the parties as to the method by which collective bargaining is to be conducted with regard to the bargaining unit, or

    (b) anything effective as, or as if contained in, a legally enforceable contract and relating to the method by which collective bargaining is to be conducted with regard to the bargaining unit.

Application to CAC to specify method

58.—(1) This paragraph applies if the parties make an agreement for recognition.

(2) The parties may in the negotiation period conduct negotiations with a view to agreeing a method by which they will conduct collective bargaining.

(3) If no agreement is made in the negotiation period the employer or the union (or unions) may apply to the CAC for assistance.

(4) The negotiation period is—

    (a) the period of 30 working days starting with the start day, or

    (b) such longer period (so starting) as the parties may from time to time agree.

(5) The start day is the day after that on which the agreement is made.

59.—(1) This paragraph applies if—

    (a) the parties to an agreement for recognition agree a method by which they will conduct collective bargaining, and

    (b) one or more of the parties fails to carry out the agreement as to a method.

(2) The employer or the union (or unions) may apply to the CAC for assistance.

60.—(1) This paragraph applies if an application for assistance is made to the CAC under paragraph 58 or 59.

(2) The application is not admissible unless the conditions in sub-paragraphs (3) and (4) are satisfied.

(3) The condition is that the employer, taken with any associated employer or employers, must—

    (a) employ at least 21 workers on the day the application is made, or

    (b) employ an average of at least 21 workers in the 13 weeks ending with that day.

(4) The condition is that the union (or every union) has a certificate under section 6 that it is independent.

(5) To find the average under sub-paragraph (3)(b)—

    (a) take the number of workers employed in each of the 13 weeks (including workers not employed for the whole of the week);

    (b) aggregate the 13 numbers;

    (c) divide the aggregate by 13.

(6) For the purposes of sub-paragraph (3)(a) any worker employed by an associated company incorporated outside Great Britain must be ignored unless the day the application was made fell within a period during which he ordinarily worked in Great Britain.

(7) For the purposes of sub-paragraph (3)(b) any worker employed by an associated company incorporated outside Great Britain must be ignored in relation to a week unless the whole or any part of that week fell within a period during which he ordinarily worked in Great Britain.

(8) For the purposes of sub-paragraphs (6) and (7) a worker who is employed on board a ship registered in the register maintained under section 8 of the Merchant Shipping Act 1995 shall be treated as ordinarily working in Great Britain unless—

    (a) the ship's entry in the register specifies a port outside Great Britain as the port to which the vessel is to be treated as belonging,

    (b) the employment is wholly outside Great Britain, or

    (c) the worker is not ordinarily resident in Great Britain.

(9) An order made under paragraph 7(6) may also—

    (a) provide that sub-paragraphs (2), (3) and (5) to (8) of this paragraph are not to apply, or are not to apply in specified circumstances, or

    (b) vary the number of workers for the time being specified in sub-paragraph (3).

61.—(1) An application to the CAC is not admissible unless—

    (a) it is made in such form as the CAC specifies, and
    (b) it is supported by such documents as the CAC specifies.

(2) An application which is made by a union (or unions) to the CAC is not admissible unless the union gives (or unions give) to the employer—

    (a) notice of the application, and
    (b) a copy of the application and any documents supporting it.

(3) An application which is made by an employer to the CAC is not admissible unless the employer gives to the union (or each of the unions)—

    (a) notice of the application, and
    (b) a copy of the application and any documents supporting it.

CAC's response to application

62.—(1) The CAC must give notice to the parties of receipt of an application under paragraph 58 or 59.

(2) Within the acceptance period the CAC must decide whether the application is admissible within the terms of paragraphs 60 and 61.

(3) In deciding whether an application is admissible the CAC must consider any evidence which it has been given by the employer or the union (or unions).

(4) If the CAC decides that the application is not admissible—

    (a) the CAC must give notice of its decision to the parties,
    (b) the CAC must not accept the application, and
    (c) no further steps are to be taken under this Part of this Schedule.

(5) If the CAC decides that the application is admissible it must—

    (a) accept the application, and
    (b) give notice of the acceptance to the parties.

(6) The acceptance period is—

    (a) the period of 10 working days starting with the day after that on which the CAC receives the application, or
    (b) such longer period (so starting) as the CAC may specify to the parties by notice containing reasons for the extension.

63.—(1) If the CAC accepts an application it must try to help the parties to reach in the agreement period an agreement on a method by which they will conduct collective bargaining.

(2) If at the end of the agreement period the parties have not made such an agreement the CAC must specify to the parties the method by which they are to conduct collective bargaining.

(3) Any method specified under sub-paragraph (2) is to have effect as if it were contained in a legally enforceable contract made by the parties.

(4) But if the parties agree in writing—

(a) that sub-paragraph (3) shall not apply, or shall not apply to particular parts of the method specified by the CAC, or

(b) to vary or replace the method specified by the CAC,

the written agreement shall have effect as a legally enforceable contract made by the parties.

(5) Specific performance shall be the only remedy available for breach of anything which is a legally enforceable contract by virtue of this paragraph.

(6) If the CAC accepts an application, the applicant may not withdraw it after the end of the agreement period.

(7) If at any time before a specification is made under sub-paragraph (2) the parties jointly apply to the CAC requesting it to stop taking steps under this paragraph, the CAC must comply with the request.

(8) The agreement period is—

(a) the period of 20 working days starting with the day after that on which the CAC gives notice of acceptance of the application, or

(b) such longer period (so starting) as the parties may from time to time agree.

PART III

CHANGES AFFECTING BARGAINING UNIT

Introduction

64.—(1) This Part of this Schedule applies if—

(a) the CAC has issued a declaration that a union is (or unions are) recognised as entitled to conduct collective bargaining on behalf of a bargaining unit, and

(b) provisions relating to the collective bargaining method apply in relation to the unit.

(2) In such a case, in this Part of this Schedule—

(a) references to the original unit are to the bargaining unit on whose behalf the union is (or unions are) recognised as entitled to conduct collective bargaining, and

(b) references to the bargaining arrangements are to the declaration and to the provisions relating to the collective bargaining method which apply in relation to the original unit.

(3) For this purpose provisions relating to the collective bargaining method are—

(a) the parties' agreement as to the method by which collective bargaining is to be conducted with regard to the original unit,

(b) anything effective as, or as if contained in, a legally enforceable contract and relating to the method by which collective bargaining is to be conducted with regard to the original unit, or

(c) any provision of this Part of this Schedule that a method of collective bargaining is to have effect with regard to the original unit.

65. References in this Part of this Schedule to the parties are to the employer and the union (or unions) concerned.

Either party believes unit no longer appropriate

66.—(1) This paragraph applies if the employer believes or the union believes (or unions believe) that the original unit is no longer an appropriate bargaining unit.

(2) The employer or union (or unions) may apply to the CAC to make a decision as to what is an appropriate bargaining unit.

67.—(1) An application under paragraph 66 is not admissible unless the CAC decides that it is likely that the original unit is no longer appropriate by reason of any of the matters specified in sub-paragraph (2).

(2) The matters are—

- (a) a change in the organisation or structure of the business carried on by the employer;
- (b) a change in the activities pursued by the employer in the course of the business carried on by him;
- (c) a substantial change in the number of workers employed in the original unit.

68.—(1) The CAC must give notice to the parties of receipt of an application under paragraph 66.

(2) Within the acceptance period the CAC must decide whether the application is admissible within the terms of paragraphs 67 and 92.

(3) In deciding whether the application is admissible the CAC must consider any evidence which it has been given by the employer or the union (or unions).

(4) If the CAC decides that the application is not admissible—

- (a) the CAC must give notice of its decision to the parties,
- (b) the CAC must not accept the application, and
- (c) no further steps are to be taken under this Part of this Schedule.

(5) If the CAC decides that the application is admissible it must—

- (a) accept the application, and
- (b) give notice of the acceptance to the parties.

(6) The acceptance period is—

- (a) the period of 10 working days starting with the day after that on which the CAC receives the application, or
- (b) such longer period (so starting) as the CAC may specify to the parties by notice containing reasons for the extension.

69.—(1) This paragraph applies if—

- (a) the CAC gives notice of acceptance of the application, and
- (b) before the end of the first period the parties agree a bargaining unit or units (the new unit or units) differing from the original unit and inform the CAC of their agreement.

(2) If in the CAC's opinion the new unit (or any of the new units) contains at least one worker falling within an outside bargaining unit no further steps are to be taken under this Part of this Schedule.

(3) If sub-paragraph (2) does not apply—

(a) the CAC must issue a declaration that the union is (or unions are) recognised as entitled to conduct collective bargaining on behalf of the new unit or units;

(b) so far as it affects workers in the new unit (or units) who fall within the original unit, the declaration shall have effect in place of any declaration that the union is (or unions are) recognised as entitled to conduct collective bargaining on behalf of the original unit;

(e) the method of collective bargaining relating to the original unit shall have effect in relation to the new unit or units, with any modifications which the CAC considers necessary to take account of the change of bargaining unit and specifies in the declaration.

(4) The first period is—

(a) the period of 10 working days starting with the day after that on which the CAC gives notice of acceptance of the application, or

(b) such longer period (so starting) as the parties may from time to time agree and notify to the CAC.

(5) An outside bargaining unit is a bargaining unit which fulfils these conditions—

(a) it is not the original unit;

(b) a union is (or unions are) recognised as entitled to conduct collective bargaining on its behalf;

(c) the union (or at least one of the unions) is not a party referred to in paragraph 64.

70.—(1) This paragraph applies if—

(a) the CAC gives notice of acceptance of the application, and

(b) the parties do not inform the CAC before the end of the first period that they have agreed a bargaining unit or units differing from the original unit.

(2) During the second period—

(a) the CAC must decide whether or not the original unit continues to be an appropriate bargaining unit;

(b) if the CAC decides that the original unit does not so continue, it must decide what other bargaining unit is or units are appropriate;

(c) the CAC must give notice to the parties of its decision or decisions under paragraphs (a) and (b).

(3) In deciding whether or not the original unit continues to be an appropriate bargaining unit the CAC must take into account only these matters—

(a) any change in the organisation or structure of the business carried on by the employer;

(b) any change in the activities pursued by the employer in the course of the business carried on by him;

(c) any substantial change in the number of workers employed in the original unit.

(4) In deciding what other bargaining unit is or units are appropriate the CAC must take these matters into account—

(a) the need for the unit or units to be compatible with effective management;
(b) the matters listed in sub-paragraph (5), so far as they do not conflict with that need.

(5) The matters are—

(a) the views of the employer and of the union (or unions);
(b) existing national and local bargaining arrangements;
(c) the desirability of avoiding small fragmented bargaining units within an undertaking;
(d) the characteristics of workers falling within the original unit and of any other employees of the employer whom the CAC considers relevant;
(e) the location of workers.

(6) If the CAC decides that two or more bargaining units are appropriate its decision must be such that no worker falls within more than one of them.

(7) The second period is—

(a) the period of 10 working days starting with the day after that on which the first period ends, or
(b) such longer period (so starting) as the CAC may specify to the parties by notice containing reasons for the extension.

71. If the CAC gives notice under paragraph 70 of a decision that the original unit continues to be an appropriate bargaining unit no further steps are to be taken under this Part of this Schedule.

72. Paragraph 82 applies if the CAC gives notice under paragraph 70 of—

(a) a decision that the original unit is no longer an appropriate bargaining unit, and
(b) a decision as to the bargaining unit which is (or units which are) appropriate.

73.—(1) This paragraph applies if—

(a) the parties agree under paragraph 69 a bargaining unit or units differing from the original unit,
(b) paragraph 69(2) does not apply, and
(c) at least one worker falling within the original unit does not fall within the new unit (or any of the new units).

(2) In such a case—

(a) the CAC must issue a declaration that the bargaining arrangements, so far as relating to the worker or workers mentioned in sub-paragraph (1)(c), are to cease to have effect on a date specified by the CAC in the declaration, and
(b) the bargaining arrangements shall cease to have effect accordingly.

Employer believes unit has ceased to exist

74.—(1) If the employer—

    (a)   believes that the original unit has ceased to exist, and

    (b)   wishes the bargaining arrangements to cease to have effect,

he must give the union (or each of the unions) a notice complying with sub-paragraph (2) and must give a copy of the notice to the CAC.

(2) A notice complies with this sub-paragraph if it—

    (a)   identifies the unit and the bargaining arrangements,

    (b)   states the date on which the notice is given,

    (c)   states that the unit has ceased to exist, and

    (d)   states that the bargaining arrangements are to cease to have effect on a date which is specified in the notice and which falls after the end of the period of 35 working days starting with the day after that on which the notice is given.

(3) Within the validation period the CAC must decide whether the notice complies with sub-paragraph (2).

(4) If the CAC decides that the notice does not comply with sub-paragraph (2).

    (a)   the CAC must give the parties notice of its decision, and

    (b)   the employer's notice shall be treated as not having been given.

(5) If the CAC decides that the notice complies with sub-paragraph (2) it must give the parties notice of the decision.

(6) The bargaining arrangements shall cease to have effect on the date specified under sub-paragraph (2)(d) if—

    (a)   the CAC gives notice under sub-paragraph (5), and

    (b)   the union does not (or unions do not) apply to the CAC under paragraph 75.

(7) The validation period is—

    (a)   the period of 10 working days starting with the day after that on which the CAC receives the copy of the notice, or

    (b)   such longer period (so starting) as the CAC may specify to the parties by notice containing reasons for the extension.

75.—(1) Paragraph 76 applies if—

    (a)   the CAC gives notice under paragraph 74(5), and

    (b)   within the period of 10 working days starting with the day after that on which the notice is given the union makes (or unions make) an application to the CAC for a decision on the questions specified in sub-paragraph (2).

(2) The questions are—

    (a)   whether the original unit has ceased to exist;

    (b)   whether the original unit is no longer appropriate by reason of any of the matters specified in sub-paragraph (3).

(3) The matters are—

    (a)   a change in the organisation or structure of the business carried on by the employer;

    (b)   a change in the activities pursued by the employer in the course of the business carried on by him;

    (c)   a substantial change in the number of workers employed in the original unit.

76.—(1) The CAC must give notice to the parties of receipt of an application under paragraph 75.

(2) Within the acceptance period the CAC must decide whether the application is admissible within the terms of paragraph 92.

(3) In deciding whether the application is admissible the CAC must consider any evidence which it has been given by the employer or the union (or unions).

(4) If the CAC decides that the application is not admissible—

    (a)   the CAC must give notice of its decision to the parties,

    (b)   the CAC must not accept the application, and

    (c)   no further steps are to be taken under this Part of this Schedule.

(5) If the CAC decides that the application is admissible it must—

    (a)   accept the application, and

    (b)   give notice of the acceptance to the parties.

(6) The acceptance period is—

    (a)   the period of 10 working days starting with the day after that on which the CAC receives the application, or

    (b)   such longer period (so starting) as the CAC may specify to the parties by notice containing reasons for the extension.

77.—(1) If the CAC accepts an application it—

    (a)   must give the employer and the union (or unions) an opportunity to put their views on the questions in relation to which the application was made;

    (b)   must decide the questions before the end of the decision period.

(2) If the CAC decides that the original unit has ceased to exist—

    (a)   the CAC must give the parties notice of its decision, and

    (b)   the bargaining arrangements shall cease to have effect on the termination date.

(3) If the CAC decides that the original unit has not ceased to exist, and that it is not the case that the original unit is no longer appropriate by reason of any of the matters specified in paragraph 75(3)—

    (a)   the CAC must give the parties notice of its decision, and

    (b)   the employer's notice shall be treated as not having been given.

(4) If the CAC decides that the original unit has not ceased to exist, and that the original unit is no longer appropriate by reason of any of the matters specified in paragraph 75(3), the CAC must give the parties notice of its decision.

(5) The decision period is—

(a) the period of 10 working days starting with the day after that on which the CAC gives notice of acceptance of the application, or

(b) such longer period (so starting) as the CAC may specify to the parties by notice containing reasons for the extension.

(6) The termination date is the later of—

(a) the date specified under paragraph 74(2)(d), and

(b) the day after the last day of the decision period.

78.—(1) This paragraph applies if—

(a) the CAC gives notice under paragraph 77(4), and

(b) before the end of the first period the parties agree a bargaining unit or units (the new unit or units) differing from the original unit and inform the CAC of their agreement.

(2) If in the CAC's opinion the new unit (or any of the new units) contains at least one worker falling within an outside bargaining unit no further steps are to be taken under this Part of this Schedule.

(3) If sub-paragraph (2) does not apply—

(a) the CAC must issue a declaration that the union is (or unions are) recognised as entitled to conduct collective bargaining on behalf of the new unit or units;

(b) so far as it affects workers in the new unit (or units) who fall within the original unit, the declaration shall have effect in place of any declaration that the union is (or unions are) recognised as entitled to conduct collective bargaining on behalf of the original unit;

(c) the method of collective bargaining relating to the original unit shall have effect in relation to the new unit or units, with any modifications which the CAC considers necessary to take account of the change of bargaining unit and specifies in the declaration.

(4) The first period is—

(a) the period of 10 working days starting with the day after that on which the CAC gives notice under paragraph 77(4), or

(b) such longer period (so starting) as the parties may from time to time agree and notify to the CAC.

(5) An outside bargaining unit is a bargaining unit which fulfils these conditions—

(a) it is not the original unit;

(b) a union is (or unions are) recognised as entitled to conduct collective bargaining on its behalf;

(c) the union (or at least one of the unions) is not a party referred to in paragraph 64.

79.—(1) This paragraph applies if—

(a) the CAC gives notice under paragraph 77(4), and

(b) the parties do not inform the CAC before the end of the first period that they have agreed a bargaining unit or units differing from the original unit.

(2) During the second period the CAC—

(a) must decide what other bargaining unit is or units are appropriate;
(b) must give notice of its decision to the parties.

(3) In deciding what other bargaining unit is or units are appropriate, the CAC must take these matters into account—

(a) the need for the unit or units to be compatible with effective management;
(b) the matters listed in sub-paragraph (4), so far as they do not conflict with that need.

(4) The matters are—

(a) the views of the employer and of the union (or unions);
(b) existing national and local bargaining arrangements;
(c) the desirability of avoiding small fragmented bargaining units within an undertaking;
(d) the characteristics of workers falling within the original unit and of any other employees of the employer whom the CAC considers relevant;
(e) the location of workers.

(5) If the CAC decides that two or more bargaining units are appropriate its decision must be such that no worker falls within more than one of them.

(6) The second period is—

(a) the period of 10 working days starting with the day after that on which the first period ends, or
(b) such longer period (so starting) as the CAC may specify to the parties by notice containing reasons for the extension.

80. Paragraph 82 applies if the CAC gives notice under paragraph 79 of a decision as to the bargaining unit which is (or units which are) appropriate.

81.—(1) This paragraph applies if—

(a) the parties agree under paragraph 78 a bargaining unit or units differing from the original unit,
(b) paragraph 78(2) does not apply, and
(c) at least one worker falling within the original unit does not fall within the new unit (or any of the new units).

(2) In such a case—

(a) the CAC must issue a declaration that the bargaining arrangements, so far as relating to the worker or workers mentioned in sub-paragraph (1)(c), are to cease to have effect on a date specified by the CAC in the declaration, and
(b) the bargaining arrangements shall cease to have effect accordingly.

Position where CAC decides new unit

82.—(1) This paragraph applies if the CAC gives notice under paragraph 70 of—

(a) a decision that the original unit is no longer an appropriate bargaining unit, and

    (b) a decision as to the bargaining unit which is (or units which are) appropriate.

(2) This paragraph also applies if the CAC gives notice under paragraph 79 of a decision as to the bargaining unit which is (or units which are) appropriate.

(3) The CAC—

    (a) must proceed as stated in paragraphs 83 to 89 with regard to the appropriate unit (if there is one only), or
    (b) must proceed as stated in paragraphs 83 to 89 with regard to each appropriate unit separately (if there are two or more).

(4) References in those paragraphs to the new unit are to the appropriate unit under consideration.

83.—(1) This paragraph applies if in the CAC's opinion the new unit contains at least one worker falling within a statutory outside bargaining unit.

(2) In such a case—

    (a) the CAC must issue a declaration that the relevant bargaining arrangements, so far as relating to workers falling within the new unit are to cease to have effect on a date specified by the CAC in the declaration, and
    (b) the relevant bargaining arrangements shall cease to have effect accordingly.

(3) The relevant bargaining arrangements are—

    (a) the bargaining arrangements relating to the original unit, and
    (b) the bargaining arrangements relating to each statutory outside bargaining unit containing workers who fall within the new unit.

(4) The bargaining arrangements relating to the original unit are the bargaining arrangements as defined in paragraph 64.

(5) The bargaining arrangements relating to an outside unit are—

    (a) the declaration recognising a union (or unions) as entitled to conduct collective bargaining on behalf of the workers constituting the outside unit, and
    (b) the provisions relating to the collective bargaining method.

(6) For this purpose the provisions relating to the collective bargaining method are—

    (a) any agreement by the employer and the union (or unions) as to the method by which collective bargaining is to be conducted with regard to the outside unit,
    (b) anything effective as, or as if contained in, a legally enforceable contract and relating to the method by which collective bargaining is to be conducted with regard to the outside unit, or
    (c) any provision of this Part of this Schedule that a method of collective bargaining is to have effect with regard to the outside unit.

(7) A statutory outside bargaining unit is a bargaining unit which fulfils these conditions—

    (a) it is not the original unit;

    (b) a union is (or unions are) recognised as entitled to conduct collective bargaining on its behalf by virtue of a declaration of the CAC;

    (c) the union (or at least one of the unions) is not a party referred to in paragraph 64.

(8) The date specified under sub-paragraph (1)(a) must be—

    (a) the date on which the relevant period expires, or

    (b) if the CAC believes that to maintain the relevant bargaining arrangements would be impracticable or contrary to the interests of good industrial relations, the date after the date on which the declaration is issued;

and the relevant period is the period of 65 working days starting with the day after that on which the declaration is issued.

84.—(1) This paragraph applies if in the CAC's opinion the new unit contains—

    (a) at least one worker falling within a voluntary outside bargaining unit, but

    (b) no worker falling within a statutory outside bargaining unit.

(2) In such a case—

    (a) the CAC must issue a declaration that the original bargaining arrangements, so far as relating to workers falling within the new unit, are to cease to have effect on a date specified by the CAC in the declaration, and

    (b) the original bargaining arrangements shall cease to have effect accordingly.

(3) The original bargaining arrangements are the bargaining arrangements as defined in paragraph 64.

(4) A voluntary outside bargaining unit is a bargaining unit which fulfils these conditions—

    (a) it is not the original unit;

    (b) a union is (or unions are) recognised as entitled to conduct collective bargaining on its behalf by virtue of an agreement with the employer;

    (c) the union (or at least one of the unions) is not a party referred to in paragraph 64.

(5) The date specified under sub-paragraph (2)(a) must be—

    (a) the date on which the relevant period expires, or

    (b) if the CAC believes that to maintain the original bargaining arrangements would be impracticable or contrary to the interests of good industrial relations, the date after the date on which the declaration is issued;

and the relevant period is the period of 65 working days starting with the day after that on which the declaration is issued.

85.—(1) If the CAC's opinion is not that mentioned in paragraph 83(1) or 84(1) it must—

    (a)   decide whether the difference between the original unit and the new unit is such that the support of the union (or unions) within the new unit needs to be assessed, and

    (b)   inform the parties of its decision.

(2) If the CAC's decision is that such support does not need to be assessed—

    (a)   the CAC must issue a declaration that the union is (or unions are) recognised as entitled to conduct collective bargaining on behalf of the new unit;

    (b)   so far as it affects workers in the new unit who fall within the original unit, the declaration shall have effect in place of any declaration that the union is (or unions are) recognised as entitled to conduct collective bargaining on behalf of the original unit;

    (c)   the method of collective bargaining relating to the original unit shall have effect in relation to the new unit, with any modifications which the CAC considers necessary to take account of the change of bargaining unit and specifies in the declaration.

86.—(1) This paragraph applies if the CAC decides under paragraph 85(1) that the support of the union (or unions) within the new unit needs to be assessed.

(2) The CAC must decide these questions—

    (a)   whether members of the union (or unions) constitute at least 10 per cent of the workers constituting the new unit;

    (b)   whether a majority of the workers constituting the new unit would be likely to favour recognition of the union (or unions) as entitled to conduct collective bargaining on behalf of the new unit.

(3) If the CAC decides one or both of the questions in the negative—

    (a)   the CAC must issue a declaration that the bargaining arrangements, so far as relating to workers falling within the new unit, are to cease to have effect on a date specified by the CAC in the declaration, and

    (b)   the bargaining arrangements shall cease to have effect accordingly.

87.—(1) This paragraph applies if—

    (a)   the CAC decides both the questions in paragraph 86(2) in the affirmative, and

    (b)   the CAC is satisfied that a majority of the workers constituting the new unit are members of the union (or unions).

(2) The CAC must issue a declaration that the union is (or unions are) recognised as entitled to conduct collective bargaining on behalf of the workers constituting the new unit.

(3) But if any of the three qualifying conditions is fulfilled, instead of issuing a declaration under sub-paragraph (2) the CAC must give notice to the parties that it intends to arrange for the holding of a secret ballot in which the workers constituting the new unit are asked whether they want the union (or unions) to conduct collective bargaining on their behalf.

(4) These are the three qualifying conditions—

    (a)   the CAC is satisfied that a ballot should be held in the interests of good industrial relations;

   (b) a significant number of the union members within the new unit inform the CAC that they do not want the union (or unions) to conduct collective bargaining on their behalf;

   (c) membership evidence is produced which leads the CAC to conclude that there are doubts whether a significant number of the union members within the new unit want the union (or unions) to conduct collective bargaining on their behalf.

(5) For the purposes of sub-paragraph (4)(c) membership evidence is—

   (a) evidence about the circumstances in which union members became members;

   (b) evidence about the length of time for which union members have been members, in a case where the CAC is satisfied that such evidence should be taken into account.

(6) If the CAC issues a declaration under sub-paragraph (2)—

   (a) so far as it affects workers in the new unit who fall within the original unit, the declaration shall have effect in place of any declaration that the union is (or unions are) recognised as entitled to conduct collective bargaining on behalf of the original unit;

   (b) the method of collective bargaining relating to the original unit shall have effect in relation to the new unit, with any modifications which the CAC considers necessary to take account of the change of bargaining unit and specifies in the declaration.

88.—(1) This paragraph applies if—

   (a) the CAC decides both the questions in paragraph 86(2) in the affirmative, and

   (b) the CAC is not satisfied that a majority of the workers constituting the new unit are members of the union (or unions).

(2) The CAC must give notice to the parties that it intends to arrange for the holding of a secret ballot in which the workers constituting the new unit are asked whether they want the union (or unions) to conduct collective bargaining on their behalf.

89.—(1) If the CAC gives notice under paragraph 87(3) or 88(2) the union (or unions) may within the notification period notify the CAC that the union does not (or unions do not) want the CAC to arrange for the holding of the ballot; and the notification period is the period of 10 working days starting with the day after that on which the union (or last of the unions) receives the CAC's notice.

(2) If the CAC is so notified—

   (a) it must not arrange for the holding of the ballot,

   (b) it must inform the parties that it will not arrange for the holding of the ballot, and why,

   (c) it must issue a declaration that the bargaining arrangements, so far as relating to workers falling within the new unit, are to cease to have effect on a date specified by it in the declaration, and

   (d) the bargaining arrangements shall cease to have effect accordingly.

(3) If the CAC is not so notified it must arrange for the holding of the ballot.

(4) Paragraph 25 applies if the CAC arranges under this paragraph for the holding of a ballot (as well as if the CAC arranges under paragraph 24 for the holding of a ballot).

(5) Paragraphs 26 to 29 apply accordingly, but as if references to the bargaining unit were references to the new unit.

(6) If as a result of the ballot the CAC issues a declaration that the union is (or unions are) recognised as entitled to conduct collective bargaining on behalf of the new unit—

(a) so far as it affects workers in the new unit who fall within the original unit, the declaration shall have effect in place of any declaration that the union is (or unions are) recognised as entitled to conduct collective bargaining on behalf of the original unit;

(b) the method of collective bargaining relating to the original unit shall have effect in relation to the new unit, with any modifications which the CAC considers necessary to take account of the change of bargaining unit and specifies in the declaration.

(7) If as a result of the ballot the CAC issues a declaration that the union is (or unions are) not entitled to be recognised as entitled to conduct collective bargaining on behalf of the new unit—

(a) the CAC must state in the declaration the date on which the bargaining arrangements, so far as relating to workers falling within the new unit, are to cease to have effect, and

(b) the bargaining arrangements shall cease to have effect accordingly.

(8) Paragraphs (a) and (b) of sub-paragraph (6) also apply if the CAC issues a declaration under paragraph 27(2).

Residual workers

90.—(1) This paragraph applies if—

(a) the CAC decides an appropriate bargaining unit or units under paragraph 70 or 79, and

(b) at least one worker falling within the original unit does not fall within the new unit (or any of the new units).

(2) In such a case—

(a) the CAC must issue a declaration that the bargaining arrangements, so far as relating to the worker or workers mentioned in sub-paragraph (1)(b), are to cease to have effect on a date specified by the CAC in the declaration, and

(b) the bargaining arrangements shall cease to have effect accordingly.

91.—(1) This paragraph applies if—

(a) the CAC has proceeded as stated in paragraphs 83 to 89 with regard to the new unit (if there is one only) or with regard to each new unit (if there are two or more), and

(b) in so doing the CAC has issued one or more declarations under paragraph 83.

(2) The CAC must—

    (a) consider each declaration issued under paragraph 83, and

    (b) in relation to each declaration, identify each statutory outside bargaining unit which contains at least one worker who also falls within the new unit to which the declaration relates;

and in this paragraph each statutory outside bargaining unit so identified is referred to as a parent unit.

(3) The CAC must then—

    (a) consider each parent unit, and

    (b) in relation to each parent unit, identify any workers who fall within the parent unit but who do not fall within the new unit (or any of the new units);

and in this paragraph the workers so identified in relation to a parent unit are referred to as a residual unit.

(4) In relation to each residual unit, the CAC must issue a declaration that the outside union is (or outside unions are) recognised as entitled to conduct collective bargaining on its behalf.

(5) But no such declaration shall be issued in relation to a residual unit if the CAC has received an application under paragraph 66 or 75 in relation to its parent unit.

(6) In this paragraph references to the outside union (or to outside unions) in relation to a residual unit are to the union which is (or unions which are) recognised as entitled to conduct collective bargaining on behalf of its parent unit.

(7) If the CAC issues a declaration under sub-paragraph (4)—

    (a) the declaration shall have effect in place of the existing declaration that the outside union is (or outside unions are) recognised as entitled to conduct collective bargaining on behalf of the parent unit, so far as the existing declaration relates to the residual unit;

    (b) if there is a method of collective bargaining relating to the parent unit, it shall have effect in relation to the residual unit with any modifications which the CAC considers necessary to take account of the change of bargaining unit and specifies in the declaration.

Applications under this Part

92.—(1) An application to the CAC under this Part of this Schedule is not admissible unless—

    (a) it is made in such form as the CAC specifies, and

    (b) it is supported by such documents as the CAC specifies.

(2) An application which is made by a union (or unions) to the CAC under this Part of this Schedule is not admissible unless the union gives (or unions give) to the employer—

    (a) notice of the application, and

(b) a copy of the application and any documents supporting it.

(3) An application which is made by an employer to the CAC under this Part of this Schedule is not admissible unless the employer gives to the union (or each of the unions)—

(a) notice of the application, and
(b) a copy of the application and any documents supporting it.

Withdrawal of application

93.—(1) If an application under paragraph 66 or 75 is accepted by the CAC, the applicant (or applicants) may not withdraw the application—

(a) after the CAC issues a declaration under paragraph 69(3) or 78(3),
(b) after the CAC decides under paragraph 77(2) or 77(3),
(c) after the CAC issues a declaration under paragraph 83(1), 85(2), 86(3) or 87(2) in relation to the new unit (where there is only one) or a declaration under any of those paragraphs in relation to any of the new units (where there is more than one),
(d) after the union has (or unions have) notified the CAC under paragraph 89(1) in relation to the new unit (where there is only one) or any of the new units (where there is more than one), or
(e) after the end of the notification period referred to in paragraph 89(1) and relating to the new unit (where there is only one) or any of the new units (where there is more than one).

(2) If an application is withdrawn by the applicant (or applicants)—

(a) the CAC must give notice of the withdrawal to the other party (or parties), and
(b) no further steps are to be taken under this Part of this Schedule.

Meaning of collective bargaining

94.—(1) This paragraph applies for the purposes of this Part of this Schedule.

(2) Except in relation to paragraphs 69(5), 78(5) and 83(6), the meaning of collective bargaining given by section 178(1) shall not apply.

(3) In relation to a new unit references to collective bargaining are to negotiations relating to the matters which were the subject of collective bargaining in relation to the corresponding original unit; and the corresponding original unit is the unit which was the subject of an application under paragraph 66 or 75 in consequence of which the new unit was agreed by the parties or decided by the CAC.

(4) But if the parties agree matters as the subject of collective bargaining in relation to the new unit, references to collective bargaining in relation to that unit are to negotiations relating to the agreed matters; and this is the case whether the agreement is made before or after the time when the CAC issues a declaration that the union is (or unions are) recognised as entitled to conduct collective bargaining on behalf of the new unit.

(5) In relation to a residual unit in relation to which a declaration is issued under paragraph 91, references to collective bargaining are to negotiations relating to the matters which were the subject of collective bargaining in relation to the corresponding parent unit.

(6) In construing paragraphs 69(3)(c), 78(3)(c), 85(2)(c), 87(6)(b) and 89(6)(b)—

    (a)   sub-paragraphs (3) and (4) do not apply, and

    (b)   references to collective bargaining are to negotiations relating to pay, hours and holidays.

Method of collective bargaining

95.—(1) This paragraph applies for the purposes of this Part of this Schedule.

(2) Where a method of collective bargaining has effect in relation to a new unit, that method shall have effect as if it were contained in a legally enforceable contract made by the parties.

(3) But if the parties agree in writing—

    (a)   that sub-paragraph (2) shall not apply, or shall not apply to particular parts of the method, or

    (b)   to vary or replace the method,

the written agreement shall have effect as a legally enforceable contract made by the parties.

(4) Specific performance shall be the only remedy available for breach of anything which is a legally enforceable contract by virtue of this paragraph.

PART IV

DERECOGNITION: GENERAL

Introduction

96.—(1) This Part of this Schedule applies if the CAC has issued a declaration that a union is (or unions are) recognised as entitled to conduct collective bargaining on behalf of a bargaining unit.

(2) In such a case references in this Part of this Schedule to the bargaining arrangements are to the declaration and to the provisions relating to the collective bargaining method.

(3) For this purpose the provisions relating to the collective bargaining method are—

    (a)   the parties' agreement as to the method by which collective bargaining is to be conducted,

    (b)   anything effective as, or as if contained in, a legally enforceable contract and relating to the method by which collective bargaining is to be conducted, or

    (c)   any provision of Part III of this Schedule that a method of collective bargaining is to have effect.

97. For the purposes of this Part of this Schedule the relevant date is the date of the expiry of the period of 3 years starting with the date of the CAC's declaration.

98. References in this Part of this Schedule to the parties are to the employer and the union (or unions) concerned.

Employer employs fewer than 21 workers

99.—(1) This paragraph applies if—

   (a) the employer believes that he, taken with any associated employer or employers, employed an average of fewer than 21 workers in any period of 13 weeks, and

   (b) that period ends on or after the relevant date.

(2) If the employer wishes the bargaining arrangements to cease to have effect, he must give the union (or each of the unions) a notice complying with sub-paragraph (3) and must give a copy of the notice to the CAC.

(3) A notice complies with this sub-paragraph if it—

   (a) identifies the bargaining arrangements,

   (b) specifies the period of 13 weeks in question,

   (c) states the date on which the notice is given,

   (d) is given within the period of 5 working days starting with the day after the last day of the specified period of 13 weeks,

   (e) states that the employer, taken with any associated employer or employers, employed an average of fewer than 21 workers in the specified period of 13 weeks, and

   (f) states that the bargaining arrangements are to cease to have effect on a date which is specified in the notice and which falls after the end of the period of 35 working days starting with the day after that on which the notice is given.

(4) To find the average number of workers employed by the employer, taken with any associated employer or employers, in the specified period of 13 weeks—

   (a) take the number of workers employed in each of the 13 weeks (including workers not employed for the whole of the week);

   (b) aggregate the 13 numbers;

   (c) divide the aggregate by 13.

(5) For the purposes of sub-paragraph (1)(a) any worker employed by an associated company incorporated outside Great Britain must be ignored in relation to a week unless the whole or any part of that week fell within a period during which he ordinarily worked in Great Britain.

(6) For the purposes of sub-paragraph (5) a worker who is employed on board a ship registered in the register maintained under section 8 of the Merchant Shipping Act 1995 shall be treated as ordinarily working in Great Britain unless—

   (a) the ship's entry in the register specifies a port outside Great Britain as the port to which the vessel is to be treated as belonging,

   (b) the employment is wholly outside Great Britain, or

   (c) the worker is not ordinarily resident in Great Britain.

(7) An order made under paragraph 7(6) may also—

   (a) provide that sub-paragraphs (1) to (6) of this paragraph and paragraphs 100 to 103 are not to apply, or are not to apply in specified circumstances, or

   (b) vary the number of workers for the time being specified in sub-paragraphs (1)(a) and (3)(e).

100.—(1) Within the validation period the CAC must decide whether the notice complies with paragraph 99(3).

(2) If the CAC decides that the notice does not comply with paragraph 99(3)—

    (a) the CAC must give the parties notice of its decision, and

    (b) the employer's notice shall be treated as not having been given.

(3) If the CAC decides that the notice complies with paragraph 99(3) it must give the parties notice of the decision.

(4) The bargaining arrangements shall cease to have effect on the date specified under paragraph 99(3)(f) if—

    (a) the CAC gives notice under sub-paragraph (3), and

    (b) the union does not (or unions do not) apply to the CAC under paragraph 101.

(5) The validation period is—

    (a) the period of 10 working days starting with the day after that on which the CAC receives the copy of the notice, or

    (b) such longer period (so starting) as the CAC may specify to the parties by notice containing reasons for the extension.

101.—(1) This paragraph applies if—

    (a) the CAC gives notice under paragraph 100(3), and

    (b) within the period of 10 working days starting with the day after that on which the notice is given, the union makes (or unions make) an application to the CAC for a decision whether the period of 13 weeks specified under paragraph 99(3)(b) ends on or after the relevant date and whether the statement made under paragraph 99(3)(e) is correct.

(2) An application is not admissible unless—

    (a) it is made in such form as the CAC specifies, and

    (b) it is supported by such documents as the CAC specifies.

(3) An application is not admissible unless the union gives (or unions give) to the employer—

    (a) notice of the application, and

    (b) a copy of the application and any documents supporting it.

(4) An application is not admissible if—

    (a) a relevant application was made within the period of 3 years prior to the date of the application,

    (b) the relevant application and the application relate to the same bargaining unit, and

    (c) the CAC accepted the relevant application.

(5) A relevant application is an application made to the CAC—

    (a) by the union (or the unions) under this paragraph,

    (b) by the employer under paragraph 106, 107 or 128, or

(c) by a worker (or workers) under paragraph 112.

102.—(1) The CAC must give notice to the parties of receipt of an application under paragraph 101.

(2) Within the acceptance period the CAC must decide whether the application is admissible within the terms of paragraph 101.

(3) In deciding whether an application is admissible the CAC must consider any evidence which it has been given by the employer or the union (or unions).

(4) If the CAC decides that the application is not admissible—

(a) the CAC must give notice of its decision to the parties,
(b) the CAC must not accept the application,
(c) no further steps are to be taken under this Part of this Schedule, and
(d) the bargaining arrangements shall cease to have effect on the date specified under paragraph 99(3)(f).

(5) If the CAC decides that the application is admissible it must—

(a) accept the application, and
(b) give notice of the acceptance to the parties.

(6) The acceptance period is—

(a) the period of 10 working days starting with the day after that on which the CAC receives the application, or
(b) such longer period (so starting) as the CAC may specify to the parties by notice containing reasons for the extension.

103.—(1) If the CAC accepts an application it—

(a) must give the employer and the union (or unions) an opportunity to put their views on the questions whether the period of 13 weeks specified under paragraph 99(3)(b) ends on or after the relevant date and whether the statement made under paragraph 99(3)(e) is correct;
(b) must decide the questions within the decision period and must give reasons for the decision.

(2) If the CAC decides that the period of 13 weeks specified under paragraph 99(3)(b) ends on or after the relevant date and that the statement made under paragraph 99(3)(e) is correct the bargaining arrangements shall cease to have effect on the termination date.

(3) If the CAC decides that the period of 13 weeks specified under paragraph 99(3)(b) does not end on or after the relevant date or that the statement made under paragraph 99(3)(e) is not correct, the notice under paragraph 99 shall be treated as not having been given.

(4) The decision period is—

(a) the period of 10 working days starting with the day after that on which the CAC gives notice of acceptance of the application, or
(b) such longer period (so starting) as the CAC may specify to the parties by notice containing reasons for the extension.

(5) The termination date is the later of—

    (a)   the date specified under paragraph 99(3)(f), and

    (b)   the day after the last day of the decision period.

Employer's request to end arrangements

104.—(1) This paragraph and paragraphs 105 to 111 apply if after the relevant date the employer requests the union (or each of the unions) to agree to end the bargaining arrangements.

(2) The request is not valid unless it—

    (a)   is in writing,

    (b)   is received by the union (or each of the unions),

    (c)   identifies the bargaining arrangements, and

    (d)   states that it is made under this Schedule.

105.—(1) If before the end of the first period the parties agree to end the bargaining arrangements no further steps are to be taken under this Part of this Schedule.

(2) Sub-paragraph (3) applies if before the end of the first period—

    (a)   the union informs the employer that the union does not accept the request but is willing to negotiate, or

    (b)   the unions inform the employer that the unions do not accept the request but are willing to negotiate.

(3) The parties may conduct negotiations with a view to agreeing to end the bargaining arrangements.

(4) If such an agreement is made before the end of the second period no further steps are to be taken under this Part of this Schedule.

(5) The employer and the union (or unions) may request ACAS to assist in conducting the negotiations.

(6) The first period is the period of 10 working days starting with the day after—

    (a)   the day on which the union receives the request, or

    (b)   the last day on which any of the unions receives the request.

(7) The second period is—

    (a)   the period of 20 working days starting with the day after that on which the first period ends, or

    (b)   such longer period (so starting) as the parties may from time to time agree.

106.—(1) This paragraph applies if—

    (a)   before the end of the first period the union fails (or unions fail) to respond to the request, or

    (b)   before the end of the first period the union informs the employer that it does not (or unions inform the employer that they do not) accept the request (without indicating a willingness to negotiate).

(2) The employer may apply to the CAC for the holding of a secret ballot to decide whether the bargaining arrangements should be ended.

107.—(1) This paragraph applies if—

(a) the union informs (or unions inform) the employer under paragraph 105(2), and

(b) no agreement is made before the end of the second period.

(2) The employer may apply to the CAC for the holding of a secret ballot to decide whether the bargaining arrangements should be ended.

(3) But no application may be made if within the period of 10 working days starting with the day after that on which the union informs (or unions inform) the employer under paragraph 105(2) the union proposes (or unions propose) that ACAS be requested to assist in conducting the negotiations and—

(a) the employer rejects the proposal, or

(b) the employer fails to accept the proposal within the period of 10 working days starting with the day after that on which the union makes (or unions make) the proposal.

108.—(1) An application under paragraph 106 or 107 is not admissible unless—

(a) it is made in such form as the CAC specifies, and

(b) it is supported by such documents as the CAC specifies.

(2) An application under paragraph 106 or 107 is not admissible unless the employer gives to the union (or each of the unions)—

(a) notice of the application, and

(b) a copy of the application and any documents supporting it.

109.—(1) An application under paragraph 106 or 107 is not admissible if—

(a) a relevant application was made within the period of 3 years prior to the date of the application under paragraph 106 or 107,

(b) the relevant application and the application under paragraph 106 or 107 relate to the same bargaining unit, and

(c) the CAC accepted the relevant application.

(2) A relevant application is an application made to the CAC—

(a) by the union (or the unions) under paragraph 101,

(b) by the employer under paragraph 106, 107 or 128, or

(c) by a worker (or workers) under paragraph 112.

110.—(1) An application under paragraph 106 or 107 is not admissible unless the CAC decides that—

(a) at least 10 per cent of the workers constituting the bargaining unit favour an end of the bargaining arrangements, and

(b) a majority of the workers constituting the bargaining unit would be likely to favour an end of the bargaining arrangements.

(2) The CAC must give reasons for the decision.

111.—(1) The CAC must give notice to the parties of receipt of an application under paragraph 106 or 107.

(2) Within the acceptance period the CAC must decide whether—

(a) the request is valid within the terms of paragraph 104, and

   (b) the application is made in accordance with paragraph 106 or 107 and admissible within the terms of paragraphs 108 to 110.

(3) In deciding those questions the CAC must consider any evidence which it has been given by the employer or the union (or unions).

(4) If the CAC decides that the request is not valid or the application is not made in accordance with paragraph 106 or 107 or is not admissible—

   (a) the CAC must give notice of its decision to the parties,

   (b) the CAC must not accept the application, and

   (c) no further steps are to be taken under this Part of this Schedule.

(5) If the CAC decides that the request is valid and the application is made in accordance with paragraph 106 or 107 and is admissible it must—

   (a) accept the application, and

   (b) give notice of the acceptance to the parties.

(6) The acceptance period is—

   (a) the period of 10 working days starting with the day after that on which the CAC receives the application, or

   (b) such longer period (so starting) as the CAC may specify to the parties by notice containing reasons for the extension.

Workers' application to end arrangements

112.—(1) A worker or workers falling within the bargaining unit may after the relevant date apply to the CAC to have the bargaining arrangements ended.

(2) An application is not admissible unless—

   (a) it is made in such form as the CAC specifies, and

   (b) it is supported by such documents as the CAC specifies.

(3) An application is not admissible unless the worker gives (or workers give) to the employer and to the union (or each of the unions)—

   (a) notice of the application, and

   (b) a copy of the application and any documents supporting it.

113.—(1) An application under paragraph 112 is not admissible if—

   (a) a relevant application was made within the period of 3 years prior to the date of the application under paragraph 112,

   (b) the relevant application and the application under paragraph 112 relate to the same bargaining unit, and

   (c) the CAC accepted the relevant application.

(2) A relevant application is an application made to the CAC—

   (a) by the union (or the unions) under paragraph 101,

   (b) by the employer under paragraph 106, 107 or 128, or

   (c) by a worker (or workers) under paragraph 112.

114.—(1) An application under paragraph 112 is not admissible unless the CAC decides that—

(a) at least 10 per cent of the workers constituting the bargaining unit favour an end of the bargaining arrangements, and

(b) a majority of the workers constituting the bargaining unit would be likely to favour an end of the bargaining arrangements.

(2) The CAC must give reasons for the decision.

115.—(1) The CAC must give notice to the worker (or workers), the employer and the union (or unions) of receipt of an application under paragraph 112.

(2) Within the acceptance period the CAC must decide whether the application is admissible within the terms of paragraphs 112 to 114.

(3) In deciding whether the application is admissible the CAC must consider any evidence which it has been given by the employer, the union (or unions) or any of the workers falling within the bargaining unit.

(4) If the CAC decides that the application is not admissible—

(a) the CAC must give notice of its decision to the worker (or workers), the employer and the union (or unions),

(b) the CAC must not accept the application, and

(c) no further steps are to be taken under this Part of this Schedule.

(5) If the CAC decides that the application is admissible it must—

(a) accept the application, and

(b) give notice of the acceptance to the worker (or workers), the employer and the union (or unions).

(6) The acceptance period is—

(a) the period of 10 working days starting with the day after that on which the CAC receives the application, or

(b) such longer period (so starting) as the CAC may specify to the worker (or workers), the employer and the union (or unions) by notice containing reasons for the extension.

116.—(1) If the CAC accepts the application, in the negotiation period the CAC must help the employer, the union (or unions) and the worker (or workers) with a view to—

(a) the employer and the union (or unions) agreeing to end the bargaining arrangements, or

(b) the worker (or workers) withdrawing the application.

(2) The negotiation period is—

(a) the period of 20 working days starting with the day after that on which the CAC gives notice of acceptance of the application, or

(b) such longer period (so starting) as the CAC may decide with the consent of the worker (or workers), the employer and the union (or unions).

Ballot on derecognition

117.—(1) This paragraph applies if the CAC accepts an application under paragraph 106 or 107.

(2) This paragraph also applies if—

(a) the CAC accepts an application under paragraph 112, and

(b) in the period mentioned in paragraph 116(1) there is no agreement or withdrawal as there described.

(3) The CAC must arrange for the holding of a secret ballot in which the workers constituting the bargaining unit are asked whether the bargaining arrangements should be ended.

(4) The ballot must be conducted by a qualified independent person appointed by the CAC.

(5) The ballot must be conducted within—

(a) the period of 20 working days starting with the day after that on which the qualified independent person is appointed, or

(b) such longer period (so starting) as the CAC may decide.

(6) The ballot must be conducted—

(a) at a workplace or workplaces decided by the CAC,

(b) by post, or

(c) by a combination of the methods described in sub-paragraphs (a) and (b),

depending on the CAC's preference.

(7) In deciding how the ballot is to be conducted the CAC must take into account—

(a) the likelihood of the ballot being affected by unfairness or malpractice if it were conducted at a workplace or workplaces;

(b) costs and practicality;

(c) such other matters as the CAC considers appropriate.

(8) The CAC may not decide that the ballot is to be conducted as mentioned in sub-paragraph (6)(c) unless there are special factors making such a decision appropriate; and special factors include—

(a) factors arising from the location of workers or the nature of their employment;

(b) factors put to the CAC by the employer or the union (or unions).

(9) A person is a qualified independent person if—

(a) he satisfies such conditions as may be specified for the purposes of this paragraph by order of the Secretary of State or is himself so specified, and

(b) there are no grounds for believing either that he will carry out any functions conferred on him in relation to the ballot otherwise than competently or that his independence in relation to the ballot might reasonably be called into question.

(10) An order under sub-paragraph (9)(a) shall be made by statutory instrument subject to annulment in pursuance of a resolution of either House of Parliament.

(11) As soon as is reasonably practicable after the CAC is required under subparagraph (3) to arrange for the holding of a ballot it must inform the employer and the union (or unions)—

(a) that it is so required;

(b) of the name of the person appointed to conduct the ballot and the date of his appointment;

(c) of the period within which the ballot must be conducted;

(d) whether the ballot is to be conducted by post or at a workplace or workplaces;

(e) of the workplace or workplaces concerned (if the ballot is to be conducted at a workplace or workplaces).

118.—(1) An employer who is informed by the CAC under paragraph 117(11) must comply with the following three duties.

(2) The first duty is to co-operate generally, in connection with the ballot, with the union (or unions) and the person appointed to conduct the ballot; and the second and third duties are not to prejudice the generality of this.

(3) The second duty is to give to the union (or unions) such access to the workers constituting the bargaining unit as is reasonable to enable the union (or unions) to inform the workers of the object of the ballot and to seek their support and their opinions on the issues involved.

(4) The third duty is to do the following (so far as it is reasonable to expect the employer to do so)—

(a) to give to the CAC, within the period of 10 working days starting with the day after that on which the employer is informed under paragraph 117(11), the names and home addresses of the workers constituting the bargaining unit;

(b) to give to the CAC, as soon as is reasonably practicable, the name and home address of any worker who joins the unit after the employer has complied with paragraph (a);

(c) to inform the CAC, as soon as is reasonably practicable, of any worker whose name has been given to the CAC under paragraph (a) or (b) but who ceases to be within the unit.

(5) As soon as is reasonably practicable after the CAC receives any information under sub-paragraph (4) it must pass it on to the person appointed to conduct the ballot.

(6) If asked to do so by the union (or unions) the person appointed to conduct the ballot must send to any worker—

(a) whose name and home address have been given under sub-paragraph (5), and

(b) who is still within the unit (so far as the person so appointed is aware),

any information supplied by the union (or unions) to the person so appointed.

(7) The duty under sub-paragraph (6) does not apply unless the union bears (or unions bear) the cost of sending the information.

(8) Each of the following powers shall be taken to include power to issue Codes of Practice about reasonable access for the purposes of sub-paragraph (3)—

(a) the power of ACAS under section 199(1);

(b) the power of the Secretary of State under section 203(1)(a).

119.—(1) If the CAC is satisfied that the employer has failed to fulfil any of the three duties imposed by paragraph 118, and the ballot has not been held, the CAC may order the employer—

    (a) to take such steps to remedy the failure as the CAC considers reasonable and specifies in the order, and

    (b) to do so within such period as the CAC considers reasonable and specifies in the order.

(2) If—

    (a) the ballot has been arranged in consequence of an application under paragraph 106 or 107,

    (b) the CAC is satisfied that the employer has failed to comply with an order under sub-paragraph (1), and

    (c) the ballot has not been held,

the CAC may refuse the application.

(3) If—

    (a) the ballot has been arranged in consequence of an application under paragraph 112, and

    (b) the ballot has not been held,

an order under sub-paragraph (1), on being recorded in the county court, may be enforced in the same way as an order of that court.

(4) If the CAC refuses an application under sub-paragraph (2) it shall take steps to cancel the holding of the ballot; and if the ballot is held it shall have no effect.

120.—(1) This paragraph applies if the holding of a ballot has been arranged under paragraph 117(3) whether or not it has been cancelled.

(2) The gross costs of the ballot shall be borne—

    (a) as to half, by the employer, and

    (b) as to half, by the union (or unions).

(3) If there is more than one union they shall bear their half of the gross costs—

    (a) in such proportions as they jointly indicate to the person appointed to conduct the ballot, or

    (b) in the absence of such an indication, in equal shares.

(4) The person appointed to conduct the ballot may send to the employer and the union (or each of the unions) a demand stating—

    (a) the gross costs of the ballot, and

    (b) the amount of the gross costs to be borne by the recipient.

(5) In such a case the recipient must pay the amount stated to the person sending the demand, and must do so within the period of 15 working days starting with the day after that on which the demand is received.

(6) In England and Wales, if the amount stated is not paid in accordance with sub-paragraph (5) it shall, if a county court so orders, be recoverable by execution issued from that court or otherwise as if it were payable under an order of that court.

(7) References to the costs of the ballot are to—

    (a)   the costs wholly, exclusively and necessarily incurred in connection with the ballot by the person appointed to conduct it,

    (b)   such reasonable amount as the person appointed to conduct the ballot charges for his services, and

    (c)   such other costs as the employer and the union (or unions) agree.

121.—(1) As soon as is reasonably practicable after the CAC is informed of the result of a ballot by the person conducting it, the CAC must act under this paragraph.

(2) The CAC must inform the employer and the union (or unions) of the result of the ballot.

(3) If the result is that the proposition that the bargaining arrangements should be ended is supported by—

    (a)   a majority of the workers voting, and

    (b)   at least 40 per cent of the workers constituting the bargaining unit,

the CAC must issue a declaration that the bargaining arrangements are to cease to have effect on a date specified by the CAC in the declaration.

(4) If the result is otherwise the CAC must refuse the application under paragraph 106, 107 or 112.

(5) If a declaration is issued under sub-paragraph (3) the bargaining arrangements shall cease to have effect accordingly.

(6) The Secretary of State may by order amend sub-paragraph (3) so as to specify a different degree of support; and different provision may be made for different circumstances.

(7) An order under sub-paragraph (6) shall be made by statutory instrument.

(8) No such order shall be made unless a draft of it has been laid before Parliament and approved by a resolution of each House of Parliament.

PART V

DERECOGNITION WHERE RECOGNITION AUTOMATIC

Introduction

122.—(1) This Part of this Schedule applies if—

    (a)   the CAC has issued a declaration under paragraph 22(2) that a union is (or unions are) recognised as entitled to conduct collective bargaining on behalf of a bargaining unit, and

    (b)   the parties have agreed under paragraph 30 or 31 a method by which they will conduct collective bargaining.

(2) In such a case references in this Part of this Schedule to the bargaining arrangements are to—

    (a)   the declaration, and

    (b)   the parties' agreement.

123.—(1) This Part of this Schedule also applies if—

    (a) the CAC has issued a declaration under paragraph 22(2) that a union is (or unions are) recognised as entitled to conduct collective bargaining on behalf of a bargaining unit, and

    (b) the CAC has specified to the parties under paragraph 31(3) the method by which they are to conduct collective bargaining.

(2) In such a case references in this Part of this Schedule to the bargaining arrangements are to—

    (a) the declaration, and

    (b) anything effective as, or as if contained in, a legally enforceable contract by virtue of paragraph 31.

124.—(1) This Part of this Schedule also applies if the CAC has issued a declaration under paragraph 87(2) that a union is (or unions are) recognised as entitled to conduct collective bargaining on behalf of a bargaining unit.

(2) In such a case references in this Part of this Schedule to the bargaining arrangements are to—

    (a) the declaration, and

    (b) paragraph 87(6)(b).

125. For the purposes of this Part of this Schedule the relevant date is the date of the expiry of the period of 3 years starting with the date of the CAC's declaration.

126. References in this Part of this Schedule to the parties are to the employer and the union (or unions) concerned.

Employer's request to end arrangements

127.—(1) The employer may after the relevant date request the union (or each of the unions) to agree to end the bargaining arrangements.

(2) The request is not valid unless it—

    (a) is in writing,

    (b) is received by the union (or each of the unions),

    (c) identifies the bargaining arrangements,

    (d) states that it is made under this Schedule, and

    (e) states that fewer than half of the workers constituting the bargaining unit are members of the union (or unions).

128.—(1) If before the end of the negotiation period the parties agree to end the bargaining arrangements no further steps are to be taken under this Part of this Schedule.

(2) If no such agreement is made before the end of the negotiation period, the employer may apply to the CAC for the holding of a secret ballot to decide whether the bargaining arrangements should be ended.

(3) The negotiation period is the period of 10 working days starting with the day after—

    (a) the day on which the union receives the request, or

    (b) the last day on which any of the unions receives the request;

or such longer period (so starting) as the parties may from time to time agree.

129.—(1) An application under paragraph 128 is not admissible unless—

(a) it is made in such form as the CAC specifies, and

(b) it is supported by such documents as the CAC specifies.

(2) An application under paragraph 128 is not admissible unless the employer gives to the union (or each of the unions)—

(a) notice of the application, and

(b) a copy of the application and any documents supporting it.

130.—(1) An application under paragraph 128 is not admissible if—

(a) a relevant application was made within the period of 3 years prior to the date of the application under paragraph 128,

(b) the relevant application and the application under paragraph 128 relate to the same bargaining unit, and

(c) the CAC accepted the relevant application.

(2) A relevant application is an application made to the CAC—

(a) by the union (or the unions) under paragraph 101,

(b) by the employer under paragraph 106, 107 or 128, or

(c) by a worker (or workers) under paragraph 112.

131.—(1) An application under paragraph 128 is not admissible unless the CAC is satisfied that fewer than half of the workers constituting the bargaining unit are members of the union (or unions).

(2) The CAC must give reasons for the decision.

132.—(1) The CAC must give notice to the parties of receipt of an application under paragraph 128.

(2) Within the acceptance period the CAC must decide whether—

(a) the request is valid within the terms of paragraph 127, and

(b) the application is admissible within the terms of paragraphs 129 to 131.

(3) In deciding those questions the CAC must consider any evidence which it has been given by the parties.

(4) If the CAC decides that the request is not valid or the application is not admissible—

(a) the CAC must give notice of its decision to the parties,

(b) the CAC must not accept the application, and

(c) no further steps are to be taken under this Part of this Schedule.

(5) If the CAC decides that the request is valid and the application is admissible it must—

(a) accept the application, and

(b) give notice of the acceptance to the parties.

(6) The acceptance period is—

(a) the period of 10 working days starting with the day after that on which the CAC receives the application, or

(b) such longer period (so starting) as the CAC may specify to the parties by notice containing reasons for the extension.

Ballot on derecognition

133.—(1) Paragraph 117 applies if the CAC accepts an application under paragraph 128 (as well as in the cases mentioned in paragraph 117(1) and (2)).

(2) Paragraphs 118 to 121 apply accordingly, but as if—

(a) the reference in paragraph 119(2)(a) to paragraph 106 or 107 were to paragraph 106, 107 or 128;
(b) the reference in paragraph 121(4) to paragraph 106, 107 or 112 were to paragraph 106, 107, 112 or 128.

PART VI

DERECOGNITION WHERE UNION NOT INDEPENDENT

Introduction

134.—(1) This Part of this Schedule applies if—

(a) an employer and a union (or unions) have agreed that the union is (or unions are) recognised as entitled to conduct collective bargaining on behalf of a group or groups of workers, and
(b) the union does not have (or none of the unions has) a certificate under section 6 that it is independent.

(2) In such a case references in this Part of this Schedule to the bargaining arrangements are to—

(a) the parties' agreement mentioned in sub-paragraph (1)(a), and
(b) any agreement between the parties as to the method by which they will conduct collective bargaining.

135. In this Part of this Schedule—

(a) references to the parties are to the employer and the union (or unions);
(b) references to the bargaining unit are to the group of workers referred to in paragraph 134(1)(a) (or the groups taken together).

136. The meaning of collective bargaining given by section 178(1) shall not apply in relation to this Part of this Schedule.

Workers' application to end arrangements

137.—(1) A worker or workers falling within the bargaining unit may apply to the CAC to have the bargaining arrangements ended.

(2) An application is not admissible unless—

(a) it is made in such form as the CAC specifies, and
(b) it is supported by such documents as the CAC specifies.

(3) An application is not admissible unless the worker gives (or workers give) to the employer and to the union (or each of the unions)—

(a) notice of the application, and

(b) a copy of the application and any documents supporting it.

138. An application under paragraph 137 is not admissible if the CAC is satisfied that any of the unions has a certificate under section 6 that it is independent.

139.—(1) An application under paragraph 137 is not admissible unless the CAC decides that—

    (a) at least 10 per cent of the workers constituting the bargaining unit favour an end of the bargaining arrangements, and

    (b) a majority of the workers constituting the bargaining unit would be likely to favour an end of the bargaining arrangements.

(2) The CAC must give reasons for the decision.

140. An application under paragraph 137 is not admissible if the CAC is satisfied that—

    (a) the union (or any of the unions) has made an application to the Certification Officer under section 6 for a certificate that it is independent, and

    (b) the Certification Officer has not come to a decision on the application (or each of the applications).

141.—(1) The CAC must give notice to the worker (or workers), the employer and the union (or unions) of receipt of an application under paragraph 137.

(2) Within the acceptance period the CAC must decide whether the application is admissible within the terms of paragraphs 137 to 140.

(3) In deciding whether the application is admissible the CAC must consider any evidence which it has been given by the employer, the union (or unions) or any of the workers falling within the bargaining unit.

(4) If the CAC decides that the application is not admissible—

    (a) the CAC must give notice of its decision to the worker (or workers), the employer and the union (or unions),

    (b) the CAC must not accept the application, and

    (c) no further steps are to be taken under this Part of this Schedule.

(5) If the CAC decides that the application is admissible it must—

    (a) accept the application, and

    (b) give notice of the acceptance to the worker (or workers), the employer and the union (or unions).

(6) The acceptance period is—

    (a) the period of 10 working days starting with the day after that on which the CAC receives the application, or

    (b) such longer period (so starting) as the CAC may specify to the worker (or workers), the employer and the union (or unions) by notice containing reasons for the extension.

142.—(1) If the CAC accepts the application, in the negotiation period the CAC must help the employer, the union (or unions) and the worker (or workers) with a view to—

   (a) the employer and the union (or unions) agreeing to end the bargaining arrangements, or

   (b) the worker (or workers) withdrawing the application.

(2) The negotiation period is—

   (a) the period of 20 working days starting with the day after that on which the CAC gives notice of acceptance of the application, or

   (b) such longer period (so starting) as the CAC may decide with the consent of the worker (or workers), the employer and the union (or unions).

143.—(1) This paragraph applies if—

   (a) the CAC accepts an application under paragraph 137,

   (b) during the period mentioned in paragraph 142(1) or 145(3) the CAC is satisfied that the union (or each of the unions) has made an application to the Certification Officer under section 6 for a certificate that it is independent, that the application (or each of the applications) to the Certification Officer was made before the application under paragraph 137 and that the Certification Officer has not come to a decision on the application (or each of the applications), and

   (c) at the time the CAC is so satisfied there has been no agreement or withdrawal as described in paragraph 142(1) or 145(3).

(2) In such a case paragraph 142(1) or 145(3) shall cease to apply from the time when the CAC is satisfied as mentioned in sub-paragraph (1)(b).

144.—(1) This paragraph applies if the CAC is subsequently satisfied that—

   (a) the Certification Officer has come to a decision on the application (or each of the applications) mentioned in paragraph 143(1)(b), and

   (b) his decision is that the union (or any of the unions) which made an application under section 6 is independent.

(2) In such a case—

   (a) the CAC must give the worker (or workers), the employer and the union (or unions) notice that it is so satisfied, and

   (b) the application under paragraph 137 shall be treated as not having been made.

145.—(1) This paragraph applies if the CAC is subsequently satisfied that—

   (a) the Certification Officer has come to a decision on the application (or each of the applications) mentioned in paragraph 143(1)(b), and

   (b) his decision is that the union (or each of the unions) which made an application under section 6 is not independent.

(2) The CAC must give the worker (or workers), the employer and the union (or unions) notice that it is so satisfied.

(3) In the new negotiation period the CAC must help the employer, the union (or unions) and the worker (or workers) with a view to—

   (a) the employer and the union (or unions) agreeing to end the bargaining arrangements, or

   (b) the worker (or workers) withdrawing the application.

(4) The new negotiation period is—

(a) the period of 20 working days starting with the day after that on which the CAC gives notice under sub-paragraph (2), or

(b) such longer period (so starting) as the CAC may decide with the consent of the worker (or workers), the employer and the union (or unions).

146.—(1) This paragraph applies if—

(a) the CAC accepts an application under paragraph 137,

(b) paragraph 143 does not apply, and

(c) during the relevant period the CAC is satisfied that a certificate of independence has been issued to the union (or any of the unions) under section 6.

(2) In such a case the relevant period is the period starting with the first day of the negotiation period (as defined in paragraph 142(2)) and ending with the first of the following to occur—

(a) any agreement by the employer and the union (or unions) to end the bargaining arrangements;

(b) any withdrawal of the application by the worker (or workers);

(c) the CAC being informed of the result of a relevant ballot by the person conducting it;

and a relevant ballot is a ballot held by virtue of this Part of this Schedule.

(3) This paragraph also applies if—

(a) the CAC gives notice under paragraph 145(2), and

(b) during the relevant period the CAC is satisfied that a certificate of independence has been issued to the union (or any of the unions) under section 6.

(4) In such a case, the relevant period is the period starting with the first day of the new negotiation period (as defined in paragraph 145(4)) and ending with the first of the following to occur—

(a) any agreement by the employer and the union (or unions) to end the bargaining arrangements;

(b) any withdrawal of the application by the worker (or workers);

(c) the CAC being informed of the result of a relevant ballot by the person conducting it;

and a relevant ballot is a ballot held by virtue of this Part of this Schedule.

(5) If this paragraph applies—

(a) the CAC must give the worker (or workers), the employer and the union (or unions) notice that it is satisfied as mentioned in sub-paragraph (1)(c) or (3)(b), and

(b) the application under paragraph 137 shall be treated as not having been made.

Ballot on derecognition

147.—(1) Paragraph 117 applies if—

(a) the CAC accepts an application under paragraph 137, and

(b) in the period mentioned in paragraph 142(1) or 145(3) there is no agreement or withdrawal as there described,

(as well as in the cases mentioned in paragraph 117(1) and (2)).

(2) Paragraphs 118 to 121 apply accordingly, but as if—

(a) the reference in paragraph 119(3)(a) to paragraph 112 were to paragraph 112 or 137;

(b) the reference in paragraph 121(4) to paragraph 106, 107 or 112 were to paragraph 106, 107, 112 or 137.

(c) the reference in paragraph 119(4) to the CAC refusing an application under paragraph 119(2) included a reference to it being required to give notice under paragraph 146(5).

Derecognition: other cases

148.—(1) This paragraph applies if as a result of a declaration by the CAC another union is (or other unions are) recognised as entitled to conduct collective bargaining on behalf of a group of workers at least one of whom falls within the bargaining unit.

(2) The CAC must issue a declaration that the bargaining arrangements are to cease to have effect on a date specified by the CAC in the declaration.

(3) If a declaration is issued under sub-paragraph (2) the bargaining arrangements shall cease to have effect accordingly.

(4) It is for the CAC to decide whether sub-paragraph (1) is fulfilled, but in deciding the CAC may take account of the views of any person it believes has an interest in the matter.

PART VII

LOSS OF INDEPENDENCE

Introduction

149.—(1) This Part of this Schedule applies if the CAC has issued a declaration that a union is (or unions are) recognised as entitled to conduct collective bargaining on behalf of a bargaining unit.

(2) In such a case references in this Part of this Schedule to the bargaining arrangements are to the declaration and to the provisions relating to the collective bargaining method.

(3) For this purpose the provisions relating to the collective bargaining method are—

(a) the parties' agreement as to the method by which collective bargaining is to be conducted,

(b) anything effective as, or as if contained in, a legally enforceable contract and relating to the method by which collective bargaining is to be conducted, or

(c) any provision of Part III of this Schedule that a method of collective bargaining is to have effect.

150.—(1) This Part of this Schedule also applies if—

    (a) the parties have agreed that a union is (or unions are) recognised as entitled to conduct collective bargaining on behalf of a bargaining unit,

    (b) the CAC has specified to the parties under paragraph 63(2) the method by which they are to conduct collective bargaining, and

    (c) the parties have not agreed in writing to replace the method or that paragraph 63(3) shall not apply.

(2) In such a case references in this Part of this Schedule to the bargaining arrangements are to—

    (a) the parties' agreement mentioned in sub-paragraph (1)(a), and

    (b) anything effective as, or as if contained in, a legally enforceable contract by virtue of paragraph 63.

151. References in this Part of this Schedule to the parties are to the employer and the union (or unions) concerned.

Loss of certificate

152.—(1) This paragraph applies if—

    (a) only one union is a party, and

    (b) under section 7 the Certification Officer withdraws the union's certificate of independence.

(2) This paragraph also applies if—

    (a) more than one union is a party, and

    (b) under section 7 the Certification Officer withdraws the certificate of independence of each union (whether different certificates are withdrawn on the same or on different days).

(3) Sub-paragraph (4) shall apply on the day after—

    (a) the day on which the Certification Officer informs the union (or unions) of the withdrawal (or withdrawals), or

    (b) if there is more than one union, and he informs them on different days, the last of those days.

(4) The bargaining arrangements shall cease to have effect; and the parties shall be taken to agree that the union is (or unions are) recognised as entitled to conduct collective bargaining on behalf of the bargaining unit concerned.

Certificate re-issued

153.—(1) This paragraph applies if—

    (a) only one union is a party,

    (b) paragraph 152 applies, and

    (c) as a result of an appeal under section 9 against the decision to withdraw the certificate, the Certification Officer issues a certificate that the union is independent.

(2) This paragraph also applies if—

    (a) more than one union is a party,

(b) paragraph 152 applies, and

(c) as a result of an appeal under section 9 against a decision to withdraw a certificate, the Certification Officer issues a certificate that any of the unions concerned is independent.

(3) Sub-paragraph (4) shall apply, beginning with the day after—

(a) the day on which the Certification Officer issues the certificate, or

(b) if there is more than one union, the day on which he issues the first or only certificate.

(4) The bargaining arrangements shall have effect again; and paragraph 152 shall cease to apply.

Miscellaneous

154. Parts III to VI of this Schedule shall not apply in the case of the parties at any time when, by virtue of this Part of this Schedule, the bargaining arrangements do not have effect.

155. If—

(a) by virtue of paragraph 153 the bargaining arrangements have effect again beginning with a particular day, and

(b) in consequence section 70B applies in relation to the bargaining unit concerned,

for the purposes of section 70B(3) that day shall be taken to be the day on which section 70B first applies in relation to the unit.

PART VIII

DETRIMENT

Detriment

156.—(1) A worker has a right not to be subjected to any detriment by any act, or any deliberate failure to act, by his employer if the act or failure takes place on any of the grounds set out in sub-paragraph (2).

(2) The grounds are that—

(a) the worker acted with a view to obtaining or preventing recognition of a union (or unions) by the employer under this Schedule;

(b) the worker indicated that he supported or did not support recognition of a union (or unions) by the employer under this Schedule;

(c) the worker acted with a view to securing or preventing the ending under this Schedule of bargaining arrangements;

(d) the worker indicated that he supported or did not support the ending under this Schedule of bargaining arrangements;

(e) the worker influenced or sought to influence the way in which votes were to be cast by other workers in a ballot arranged under this Schedule;

(f) the worker influenced or sought to influence other workers to vote or to abstain from voting in such a ballot;

(g) the worker voted in such a ballot;

(h)　the worker proposed to do, failed to do, or proposed to decline to do, any of the things referred to in paragraphs (a) to (g).

(3) A ground does not fall within sub-paragraph (2) if it constitutes an unreasonable act or omission by the worker.

(4) This paragraph does not apply if the worker is an employee and the detriment amounts to dismissal within the meaning of the Employment Rights Act 1996.

(5) A worker may present a complaint to an employment tribunal on the ground that he has been subjected to a detriment in contravention of this paragraph.

(6) Apart from the remedy by way of complaint as mentioned in sub-paragraph (5), a worker has no remedy for infringement of the right conferred on him by this paragraph.

157.—(1) An employment tribunal shall not consider a complaint under paragraph 156 unless it is presented—

(a)　before the end of the period of 3 months starting with the date of the act or failure to which the complaint relates or, if that act or failure is part of a series of similar acts or failures (or both), the last of them, or
(b)　where the tribunal is satisfied that it was not reasonably practicable for the complaint to be presented before the end of that period, within such further period as it considers reasonable.

(2) For the purposes of sub-paragraph (1)—

(a)　where an act extends over a period, the reference to the date of the act is a reference to the last day of that period;
(b)　a failure to act shall be treated as done when it was decided on.

(3) For the purposes of sub-paragraph (2), in the absence of evidence establishing the contrary an employer must be taken to decide on a failure to act—

(a)　when he does an act inconsistent with doing the failed act, or
(b)　if he has done no such inconsistent act, when the period expires within which he might reasonably have been expected to do the failed act if it was to be done.

158. On a complaint under paragraph 156 it shall be for the employer to show the ground on which he acted or failed to act.

159.—(1) If the employment tribunal finds that a complaint under paragraph 156 is well-founded it shall make a declaration to that effect and may make an award of compensation to be paid by the employer to the complainant in respect of the act or failure complained of.

(2) The amount of the compensation awarded shall be such as the tribunal considers just and equitable in all the circumstances having regard to the infringement complained of and to any loss sustained by the complainant which is attributable to the act or failure which infringed his right.

(3) The loss shall be taken to include—

(a)　any expenses reasonably incurred by the complainant in consequence of the act or failure complained of, and

(b) loss of any benefit which he might reasonably be expected to have had but for that act or failure.

(4) In ascertaining the loss, the tribunal shall apply the same rule concerning the duty of a person to mitigate his loss as applies to damages recoverable under the common law of England and Wales or Scotland.

(5) If the tribunal finds that the act or failure complained of was to any extent caused or contributed to by action of the complainant, it shall reduce the amount of the compensation by such proportion as it considers just and equitable having regard to that finding.

160.—(1) If the employment tribunal finds that a complaint under paragraph 156 is well-founded and—

(a) the detriment of which the worker has complained is the termination of his worker's contract, but
(b) that contract was not a contract of employment,

any compensation awarded under paragraph 159 must not exceed the limit specified in sub-paragraph (2).

(2) The limit is the total of—

(a) the sum which would be the basic award for unfair dismissal, calculated in accordance with section 119 of the Employment Rights Act 1996, if the worker had been an employee and the contract terminated had been a contract of employment, and
(b) the sum for the time being specified in section 124(1) of that Act which is the limit for a compensatory award to a person calculated in accordance with section 123 of that Act.

Dismissal

161.—(1) For the purposes of Part X of the Employment Rights Act 1996 (unfair dismissal) the dismissal of an employee shall be regarded as unfair if the dismissal was made—

(a) for a reason set out in sub-paragraph (2), or
(b) for reasons the main one of which is one of those set out in sub-paragraph (2).

(2) The reasons are that—

(a) the employee acted with a view to obtaining or preventing recognition of a union (or unions) by the employer under this Schedule;
(b) the employee indicated that he supported or did not support recognition of a union (or unions) by the employer under this Schedule;
(c) the employee acted with a view to securing or preventing the ending under this Schedule of bargaining arrangements;
(d) the employee indicated that he supported or did not support the ending under this Schedule of bargaining arrangements;
(e) the employee influenced or sought to influence the way in which votes were to be cast by other workers in a ballot arranged under this Schedule;
(f) the employee influenced or sought to influence other workers to vote or to abstain from voting in such a ballot;

(g)   the employee voted in such a ballot;
(h)   the employee proposed to do, failed to do, or proposed to decline to do, any of the things referred to in paragraphs (a) to (g).

(3) A reason does not fall within sub-paragraph (2) if it constitutes an unreasonable act or omission by the employee.

Selection for redundancy

162. For the purposes of Part X of the Employment Rights Act 1996 (unfair dismissal) the dismissal of an employee shall be regarded as unfair if the reason or principal reason for the dismissal was that he was redundant but it is shown—

(a)   that the circumstances constituting the redundancy applied equally to one or more other employees in the same undertaking who held positions similar to that held by him and who have not been dismissed by the employer, and
(b)   that the reason (or, if more than one, the principal reason) why he was selected for dismissal was one falling within paragraph 161(2).

Employees with fixed-term contracts

163. Section 197(1) of the Employment Rights Act 1996 (fixed-term contracts) does not prevent Part X of that Act from applying to a dismissal which is regarded as unfair by virtue of paragraph 161 or 162.

Exclusion of requirement as to qualifying period

164. Sections 108 and 109 of the Employment Rights Act 1996 (qualifying period and upper age limit for unfair dismissal protection) do not apply to a dismissal which by virtue of paragraph 161 or 162 is regarded as unfair for the purposes of Part X of that Act.

Meaning of worker's contract

165. References in this Part of this Schedule to a worker's contract are to the contract mentioned in paragraph (a) or (b) of section 296(1) or the arrangements for the employment mentioned in paragraph (c) of section 296(1).

PART IX

GENERAL

Power to amend

166.—(1) If the CAC represents to the Secretary of State that paragraph 22 or 87 has an unsatisfactory effect and should be amended, he may by order amend it with a view to rectifying that effect.

(2) He may amend it in such way as he thinks fit, and not necessarily in a way proposed by the CAC (if it proposes one).

(3) An order under this paragraph shall be made by statutory instrument.

(4) No such order shall be made unless a draft of it has been laid before Parliament and approved by a resolution of each House of Parliament.

Guidance

167.—(1) The Secretary of State may issue guidance to the CAC on the way in which it is to exercise its functions under paragraph 22 or 87.

(2) The CAC must take into account any such guidance in exercising those functions.

(3) However, no guidance is to apply with regard to an application made to the CAC before the guidance in question was issued.

(4) The Secretary of State must—

  (a) lay before each House of Parliament any guidance issued under this paragraph, and
  (b) arrange for any such guidance to be published by such means as appear to him to be most appropriate for drawing it to the attention of persons likely to be affected by it.

Method of conducting collective bargaining

168.—(1) After consulting ACAS the Secretary of State may by order specify for the purposes of paragraphs 31(3) and 63(2) a method by which collective bargaining might be conducted.

(2) If such an order is made the CAC—

  (a) must take it into account under paragraphs 31(3) and 63(2), but
  (b) may depart from the method specified by the order to such extent as the CAC thinks it is appropriate to do so in the circumstances.

(3) An order under this paragraph shall be made by statutory instrument subject to annulment in pursuance of a resolution of either House of Parliament.

Directions about certain applications

169.—(1) The Secretary of State may make to the CAC directions as described in sub-paragraph (2) in relation to any case where—

  (a) two or more applications are made to the CAC,
  (b) each application is a relevant application,
  (c) each application relates to the same bargaining unit, and
  (d) the CAC has not accepted any of the applications.

(2) The directions are directions as to the order in which the CAC must consider the admissibility of the applications.

(3) The directions may include—

  (a) provision to deal with a case where a relevant application is made while the CAC is still considering the admissibility of another one relating to the same bargaining unit;
  (b) other incidental provisions.

(4) A relevant application is an application under paragraph 101, 106, 107, 112 or 128.

Notice of declarations

170.—(1) If the CAC issues a declaration under this Schedule it must notify the parties of the declaration and its contents.

(2) The reference here to the parties is to—

    (a) the union (or unions) concerned and the employer concerned, and

    (b) if the declaration is issued in consequence of an application by a worker or workers, the worker or workers making it.

CAC's general duty

171. In exercising functions under this Schedule in any particular case the CAC must have regard to the object of encouraging and promoting fair and efficient practices and arrangements in the workplace, so far as having regard to that object is consistent with applying other provisions of this Schedule in the case concerned.

General interpretation

172.—(1) References in this Schedule to the CAC are to the Central Arbitration Committee.

(2) For the purposes of this Schedule in its application to a part of Great Britain a working day is a day other than—

    (a) a Saturday or a Sunday,

    (b) Christmas day or Good Friday, or

    (c) a day which is a bank holiday under the Banking and Financial Dealings Act 1971 in that part of Great Britain.'

Section 2   **SCHEDULE 2**

UNION MEMBERSHIP: DETRIMENT

Introduction

1. The Trade Union and Labour Relations (Consolidation) Act 1992 shall be amended as provided in this Schedule.

Detriment

2.—(1) Section 146 (action short of dismissal on grounds related to union membership or activities) shall be amended as follows.

(2) In subsection (1) for 'have action short of dismissal taken against him as an individual by his employer' substitute 'be subjected to any detriment as an individual by any act, or any deliberate failure to act, by his employer if the act or failure takes place'.

(3) In subsection (3) for 'have action short of dismissal taken against him' substitute 'be subjected to any detriment as an individual by any act, or any deliberate failure to act, by his employer if the act or failure takes place'.

(4) In subsection (4) for 'action short of dismissal taken against him' substitute 'a detriment to which he has been subjected as an individual by an act of his employer taking place'.

(5) In subsection (5) for 'action has been taken against him' substitute 'he has been subjected to a detriment'.

(6) After subsection (5) insert—

'(6) For the purposes of this section detriment is detriment short of dismissal.'

Time limit for proceedings

3.—(1) Section 147 shall be amended as follows.

(2) Before 'An' insert '(1)'.

(3) In paragraph (a) of subsection (1) (as created by sub-paragraph (2) above) for the words from 'action to which' to 'those actions' substitute 'act or failure to which the complaint relates or, where that act or failure is part of a series of similar acts or failures (or both) the last of them'.

(4) After subsection (1) (as created by sub-paragraph (2) above) insert—

'(2) For the purposes of subsection (1)—

    (a) where an act extends over a period, the reference to the date of the act is a reference to the last day of that period;

    (b) a failure to act shall be treated as done when it was decided on.

(3) For the purposes of subsection (2), in the absence of evidence establishing the contrary an employer shall be taken to decide on a failure to act—

    (a) when he does an act inconsistent with doing the failed act, or

    (b) if he has done no such inconsistent act, when the period expires within which he might reasonably have been expected to do the failed act if it was to be done.'

Consideration of complaint

4.—(1) Section 148 shall be amended as follows.

(2) In subsection (1) for 'action was taken against the complainant' substitute 'he acted or failed to act'.

(3) In subsection (2) for 'action was taken by the employer or the purpose for which it was taken' substitute 'the employer acted or failed to act, or the purpose for which he did so'.

(4) In subsection (3)—

    (a) for 'action was taken by the employer against the complainant' substitute 'the employer acted or failed to act';

    (b) for the words from 'took the action' to 'would take' substitute 'acted or failed to act, unless it considers that no reasonable employer would act or fail to act in the way concerned'.

(5) For subsection (4) substitute—

'(4) Where the tribunal determines that—

(a) the complainant has been subjected to a detriment by an act or deliberate failure to act by his employer, and

(b) the act or failure took place in consequence of a previous act or deliberate failure to act by the employer,

paragraph (a) of subsection (3) is satisfied if the purpose mentioned in that paragraph was the purpose of the previous act or failure.'

Remedies

5. In section 149 for 'action' there shall be substituted 'act or failure'—

(a) in subsections (1), (2) and (3)(a) and (b), and

(b) in subsection (6), in the first place where 'action' occurs.

Awards against third parties

6. In section 150(1)—

(a) in paragraph (a) for 'action has been taken, against the complainant by his employer' there shall be substituted 'the complainant has been subjected to detriment by an act or failure by his employer taking place';

(b) in paragraph (b) for 'take the action' there shall be substituted 'act or fail to act in the way'.

Section 4 | **SCHEDULE 3**

BALLOTS AND NOTICES

Introduction

1. The Trade Union and Labour Relations (Consolidation) Act 1992 shall be amended as provided by this Schedule.

Support of ballot

2.—(1) Section 226 (requirement of ballot before action by trade union) shall amended as follows.

(2) In subsection (2) (industrial action to be regarded as having support of ballot only if certain conditions are fulfilled) in paragraph (a)(ii) for '231A' substitute '231', omit the word 'and' at the end of paragraph (b), and after paragraph (b) insert—

'(bb) section 232A does not prevent the industrial action from being regarded as having the support of the ballot; and'.

(3) After subsection (3) insert—

'(3A) If the requirements of section 231A fall to be satisfied in relation to an employer, as respects that employer industrial action shall not be regarded as having the support of a ballot unless those requirements are satisfied in relation to that employer.'

Documents for employers

3.—(1) Section 226A (notice of ballot and sample voting paper for employers) shall be amended as follows.

(2) In subsection (2) (c) (notice of ballot must describe employees entitled to vote) for 'describing (so that he can readily ascertain them) the employees of the employer' substitute 'containing such information in the union's possession as would help the employer to make plans and bring information to the attention of those of his employees'.

(3) After subsection (3) insert—

'(3A) These rules apply for the purposes of paragraph (c) of subsection (2)—

    (a) if the union possesses information as to the number, category or work-place of the employees concerned, a notice must contain that information (at least);

    (b) if a notice does not name any employees, that fact shall not be a ground for holding that it does not comply with paragraph (c) of subsection (2).

(3B) In subsection (3) references to employees are to employees of the employer concerned.'

Entitlement to vote

4. In section 227 (entitlement to vote in ballot) subsection (2) (position where member is denied entitlement to vote) shall be omitted.

Separate workplace ballots

5. The following shall be substituted for section 228 (separate workplace ballots)—

'228   Separate workplace ballots

(1) Subject to subsection (2), this section applies if the members entitled to vote in a ballot by virtue of section 227 do not all have the same workplace.

(2) This section does not apply if the union reasonably believes that all those members have the same workplace.

(3) Subject to section 228A, a separate ballot shall be held for each workplace; and entitlement to vote in each ballot shall be accorded equally to, and restricted to, members of the union who—

    (a) are entitled to vote by virtue of section 227, and

    (b) have that workplace.

(4) In this section and section 228A "workplace" in relation to a person who is employed means—

    (a) if the person works at or from a single set of premises, those premises, and

    (b) in any other case, the premises with which the person's employment has the closest connection.

228A   Separate workplaces: single and aggregate ballots

(1) Where section 228(3) would require separate ballots to be held for each workplace, a ballot may be held in place of some or all of the separate ballots if one of subsections (2) to (4) is satisfied in relation to it.

(2) This subsection is satisfied in relation to a ballot if the workplace of each member entitled to vote in the ballot is the workplace of at least one member of the union who is affected by the dispute.

(3) This subsection is satisfied in relation to a ballot if entitlement to vote is accorded to, and limited to, all the members of the union who—

    (a) according to the union's reasonable belief have an occupation of a particular kind or have any of a number of particular kinds of occupation, and

    (b) are employed by a particular employer, or by any of a number of particular employers, with whom the union is in dispute.

(4) This subsection is satisfied in relation to a ballot if entitlement to vote is accorded to, and limited to, all the members of the union who are employed by a particular employer, or by any of a number of particular employers, with whom the union is in dispute.

(5) For the purposes of subsection (2) the following are members of the union affected by a dispute—

    (a) if the dispute relates (wholly or partly) to a decision which the union reasonably believes the employer has made or will make concerning a matter specified in subsection (1)(a), (b) or (c) of section 244 (meaning of "trade dispute"), members whom the decision directly affects,

    (b) if the dispute relates (wholly or partly) to a matter specified in subsection (1)(d) of that section, members whom the matter directly affects,

    (c) if the dispute relates (wholly or partly) to a matter specified in subsection (1)(e) of that section, persons whose membership or non-membership is in dispute,

    (d) if the dispute relates (wholly or partly) to a matter specified in subsection (1)(f) of that section, officials of the union who have used or would use the facilities concerned in the dispute.'

Voting paper

6.—(1) Section 229 (voting paper) shall be amended as follows.

(2) After subsection (2) (voting paper must ask whether voter is prepared to take part in a strike or industrial action short of a strike) insert—

'(2A) For the purposes of subsection (2) an overtime ban and a call-out ban constitute industrial action short of a strike.'

(3) At the end of the statement in subsection (4) (statement that industrial action may be a breach of employment contract to be set out on every voting paper) insert—

'However, if you are dismissed for taking part in strike or other industrial action which is called officially and is otherwise lawful, the dismissal will be unfair if it takes place fewer than eight weeks after you started taking part in the action, and depending on the circumstances may be unfair if it takes place later.'

(4) In the definition of 'strike' in section 246 (interpretation) after 'means' there shall be inserted '(except for the purposes of section 229(2))'.

Conduct of ballot: merchant seamen

7. In section 230 (conduct of ballot) for subsections (2A) and (2B) there shall be substituted—

'(2A) Subsection (2B) applies to a merchant seaman if the trade union reasonably believes that—

 (a) he will be employed in a ship either at sea or at a place outside Great Britain at some time in the period during which votes may be cast, and

 (b) it will be convenient for him to receive a voting paper and to vote while on the ship or while at a place where the ship is rather than in accordance with subsection (2).

(2B) Where this subsection applies to a merchant seaman he shall, if it is reasonably practicable—

 (a) have a voting paper made available to him while on the ship or while at a place where the ship is, and

 (b) be given an opportunity to vote while on the ship or while at a place where the ship is.'

Inducement

8. After section 232 insert—

'232A   Inducement of member denied entitlement to vote

Industrial action shall not be regarded as having the support of a ballot if the following conditions apply in the case of any person—

 (a) he was a member of the trade union at the time when the ballot was held,

 (b) it was reasonable at that time for the trade union to believe he would be induced to take part or, as the case may be, to continue to take part in the industrial action,

 (c) he was not accorded entitlement to vote in the ballot, and

 (d) he was induced by the trade union to take part or, as the case may be to continue to take part in the industrial action.'

Disregard of certain failures

9. After section 232A there shall be inserted—

'232B   Small accidental failures to be disregarded

(1) If—

 (a) in relation to a ballot there is a failure (or there are failures) to comply with a provision mentioned in subsection (2) or with more than one of those provisions, and

 (b) the failure is accidental and on a scale which is unlikely to affect the result of the ballot or, as the case may be, the failures are accidental and taken together are on a scale which is unlikely to affect the result of the ballot,

the failure (or failures) shall be disregarded.

(2) The provisions are section 227(1), section 230(2) and section 230(2A).'

Period of ballot's effectiveness

10. In section 234 (period after which ballot ceases to be effective) for subsection (1) there shall be substituted—

'(1) Subject to the following provisions, a ballot ceases to be effective for the purposes of section 233(3)(b) in relation to industrial action by members of a trade union at the end of the period, beginning with the date of the ballot—

    (a) of four weeks, or
    (b) of such longer duration not exceeding eight weeks as is agreed between the union and the members' employer.'

Notice of industrial action

11.—(1) Section 234A (notice to employers of industrial action) shall be amended as follows.

(2) In subsection (3)(a) (notice relating to industrial action must describe employees intended to take part in industrial action) for 'describes (so that he can readily ascertain them) the employees of the employer who' substitute 'contains such information in the union's possession as would help the employer to make plans and bring information to the attention of those of his employees whom'.

(3) After subsection (5) insert—

'(5A) These rules apply for the purposes of paragraph (a) of subsection (3)—

    (a) if the union possesses information as to the number, category or work-place of the employees concerned, a notice must contain that information (at least);
    (b) if a notice does not name any employees, that fact shall not be a ground for holding that it does not comply with paragraph (a) of subsection (3).'

(4) In subsection (7)—

    (a) insert at the beginning the words 'Subject to subsections (7A) and (7B),' and
    (b) in paragraph (a) the words 'otherwise than to enable the union to comply with a court order or an undertaking given to a court' shall cease to have effect.

(5) After subsection (7) insert—

'(7A) Subsection (7) shall not apply where industrial action ceases to be authorised or endorsed in order to enable the union to comply with a court order or an undertaking given to a court.

(7B) Subsection (7) shall not apply where—

    (a) a union agrees with an employer, before industrial action ceases to be authorised or endorsed, that it will cease to be authorised or endorsed with effect from a date specified in the agreement ("the suspension date") and that it may again be authorised or endorsed with effect from a date not earlier than a date specified in the agreement ("the resumption date"),

> (b) the action ceases to be authorised or endorsed with effect from the suspension date, and
>
> (c) the action is again authorised or endorsed with effect from a date which is not earlier than the resumption date or such later date as may be agreed between the union and the employer.'

(6) In subsection (9) for 'subsection (7)' substitute 'subsections (7) to (7B)'.

Sections 7, 8 and 9   **SCHEDULE 4**

LEAVE FOR FAMILY REASONS ETC

PART I

MATERNITY LEAVE AND PARENTAL LEAVE

NEW PART VIII OF EMPLOYMENT RIGHTS ACT 1996

'PART VIII

CHAPTER I

MATERNITY LEAVE

71   Ordinary maternity leave

(1) An employee may, provided that she satisfies any conditions which may be prescribed, be absent from work at any time during an ordinary maternity leave period.

(2) An ordinary maternity leave period is a period calculated in accordance with regulations made by the Secretary of State.

(3) Regulations under subsection (2)—

     (a) shall secure that no ordinary maternity leave period is less than 18 weeks;

     (b) may allow an employee to choose, subject to any prescribed restrictions, the date on which an ordinary maternity leave period starts.

(4) Subject to section 74, an employee who exercises her right under subsection (1)—

     (a) is entitled to the benefit of the terms and conditions of employment which would have applied if she had not been absent,

     (b) is bound by any obligations arising under those terms and conditions (except in so far as they are inconsistent with subsection (1)), and

     (c) is entitled to return from leave to the job in which she was employed before her absence.

(5) In subsection (4)(a) "terms and conditions of employment"—

     (a) includes matters connected with an employee's employment whether or not they arise under her contract of employment, but

(b) does not include terms and conditions about remuneration.

(6) The Secretary of State may make regulations specifying matters which are, or are not, to be treated as remuneration for the purposes of this section.

(7) An employee's right to return under subsection (4)(c) is a right to return—

(a) with her seniority, pension rights and similar rights as they would have been if she had not been absent (subject to paragraph 5 of Schedule 5 to the Social Security Act 1989 (equal treatment under pension schemes: maternity)), and

(b) on terms and conditions not less favourable than those which would have applied if she had not been absent.

72 Compulsory maternity leave

(1) An employer shall not permit an employee who satisfies prescribed conditions to work during a compulsory maternity leave period.

(2) A compulsory maternity leave period is a period calculated in accordance with regulations made by the Secretary of State.

(3) Regulations under subsection (2) shall secure—

(a) that no compulsory leave period is less than two weeks, and

(b) that every compulsory maternity leave period falls within an ordinary maternity leave period.

(4) Subject to subsection (5), any provision of or made under the Health and Safety at Work etc Act 1974 shall apply in relation to the prohibition under subsection (1) as if it were imposed by regulations under section 15 of that Act.

(5) Section 33(1)(c) of the 1974 Act shall not apply in relation to the prohibition under subsection (1); and an employer who contravenes that subsection shall be—

(a) guilty of an offence, and

(b) liable on summary conviction to a fine not exceeding level 2 on the standard scale.

73 Additional maternity leave

(1) An employee who satisfies prescribed conditions may be absent from work at any time during an additional maternity leave period.

(2) An additional maternity leave period is a period calculated in accordance with regulations made by the Secretary of State.

(3) Regulations under subsection (2) may allow an employee to choose, subject to prescribed restrictions, the date on which an additional maternity leave period ends.

(4) Subject to section 74, an employee who exercises her right under subsection (1)—

(a) is entitled, for such purposes and to such extent as may be prescribed, to the benefit of the terms and conditions of employment which would have applied if she had not been absent,

    (b) is bound, for such purposes and to such extent as may be prescribed, by obligations arising under those terms and conditions (except in so far as they are inconsistent with subsection (1)), and

    (c) is entitled to return from leave to a job of a prescribed kind.

(5) In subsection (4)(a) "terms and conditions of employment"—

    (a) includes matters connected with an employee's employment whether or not they arise under her contract of employment, but

    (b) does not include terms and conditions about remuneration.

(6) The Secretary of State may make regulations specifying matters which are, or are not, to be treated as remuneration for the purposes of this section.

(7) The Secretary of State may make regulations making provision, in relation to the right to return under subsection (4)(c), about—

    (a) seniority, pension rights and similar rights;

    (b) terms and conditions of employment on return.

74 Redundancy and dismissal

(1) Regulations under section 71 or 73 may make provision about redundancy during an ordinary or additional maternity leave period.

(2) Regulations under section 71 or 73 may make provision about dismissal (other than by reason of redundancy) during an ordinary or additional maternity leave period.

(3) Regulations made by virtue of subsection (1) or (2) may include—

    (a) provision requiring an employer to offer alternative employment;

    (b) provision for the consequences of failure to comply with the regulations (which may include provision for a dismissal to be treated as unfair for the purposes of Part X).

(4) Regulations under section 73 may make provision—

    (a) for section 73(4)(c) not to apply in specified cases, and

    (b) about dismissal at the conclusion of an additional maternity leave period.

75 Sections 71 to 73: supplemental

(1) Regulations under section 71, 72 or 73 may—

    (a) make provision about notices to be given, evidence to be produced and other procedures to be followed by employees and employers;

    (b) make provision for the consequences of failure to give notices, to produce evidence or to comply with other procedural requirements;

    (c) make provision for the consequences of failure to act in accordance with a notice given by virtue of paragraph (a);

    (d) make special provision for cases where an employee has a right which corresponds to a right under this Chapter and which arises under her contract of employment or otherwise;

    (e) make provision modifying the effect of Chapter II of Part XIV (calculation of a week's pay) in relation to an employee who is or has been absent from work on ordinary or additional maternity leave;

(f) make provision applying, modifying or excluding an enactment, in such circumstances as may be specified and subject to any conditions specified, in relation to a person entitled to ordinary, compulsory or additional maternity leave;

(g) make different provision for different cases or circumstances.

(2) In sections 71 to 73 "prescribed" means prescribed by regulations made by the Secretary of State.

CHAPTER II

PARENTAL LEAVE

76 Entitlement to parental leave

(1) The Secretary of State shall make regulations entitling an employee who satisfies specified conditions—

(a) as to duration of employment, and

(b) as to having, or expecting to have, responsibility for a child,

to be absent from work on parental leave for the purpose of caring for a child.

(2) The regulations shall include provision for determining—

(a) the extent of an employee's entitlement to parental leave in respect of a child;

(b) when parental leave may be taken.

(3) Provision under subsection (2)(a) shall secure that where an employee is entitled to parental leave in respect of a child he is entitled to a period or total period of leave of at least three months; but this subsection is without prejudice to any provision which may be made by the regulations for cases in which—

(a) a person ceases to satisfy conditions under subsection (1);

(b) an entitlement to parental leave is transferred.

(4) Provision under subsection (2)(b) may, in particular, refer to—

(a) a child's age, or

(b) a specified period of time starting from a specified event.

(5) Regulations under subsection (1) may—

(a) specify things which are, or are not, to be taken as done for the purpose of caring for a child;

(b) require parental leave to be taken as a single period of absence in all cases or in specified cases;

(c) require parental leave to be taken as a series of periods of absence in all cases or in specified cases;

(d) require all or specified parts of a period of parental leave to be taken at or by specified times;

(e) make provision about the postponement by an employer of a period of parental leave which an employee wishes to take;

(f) specify a minimum or maximum period of absence which may be taken as part of a period of parental leave.

(g) specify a maximum aggregate of periods of parental leave which may be taken during a specified period of time.

77   Rights during and after parental leave

(1) Regulations under section 76 shall provide—

(a) that an employee who is absent on parental leave is entitled, for such purposes and to such extent as may be prescribed, to the benefit of the terms and conditions of employment which would have applied if he had not been absent,

(b) that an employee who is absent on parental leave is bound, for such purposes and to such extent as may be prescribed, by any obligations arising under those terms and conditions (except in so far as they are inconsistent with section 76(1)), and

(c) that an employee who is absent on parental leave is entitled, subject to section 78(1), to return from leave to a job of such kind as the regulations may specify.

(2) In subsection (1)(a) "terms and conditions of employment"—

(a) includes matters connected with an employee's employment whether or not they arise under a contract of employment, but

(b) does not include terms and conditions about remuneration.

(3) Regulations under section 76 may specify matters which are, or are not, to be treated as remuneration for the purposes of subsection (2)(b) above.

(4) The regulations may make provision, in relation to the right to return mentioned in subsection (1)(c), about—

(a) seniority, pension rights and similar rights;

(b) terms and conditions of employment on return.

78   Special cases

(1) Regulations under section 76 may make provision—

(a) about redundancy during a period of parental leave;

(b) about dismissal (other than by reason of redundancy) during a period of parental leave.

(2) Provision by virtue of subsection (1) may include—

(a) provision requiring an employer to offer alternative employment;

(b) provision for the consequences of failure to comply with the regulations (which may include provision for a dismissal to be treated as unfair for the purposes of Part X).

(3) Regulations under section 76 may provide for an employee to be entitled to choose to exercise all or part of his entitlement to parental leave—

(a) by varying the terms of his contract of employment as to hours of work, or

    (b) by varying his normal working practice as to hours of work,

in a way specified in or permitted by the regulations for a period specified in the regulations.

(4) Provision by virtue of subsection (3)—

    (a) may restrict an entitlement to specified circumstances;

    (b) may make an entitlement subject to specified conditions (which may include conditions relating to obtaining the employer's consent);

    (c) may include consequential and incidental provision.

(5) Regulations under section 76 may make provision permitting all or part of an employee's entitlement to parental leave in respect of a child to be transferred to another employee in specified circumstances.

(6) The reference in section 77(1)(c) to absence on parental leave includes, where appropriate, a reference to a continuous period of absence attributable partly to maternity leave and partly to parental leave.

(7) Regulations under section 76 may provide for specified provisions of the regulations not to apply in relation to an employee if any provision of his contract of employment—

    (a) confers an entitlement to absence from work for the purpose of caring for a child, and

    (b) incorporates or operates by reference to all or part of a collective agreement, or workforce agreement, of a kind specified in the regulations.

79 Supplemental

(1) Regulations under section 76 may, in particular—

    (a) make provision about notices to be given and evidence to be produced by employees to employers, by employers to employees, and by employers to other employers;

    (b) make provision requiring employers or employees to keep records;

    (c) make provision about other procedures to be followed by employees and employers;

    (d) make provision (including provision creating criminal offences) specifying the consequences of failure to give notices, to produce evidence, to keep records or to comply with other procedural requirements;

    (e) make provision specifying the consequences of failure to act in accordance with a notice given by virtue of paragraph (a);

    (f) make special provision for cases where an employee has a right which corresponds to a right conferred by the regulations and which arises under his contract of employment or otherwise;

    (g) make provision applying, modifying or excluding an enactment, in such circumstances as may be specified and subject to any conditions specified, in relation to a person entitled to parental leave;

    (h) make different provision for different cases or circumstances.

(2) The regulations may make provision modifying the effect of Chapter II of Part XIV (calculation of a week's pay) in relation to an employee who is or has been absent from work on parental leave.

(3) Without prejudice to the generality of section 76, the regulations may make any provision which appears to the Secretary of State to be necessary or expedient—

    (a) for the purpose of implementing Council Directive 96/34/EC on the framework agreement on parental leave, or

    (b) for the purpose of dealing with any matter arising out of or related to the United Kingdom's obligations under that Directive.

80 Complaint to employment tribunal

(1) An employee may present a complaint to an employment tribunal that his employer—

    (a) has unreasonably postponed a period of parental leave requested by the employee, or

    (b) has prevented or attempted to prevent the employee from taking parental leave.

(2) An employment tribunal shall not consider a complaint under this section unless it is presented—

    (a) before the end of the period of three months beginning with the date (or last date) of the matters complained of, or

    (b) within such further period as the tribunal considers reasonable in a case where it is satisfied that it was not reasonably practicable for the complaint to be presented before the end of that period of three months.

(3) Where an employment tribunal finds a complaint under this section well-founded it—

    (a) shall make a declaration to that effect, and

    (b) may make an award of compensation to be paid by the employer to the employee.

(4) The amount of compensation shall be such as the tribunal considers just and equitable in all the circumstances having regard to—

    (a) the employer's behaviour, and

    (b) any loss sustained by the employee which is attributable to the matters complained of.'

PART II

TIME OFF FOR DEPENDANTS

PROVISIONS TO BE INSERTED AFTER SECTION 57 OF THE EMPLOYMENT RIGHTS ACT 1996

'Dependants

57A Time off for dependants

(1) An employee is entitled to be permitted by his employer to take a reasonable amount of time off during the employee's working hours in order to take action which is necessary—

    (a)   to provide assistance on an occasion when a dependant falls ill, gives birth or is injured or assaulted,

    (b)   to make arrangements for the provision of care for a dependant who is ill or injured,

    (c)   in consequence of the death of a dependant,

    (d)   because of the unexpected disruption or termination of arrangements for the care of a dependant, or

    (e)   to deal with an incident which involves a child of the employee and which occurs unexpectedly in a period during which an educational establishment which the child attends is responsible for him.

(2) Subsection (1) does not apply unless the employee—

    (a)   tells his employer the reason for his absence as soon as reasonably practicable, and

    (b)   except where paragraph (a) cannot be complied with until after the employee has returned to work, tells his employer for how long he expects to be absent.

(3) Subject to subsections (4) and (5), for the purposes of this section "dependant" means, in relation to an employee—

    (a)   a spouse,

    (b)   a child,

    (c)   a parent,

    (d)   a person who lives in the same household as the employee, otherwise than by reason of being his employee, tenant, lodger or boarder.

(4) For the purposes of subsection (1)(a) or (b) "dependant" includes, in addition to the persons mentioned in subsection (3), any person who reasonably relies on the employee—

    (a)   for assistance on an occasion when the person falls ill or is injured or assaulted, or

    (b)   to make arrangements for the provision of care in the event of illness or injury.

(5) For the purposes of subsection (1)(d) "dependant" includes, in addition to the persons mentioned in subsection (3), any person who reasonably relies on the employee to make arrangements for the provision of care.

(6) A reference in this section to illness or injury includes a reference to mental illness or injury.

57B Complaint to employment tribunal

(1) An employee may present a complaint to an employment tribunal that his employer has unreasonably refused to permit him to take time off as required by section 57A.

(2) An employment tribunal shall not consider a complaint under this section unless it is presented—

    (a)   before the end of the period of three months beginning with the date when the refusal occurred, or

(b) within such further period as the tribunal considers reasonable in a case where it is satisfied that it was not reasonably practicable for the complaint to be presented before the end of that period of three months.

(3) Where an employment tribunal finds a complaint under subsection (1) well-founded, it—

(a) shall make a declaration to that effect, and
(b) may make an award of compensation to be paid by the employer to the employee.

(4) The amount of compensation shall be such as the tribunal considers just and equitable in all the circumstances having regard to—

(a) the employer's default in refusing to permit time off to be taken by the employee, and
(b) any loss sustained by the employee which is attributable to the matters complained of.'

PART III

CONSEQUENTIAL AMENDMENTS

Trade Union and Labour Relations (Consolidation) Act 1992 (c. 52)

1. The Trade Union and Labour Relations (Consolidation) Act 1992 shall be amended as follows.

2. In section 237(1A) (dismissal of those taking part in unofficial industrial action)—

(a) for the words from 'section 99(1) to (3)' to the end substitute 'or under—

(a) section 99, 100, 101A(d), 103 or 103A of the Employment Rights Act 1996 (dismissal in family, health and safety, working time, employee representative and protected disclosure cases),
(b) section 104 of that Act in its application in relation to time off under section 57A of that Act (dependants);' and

(b) at the end insert '; and a reference to a specified reason for dismissal includes a reference to specified circumstances of dismissal'.

3. In section 238(2A) (dismissal in connection with other industrial action)—

(a) for the words from 'section 99(1) to (3)' to the end substitute 'or under—

(a) section 99, 100, 101A(d) or 103 of the Employment Rights Act 1996 (dismissal in family, health and safety, working time and employee representative cases),
(b) section 104 of that Act in its application in relation to time off under section 57A of that Act (dependants);' and

(b) at the end insert '; and a reference to a specified reason for dismissal includes a reference to specified circumstances of dismissal'.

Employment Tribunals Act 1996 (c. 17)

4. In section 13(2) of the Employment Tribunals Act 1996 (costs and expenses) the following shall cease to have effect—

(a) the word 'or' after paragraph (a),

(b) paragraph (b), and

(c) the words ', or which she held before her absence,'.

Employment Rights Act 1996 (c. 18)

5. The Employment Rights Act 1996 shall be amended as follows.

6. In section 37 (contractual requirements for Sunday work: protected workers) omit the following—

(a) subsection (4),

(b) the word 'and' after subsection (5)(a), and

(c) subsection (5)(b).

7. In section 43 (contractual requirements relating to Sunday work: opting out) omit the following—

(a) subsection (4),

(b) the word 'and' after subsection (5)(a), and

(c) subsection (5)(b).

8. After section 47B (protection from detriment: disclosures) insert—

'47C Leave for family and domestic reasons

(1) An employee has the right not to be subjected to any detriment by any act, or any deliberate failure to act, by his employer done for a prescribed reason.

(2) A prescribed reason is one which is prescribed by regulations made by the Secretary of State and which relates to—

(a) pregnancy, childbirth or maternity,

(b) ordinary, compulsory or additional maternity leave,

(c) parental leave, or

(d) time off under section 57A.

(3) A reason prescribed under this section in relation to parental leave may relate to action which an employee takes, agrees to take or refuses to take under or in respect of a collective or workforce agreement.

(4) Regulations under this section may make different provision for different cases or circumstances.'

9. In section 48(1) (detriment: complaints to employment tribunals) for 'or 47A' substitute ', 47A or 47C'.

10. In section 88(1)(c) (notice period: employment with normal working hours) after 'childbirth' insert 'or on parental leave'.

11. In section 89(3)(b) (notice period: employment without normal working hours) after 'childbirth' insert 'or on parental leave'.

12. In section 92(4)(b) (right to written statement of reasons for dismissal) for 'maternity leave period' substitute 'ordinary or additional maternity leave period'.

13. Omit section 96 (failure to permit return after childbirth treated as dismissal).

14. Omit section 97(6) (effective date of termination: section 96).

15. In section 98 (fairness of dismissal)—

    (a) omit subsection (5), and

    (b) in subsection (6) for 'subsections (4) and (5)' substitute 'subsection (4)'.

16. For section 99 (unfair dismissal: pregnancy and childbirth) substitute—

'99 Leave for family reasons

(1) An employee who is dismissed shall be regarded for the purposes of this Part as unfairly dismissed if—

    (a)   the reason or principal reason for the dismissal is of a prescribed kind, or

    (b)   the dismissal takes place in prescribed circumstances.

(2) In this section "prescribed" means prescribed by regulations made by the Secretary of State.

(3) A reason or set of circumstances prescribed under this section must relate to—

    (a)   pregnancy, childbirth or maternity,

    (b)   ordinary, compulsory or additional maternity leave,

    (c)   parental leave, or

    (d)   time off under section 57A;

and it may also relate to redundancy or other factors.

(4) A reason or set of circumstances prescribed under subsection (1) satisfies subsection (3)(c) or (d) if it relates to action which an employee—

    (a)   takes,

    (b)   agrees to take, or

    (c)   refuses to take,

under or in respect of a collective or workforce agreement which deals with parental leave.

(5) Regulations under this section may—

    (a)   make different provision for different cases or circumstances;

    (b)   apply any enactment, in such circumstances as may be specified and subject to any conditions specified, in relation to persons regarded as unfairly dismissed by reason of this section.'

17. In section 105 (unfair dismissal: redundancy) omit subsection (2).

18. In section 108 (qualifying period of employment) omit subsection (3)(a).

19. In section 109 (upper age limit) omit subsection (2)(a).

20. In section 114 (order for reinstatement) omit subsection (5).

21. In section 115 (order for re-engagement) omit subsection (4).

22. In section 118(1)(b) (compensation: general) omit ', 127'.

23. In section 119 (compensation: basic award) omit subsection (6).

24. Omit section 127 (dismissal at or after end of maternity leave period).

25. Omit section 137 (failure to permit return after childbirth treated as dismissal).

26. In section 145 (redundancy payments: relevant date) omit subsection (7).

27. In section 146 (supplemental provisions) omit subsection (3).

28. In section 156 (upper age limit) omit subsection (2).

29. In section 157 (exemption orders) omit subsection (6).

30. In section 162 (amount of redundancy payment) omit subsection (7).

31. In section 192(2) (armed forces)—

(a) after paragraph (aa) insert—

'(ab) section 47C,' , and

(b) in paragraph (b) for '55 to 57' substitute '55 to 57B'.

32. In section 194(2)(c) (House of Lords staff) for 'and 47' substitute ', 47 and 47C'.

33. In section 195(2)(c) (House of Commons staff) for 'and 47' substitute ', 47 and 47C'.

34. In section 199 (mariners)—

(a) in subsection (2) for '50 to 57' substitute '47C, 50 to 57B'.
(b) in subsection (2) omit the words '(subject to subsection (3))', and
(c) omit subsection (3).

35. In section 200(1) (police officers)—

(a) after '47B,' insert '47C,',
(b) for 'to 57' substitute 'to 57B',
(c) after '93' insert 'and', and
(d) omit 'and section 137'.

36. In section 202(2) (national security)—

(a) in paragraph (b) for 'and 47' substitute ', 47 and 47C',
(b) in paragraph (c) for '55 to 57' substitute '55 to 57B', and
(c) in paragraph (g) for sub-paragraph (1) substitute—

'(i) by section 99, 100, 101A(d) or 103, or by section 104 in its application in relation to time off under section 57A,'.

37. In section 209 (power to amend Act) omit subsection (6).

38.—(1) Section 212 (weeks counted in computing period of employment) is amended as follows.

(2) Omit subsection (2).

(3) In subsection (3)—

(a) insert 'or' after paragraph (b),
(b) omit 'or' after paragraph (c), and
(c) omit paragraph (d).

(4) In subsection (4) omit 'or (subject to subsection (2)) subsection (3)(d)'.

39. In section 225(5)(b) (calculation date: rights during employment) for sub-paragraph (1) substitute—

'(i) where the day before that on which the suspension begins falls during a period of ordinary or additional maternity leave, the day before the beginning of that period,'.

40. In section 226 (rights on termination) omit subsections (3)(a) and (5)(a).

41. In section 235(1) (interpretation: other definitions) omit the definitions of 'maternity leave period' and 'notified day of return'.

42.—(1) Section 236 (orders and regulations) shall be amended as follows.

(2) In subsection (2)(a) after 'order' insert 'or regulations'.

(3) In subsection (3)—

    (a) after 'and no order' insert 'or regulations',
    (b) for '72(3), 73(5), 79(3),' substitute '47C, 71, 72, 73, 76, 99,', and
    (c) for 'or order' substitute ', order or regulations'.

Section 16   **SCHEDULE 5**

UNFAIR DISMISSAL OF STRIKING WORKERS

Trade Union and Labour Relations (Consolidation) Act 1992 (c. 52)

1. The Trade Union and Labour Relations (Consolidation) Act 1992 shall be amended as follows.

2. In section 238 (dismissals in connection with industrial action) after subsection (2A) there shall be inserted—

    '(2B) Subsection (2) does not apply in relation to an employee who is regarded as unfairly dismissed by virtue of section 238A below.'

3. The following shall be inserted after section 238—

'238A Participation in official industrial action

    (1) For the purposes of this section an employee takes protected industrial action if he commits an act which, or a series of acts each of which, he is induced to commit by an act which by virtue of section 219 is not actionable in tort.

    (2) An employee who is dismissed shall be regarded for the purposes of Part X of the Employment Rights Act 1996 (unfair dismissal) as unfairly dismissed if—

        (a) the reason (or, if more than one, the principal reason) for the dismissal is that the employee took protected industrial action, and
        (b) subsection (3), (4) or (5) applies to the dismissal.

    (3) This subsection applies to a dismissal if it takes place within the period of eight weeks beginning with the day on which the employee started to take protected industrial action.

    (4) This subsection applies to a dismissal if—

        (a) it takes place after the end of that period, and
        (b) the employee had stopped taking protected industrial action before the end of that period.

    (5) This subsection applies to a dismissal if—

        (a) it takes place after the end of that period,

    (b)   the employee had not stopped taking protected industrial action before the end of that period, and

    (c)   the employer had not taken such procedural steps as would have been reasonable for the purposes of resolving the dispute to which the protected industrial action relates.

(6) In determining whether an employer has taken those steps regard shall be had, in particular, to—

    (a)   whether the employer or a union had complied with procedures established by any applicable collective or other agreement;

    (b)   whether the employer or a union offered or agreed to commence or resume negotiations after the start of the protected industrial action;

    (c)   whether the employer or a union unreasonably refused, after the start of the protected industrial action, a request that conciliation services be used;

    (d)   whether the employer or a union unreasonably refused, after the start of the protected industrial action, a request that mediation services be used in relation to procedures to be adopted for the purposes of resolving the dispute.

(7) In determining whether an employer has taken those steps no regard shall be had to the merits of the dispute.

(8) For the purposes of this section no account shall be taken of the repudiation of any act by a trade union as mentioned in section 21 in relation to anything which occurs before the end of the next working day (within the meaning of section 237) after the day on which the repudiation takes place.'

4.—(1) Section 239 (supplementary provisions relating to unfair dismissal) shall be amended as follows.

(2) In subsection (1) for 'Sections 237 and 238' there shall be substituted 'Sections 237 to 238A'.

(3) At the end of subsection (1) there shall be added '; but sections 108 and 109 of that Act (qualifying period and age limit) shall not apply in relation to section 238A of this Act.'

(4) In subsection (2) after 'section 238' there shall be inserted 'or 238A'.

(5) At the end there shall be added—

    '(4) In relation to a complaint under section 111 of the 1996 Act (unfair dismissal: complaint to employment tribunal) that a dismissal was unfair by virtue of section 238A of this Act—

    (a)   no order shall be made under section 113 of the 1996 Act (reinstatement or re-engagement) until after the conclusion of protected industrial action by any employee in relation to the relevant dispute,

    (b)   regulations under section 7 of the Employment Tribunals Act 1996 may make provision about the adjournment and renewal of applications (including provision requiring adjournment in specified circumstances), and

    (c)   regulations under section 9 of that Act may require a pre-hearing review to be carried out in specified circumstances.'

Employment Rights Act 1996 (c. 18)

5.—(1) Section 105 of the Employment Rights Act 1996 (redundancy) shall be amended as follows.

(2) In subsection (1)(c) for 'subsections (2) to (7)' there shall be substituted 'subsections (2) to (7C).'.

(3) After subsection (7B) (inserted by Schedule 3 to the Tax Credits Act 1999) there shall be inserted—

'(7C) This subsection applies if—

(a)   the reason (or, if more than one, the principal reason) for which the employee was selected for dismissal was the reason mentioned in section 238A(2) of the Trade Union and Labour Relations (Consolidation) Act 1992 (participation in official industrial action), and

(b)   subsection (3), (4) or (5) of that section applies to the dismissal.'

Section 29   **SCHEDULE 6**

THE CERTIFICATION OFFICER

Introduction

1. The Trade Union and Labour Relations (Consolidation) Act 1992 shall be amended as provided by this Schedule.

Register of members

2. In section 24 (duty to maintain register of members' names and addresses) the second sentence of subsection (6) (application to Certification Officer does not prevent application to court) shall be omitted.

3. In section 24A (securing confidentiality of register during ballots) the second sentence of subsection (6) (application to Certification Officer does not prevent application to court) shall be omitted.

4.—(1) Section 25 (application to Certification Officer for declaration of breach of duty regarding register of members' names and addresses) shall be amended as follows.

(2) In subsection (2)(b) (duty to give opportunity to be heard where Certification Officer considers it appropriate) omit 'where he considers it appropriate,'.

(3) After subsection (5) insert—

'(5A) Where the Certification Officer makes a declaration he shall also, unless he considers that to do so would be inappropriate, make an enforcement order, that is, an order imposing on the union one or both of the following requirements—

(a)   to take such steps to remedy the declared failure, within such period, as may be specified in the order;

(b)   to abstain from such acts as may be so specified with a view to securing that a failure of the same or a similar kind does not occur in future.

(5B) Where an enforcement order has been made, any person who is a member of the union and was a member at the time it was made is entitled to enforce obedience to the order as if he had made the application on which the order was made.'

(4) After subsection (8) insert—

'(9) A declaration made by the Certification Officer under this section may be relied on as if it were a declaration made by the court.

(10) An enforcement order made by the Certification Officer under this section may be enforced in the same way as an order of the court.

(11) The following paragraphs have effect if a person applies under section 26 in relation to an alleged failure—

(a) that person may not apply under this section in relation to that failure;
(b) on an application by a different person under this section in relation to that failure, the Certification Officer shall have due regard to any declaration, order, observations or reasons made or given by the court regarding that failure and brought to the Certification Officer's notice.'

5.—(1) Section 26 (application to court for declaration of breach of duty regarding register of members' names and addresses) shall be amended as follows.

(2) Omit subsection (2) (position where application in respect of the same matter has been made to Certification Officer).

(3) After subsection (7) insert—

'(8) The following paragraphs have effect if a person applies under section 25 in relation to an alleged failure—

(a) that person may not apply under this section in relation to that failure;
(b) on an application by a different person under this section in relation to that failure, the court shall have due regard to any declaration, order, observations or reasons made or given by the Certification Officer regarding that failure and brought to the court's notice.'

Accounting records

6.—(1) Section 31 (remedy for failure to comply with request for access to accounting records) shall be amended as follows.

(2) In subsection (1) after 'the court' insert 'or to the Certification Officer'.

(3) In subsection (2) (court to make order if claim well-founded) after 'Where' insert 'on an application to it' and for 'that person' substitute 'the applicant'.

(4) After subsection (2) insert—

'(2A) On an application to him the Certification Officer shall—

(a) make such enquiries as he thinks fit, and
(b) give the applicant and the trade union an opportunity to be heard.

(2B) Where the Certification Officer is satisfied that the claim is well-founded he shall make such order as he considers appropriate for ensuring that the applicant—

(a) is allowed to inspect the records requested,

(b) is allowed to be accompanied by an accountant when making the inspection of those records, and

(c) is allowed to take, or is supplied with, such copies of, or of extracts from, the records as he may require.

(2C) In exercising his functions under this section the Certification Officer shall ensure that, so far as is reasonably practicable, an application made to him is determined within six months of being made.'

(5) In subsection (3) (court's power to grant interlocutory relief) after 'an application' insert 'to it'.

(6) After subsection (3) insert—

'(4) Where the Certification Officer requests a person to furnish information to him in connection with enquiries made by him under this section, he shall specify the date by which that information is to be furnished and, unless he considers that it would be inappropriate to do so, shall proceed with his determination of the application notwithstanding that the information has not been furnished to him by the specified date.

(5) An order made by the Certification Officer under this section may be enforced in the same way as an order of the court.

(6) If a person applies to the court under this section in relation to an alleged failure he may not apply to the Certification Officer under this section in relation to that failure.

(7) If a person applies to the Certification Officer under this section in relation to an alleged failure he may not apply to the court under this section in relation to that failure.'

Offenders

7.—(1) Section 45C (application to Certification Officer or court for declaration of breach of duty to secure positions not held by certain offenders) shall be amended as follows.

(2) In subsection (2) (Certification Officer's powers and duties) insert before paragraph (a)—

'(aa) shall make such enquiries as he thinks fit,'

(3) In subsection (2)(a) (duty to give opportunity to be heard where Certification Officer considers it appropriate) omit ', where he considers it appropriate,'.

(4) Omit subsections (3) and (4) (different applications in respect of the same matter).

(5) After subsection (5) insert—

'(5A) Where the Certification Officer makes a declaration he shall also, unless he considers that it would be inappropriate, make an order imposing on the trade union a requirement to take within such period as may be specified in the order such steps to remedy the declared failure as may be so specified.

(5B) The following paragraphs have effect if a person applies to the Certification Officer under this section in relation to an alleged failure—

(a) that person may not apply to the court under this section in relation to that failure;

(b) on an application by a different person to the court under this section in relation to that failure, the court shall have due regard to any declaration, order, observations or reasons made or given by the Certification Officer regarding that failure and brought to the court's notice.

(5C) The following paragraphs have effect if a person applies to the court under this section in relation to an alleged failure—

(a) that person may not apply to the Certification Officer under this section in relation to that failure;

(b) on an application by a different person to the Certification Officer under this section in relation to that failure, the Certification Officer shall have regard to any declaration, order, observations or reasons made or given by the court regarding that failure and brought to the Certification Officer's notice.'

(6) In subsection (6) (entitlement to enforce order) after 'been made' insert 'under subsection (5) or (5A)'.

(7) After subsection (6) insert—

'(7) Where the Certification Officer requests a person to furnish information to him in connection with enquiries made by him under this section, he shall specify the date by which that information is to be furnished and, unless he considers that it would be inappropriate to do so, shall proceed with his determination of the application notwithstanding that the information has not been furnished to him by the specified date.

(8) A declaration made by the Certification Officer under this section may be relied on as if it were a declaration made by the court.

(9) An order made by the Certification Officer under this section may be enforced in the same way as an order of the court.'

Trade union administration: appeals

8. After section 45C there shall be inserted—

'45D Appeals from Certification Officer

An appeal lies to the Employment Appeal Tribunal on any question of law arising in proceedings before or arising from any decision of the Certification Officer under section 25, 31 or 45C.'

Elections

9. In section 54 (remedy for failure to comply with the duty regarding elections) the second sentence of subsection (1) (application to Certification Officer does not prevent application to court) shall be omitted.

10.—(1) Section 55 (application to Certification Officer for declaration of breach of duty regarding elections) shall be amended as follows.

(2) In subsection (2)(b) (duty to give opportunity to be heard where Certification Officer considers it appropriate) omit 'where he considers it appropriate,' .

(3) After subsection (5) insert—

'(5A) Where the Certification Officer makes a declaration he shall also, unless he considers that to do so would be inappropriate, make an enforcement order, that is, an order imposing on the union one or more of the following requirements—

    (a)   to secure the holding of an election in accordance with the order;

    (b)   to take such other steps to remedy the declared failure as may be specified in the order;

    (c)   to abstain from such acts as may be so specified with a view to securing that a failure of the same or a similar kind does not occur in future.

The Certification Officer shall in an order imposing any such requirement as is mentioned in paragraph (a) or (b) specify the period within which the union is to comply with the requirements of the order.

(5B) Where the Certification Officer makes an order requiring the union to hold a fresh election, he shall (unless he considers that it would be inappropriate to do so in the particular circumstances of the case) require the election to be conducted in accordance with the requirements of this Chapter and such other provisions as may be made by the order.

(5C) Where an enforcement order has been made—

    (a)   any person who is a member of the union and was a member at the time the order was made, or

    (b)   any person who is or was a candidate in the election in question,

is entitled to enforce obedience to the order as if he had made the application on which the order was made.'

(4) After subsection (7) insert—

'(8) A declaration made by the Certification Officer under this section may be relied on as if it were a declaration made by the court.

(9) An enforcement order made by the Certification Officer under this section may be enforced in the same way as an order of the court.

(10) The following paragraphs have effect if a person applies under section 56 in relation to an alleged failure—

    (a)   that person may not apply under this section in relation to that failure;

    (b)   on an application by a different person under this section in relation to that failure, the Certification Officer shall have due regard to any declaration, order, observations or reasons made or given by the court regarding that failure and brought to the Certification Officer's notice.'

11.—(1) Section 56 (application to court for declaration of failure to comply with requirements regarding elections) shall be amended as follows.

(2) Omit subsection (2) (position where application in respect of the same matter has been made to the Certification Officer).

(3) After subsection (7) insert—

'(8) The following paragraphs have effect if a person applies under section 55 in relation to an alleged failure—

  (a) that person may not apply under this section in relation to that failure;
  (b) on an application by a different person under this section in relation to that failure, the court shall have due regard to any declaration, order, observations or reasons made or given by the Certification Officer regarding that failure and brought to the court's notice.'

12. After section 56 there shall be inserted—

'56A Appeals from Certification Officer

An appeal lies to the Employment Appeal Tribunal on any question of law arising in proceedings before or arising from any decision of the Certification Officer under section 55.'

Application of funds for political objects

13. After section 72 there shall be inserted—

'72A Application of funds in breach of section 71

(1) A person who is a member of a trade union and who claims that it has applied its funds in breach of section 71 may apply to the Certification Officer for a declaration that it has done so.

(2) On an application under this section the Certification Officer—

  (a) shall make such enquiries as he thinks fit,
  (b) shall give the applicant and the union an opportunity to be heard,
  (c) shall ensure that, so far as is reasonably practicable, the application is determined within six months of being made,
  (d) may make or refuse the declaration asked for,
  (e) shall, whether he makes or refuses the declaration, give reasons for his decision in writing, and
  (f) may make written observations on any matter arising from, or connected with, the proceedings.

(3) If he makes a declaration he shall specify in it—

  (a) the provisions of section 71 breached, and
  (b) the amount of the funds applied in breach.

(4) If he makes a declaration and is satisfied that the union has taken or agreed to take steps with a view to—

  (a) remedying the declared breach, or
  (b) securing that a breach of the same or any similar kind does not occur in future,

he shall specify those steps in making the declaration.

(5) If he makes a declaration he may make such order for remedying the breach as he thinks just under the circumstances.

(6) Where the Certification Officer requests a person to furnish information to him in connection with enquiries made by him under this section, he shall specify

the date by which that information is to be furnished and, unless he considers that it would be inappropriate to do so, shall proceed with his determination of the application notwithstanding that the information has not been furnished to him by the specified date.

(7) A declaration made by the Certification Officer under this section may be relied on as if it were a declaration made by the court.

(8) Where an order has been made under this section, any person who is a member of the union and was a member at the time it was made is entitled to enforce obedience to the order as if he had made the application on which the order was made.

(9) An order made by the Certification Officer under this section may be enforced in the same way as an order of the court.

(10) If a person applies to the Certification Officer under this section in relation to an alleged breach he may not apply to the court in relation to the breach; but nothing in this subsection shall prevent such a person from exercising any right to appeal against or challenge the Certification Officer's decision on the application to him.

(11) If—

    (a)   a person applies to the court in relation to an alleged breach, and
    (b)   the breach is one in relation to which he could have made an application to the Certification Officer under this section,

he may not apply to the Certification Officer under this section in relation to the breach.'

Political ballot rules

14. In section 79 (remedy for failure to comply with political ballot rules) the second sentence of subsection (1) (application to Certification Officer does not prevent application to court) shall be omitted.

15.—(1) Section 80 (application to Certification Officer for declaration of failure to comply with political ballot rules) shall be amended as follows.

(2) In subsection (2)(b) (duty to give opportunity to be heard where Certification Officer considers it appropriate) omit 'where he considers it appropriate,'.

(3) After subsection (5) insert—

'(5A) Where the Certification Officer makes a declaration he shall also, unless he considers that to do so would be inappropriate, make an enforcement order, that is, an order imposing on the union one or more of the following requirements—

    (a)   to secure the holding of a ballot in accordance with the order;
    (b)   to take such other steps to remedy the declared failure as may be specified in the order;
    (c)   to abstain from such acts as may be so specified with a view to securing that a failure of the same or a similar kind does not occur in future.

The Certification Officer shall in an order imposing any such requirement as is mentioned in paragraph (a) or (b) specify the period within which the union must comply with the requirements of the order.

(5B) Where the Certification Officer makes an order requiring the union to hold a fresh ballot, he shall (unless he considers that it would be inappropriate to do so in the particular circumstances of the case) require the ballot to be conducted in accordance with the union's political ballot rules and such other provisions as may be made by the order.

(5C) Where an enforcement order has been made, any person who is a member of the union and was a member at the time the order was made is entitled to enforce obedience to the order as if he had made the application on which the order was made.'

(4) After subsection (7) insert—

'(8) A declaration made by the Certification Officer under this section may be relied on as if it were a declaration made by the court.

(9) An enforcement order made by the Certification Officer under this section may be enforced in the same way as an order of the court.

(10) The following paragraphs have effect if a person applies under section 81 in relation to a matter—

    (a) that person may not apply under this section in relation to that matter;

    (b) on an application by a different person under this section in relation to that matter, the Certification Officer shall have due regard to any declaration, order, observations, or reasons made or given by the court regarding that matter and brought to the Certification Officer's notice.'

16.—(1) Section 81 (application to court for declaration of failure to comply with political ballot rules) shall be amended as follows.

(2) Omit subsection (2) (position where application in respect of the same matter has been made to Certification Officer).

(3) After subsection (7) insert—

'(8) The following paragraphs have effect if a person applies under section 80 in relation to a matter—

    (a) that person may not apply under this section in relation to that matter;

    (b) on an application by a different person under this section in relation to that matter, the court shall have due regard to any declaration, order, observations or reasons made or given by the Certification Officer regarding that matter and brought to the court's notice.'

Political fund

17.—(1) Section 82 (rules as to political fund) shall be amended as follows.

(2) After subsection (2) insert—

'(2A) On a complaint being made to him the Certification Officer shall make such enquiries as he thinks fit.'

(3) After subsection (3) insert—

'(3A) Where the Certification Officer requests a person to furnish information to him in connection with enquiries made by him under this section, he shall specify the date by which that information is to be furnished and, unless he considers that it would be inappropriate to do so, shall proceed with his determination of the application notwithstanding that the information has not been furnished to him by the specified date.'

Amalgamation or transfer of engagements

18.—(1) Section 103 (complaints about procedure relating to amalgamation or transfer of engagements) shall be amended as follows.

(2) After subsection (2) insert—

'(2A) On a complaint being made to him the Certification Officer shall make such enquiries as he thinks fit.'

(3) After subsection (5) insert—

'(6) Where the Certification Officer requests a person to furnish information to him in connection with enquiries made by him under this section, he shall specify the date by which that information is to be furnished and, unless he considers that it would be inappropriate to do so, shall proceed with his determination of the application notwithstanding that the information has not been furnished to him by the specified date.

(7) A declaration made by the Certification Officer under this section may be relied on as if it were a declaration made by the court.

(8) Where an order has been made under this section, any person who is a member of the union and was a member at the time it was made is entitled to enforce obedience to the order as if he had made the application on which the order was made.

(9) An order made by the Certification Officer under this section may be enforced in the same way as an order of the court.'

Breach of union rules

19. In Part I, after Chapter VII there shall be inserted—

'CHAPTER VIIA

BREACH OF RULES

108A   Right to apply to Certification Officer

(1) A person who claims that there has been a breach or threatened breach of the rules of a trade union relating to any of the matters mentioned in subsection (2) may apply to the Certification Officer for a declaration to that effect, subject to subsections (3) to (7).

(2) The matters are—

(a)   the appointment or election of a person to, or the removal of a person from, any office;

(b)   disciplinary proceedings by the union (including expulsion);

(c)   the balloting of members on any issue other than industrial action;

(d)   the constitution or proceedings of any executive committee or of any decision-making meeting;

(e) such other matters as may be specified in an order made by the Secretary of State.

(3) The applicant must be a member of the union, or have been one at the time of the alleged breach or threatened breach.

(4) A person may not apply under subsection (1) in relation to a claim if he is entitled to apply under section 80 in relation to the claim.

(5) No application may be made regarding—

(a) the dismissal of an employee of the union;
(b) disciplinary proceedings against an employee of the union.

(6) An application must be made—

(a) within the period of six months starting with the day on which the breach or threatened breach is alleged to have taken place, or
(b) if within that period any internal complaints procedure of the union is invoked to resolve the claim, within the period of six months starting with the earlier of the days specified in subsection (7).

(7) Those days are—

(a) the day on which the procedure is concluded, and
(b) the last day of the period of one year beginning with the day on which the procedure is invoked.

(8) The reference in subsection (1) to the rules of a union includes references to the rules of any branch or section of the union.

(9) In subsection (2)(c) "industrial action" means a strike or other industrial action by persons employed under contracts of employment.

(10) For the purposes of subsection (2)(d) a committee is an executive committee if—

(a) it is a committee of the union concerned and has power to make executive decisions on behalf of the union or on behalf of a constituent body,
(b) it is a committee of a major constituent body and has power to make executive decisions on behalf of that body, or
(c) it is a sub-committee of a committee falling within paragraph (a) or (b).

(11) For the purposes of subsection (2)(d) a decision-making meeting is—

(a) a meeting of members of the union concerned (or the representatives of such members) which has power to make a decision on any matter which, under the rules of the union, is final as regards the union or which, under the rules of the union or a constituent body, is final as regards that body, or
(b) a meeting of members of a major constituent body (or the representatives of such members) which has power to make a decision on any matter which, under the rules of the union or the body, is final as regards that body.

(12) For the purposes of subsections (10) and (11), in relation to the trade union concerned—

(a) a constituent body is any body which forms part of the union, including a branch, group, section or region;

(b) a major constituent body is such a body which has more than 1,000 members.

(13) Any order under subsection (2)(e) shall be made by statutory instrument; and no such order shall be made unless a draft of it has been laid before and approved by resolution of each House of Parliament.

(14) If a person applies to the Certification Officer under this section in relation to an alleged breach or threatened breach he may not apply to the court in relation to the breach or threatened breach; but nothing in this subsection shall prevent such a person from exercising any right to appeal against or challenge the Certification Officer's decision on the application to him.

(15) If—

(a) a person applies to the court in relation to an alleged breach or threatened breach, and

(b) the breach or threatened breach is one in relation to which he could have made an application to the Certification Officer under this section,

he may not apply to the Certification Officer under this section in relation to the breach or threatened breach.

108B Declarations and orders

(1) The Certification Officer may refuse to accept an application under section 108A unless he is satisfied that the applicant has taken all reasonable steps to resolve the claim by the use of any internal complaints procedure of the union.

(2) If he accepts an application under section 108A the Certification Officer—

(a) shall make such enquiries as he thinks fit,

(b) shall give the applicant and the union an opportunity to be heard,

(c) shall ensure that, so far as is reasonably practicable, the application is determined within six months of being made,

(d) may make or refuse the declaration asked for, and

(e) shall, whether he makes or refuses the declaration, give reasons for his decision in writing.

(3) Where the Certification Officer makes a declaration he shall also, unless he considers that to do so would be inappropriate, make an enforcement order, that is, an order imposing on the union one or both of the following requirements—

(a) to take such steps to remedy the breach, or withdraw the threat of a breach, as may be specified in the order;

(b) to abstain from such acts as may be so specified with a view to securing that a breach or threat of the same or a similar kind does not occur in future.

(4) The Certification Officer shall in an order imposing any such requirement as is mentioned in subsection (3)(a) specify the period within which the union is to comply with the requirement.

(5) Where the Certification Officer requests a person to furnish information to him in connection with enquiries made by him under this section, he shall specify

the date by which that information is to be furnished and, unless he considers that it would be inappropriate to do so, shall proceed with his determination of the application notwithstanding that the information has not been furnished to him by the specified date.

(6) A declaration made by the Certification Officer under this section may be relied on as if it were a declaration made by the court.

(7) Where an enforcement order has been made, any person who is a member of the union and was a member at the time it was made is entitled to enforce obedience to the order as if he had made the application on which the order was made.

(8) An enforcement order made by the Certification Officer under this section may be enforced in the same way as an order of the court.

(9) An order under section 108A(2)(e) may provide that, in relation to an application under section 108A with regard to a prescribed matter, the preceding provisions of this section shall apply with such omissions or modifications as may be specified in the order; and a prescribed matter is such matter specified under section 108A(2)(e) as is prescribed under this subsection.

108C　Appeals from Certification Officer

An appeal lies to the Employment Appeal Tribunal on any question of law arising in proceedings before or arising from any decision of the Certification Officer under this Chapter.'

Employers' associations

20.—(1) Section 132 (provisions about application of funds for political objects to apply to unincorporated employers' associations) shall be amended as follows.

(2) For 'The' substitute '(1) Subject to subsections (2) to (5), the'.

(3) After subsection (1) (as created by sub-paragraph (2)) insert—

'(2) Subsection (1) does not apply to these provisions—

    (a)　section 72A;
    (b)　in section 80, subsections (5A) to (5C) and (8) to (10);
    (c)　in section 81, subsection (8).

(3) In its application to an unincorporated employers' association, section 79 shall have effect as if at the end of subsection (1) there were inserted—

"The making of an application to the Certification Officer does not prevent the applicant, or any other person, from making an application to the court in respect of the same matter."

(4) In its application to an unincorporated employers' association, section 80(2)(b) shall have effect as if the words "where he considers it appropriate," were inserted at the beginning.

(5) In its application to an unincorporated employers' association, section 81 shall have effect as if after subsection (1) there were inserted—

"(2) If an application in respect of the same matter has been made to the Certification Officer, the court shall have due regard to any declaration, reasons or observations of his which are brought to its notice.'"

21. In section 133 (provisions about amalgamations and similar matters to apply to unincorporated employers' associations) in subsection (2)(c) after '101(3)' there shall be inserted ', 103(2A) and (6) to (9)'.

Procedure before Certification Officer

22. In section 256 (procedure before Certification Officer) for subsection (2) (provision for restricting disclosure of individual's identity) there shall be substituted—

'(2) He shall in particular make provision about the disclosure, and restriction of the disclosure, of the identity of an individual who has made or is proposing to make any such application or complaint.

(2A) Provision under subsection (2) shall be such that if the application or complaint relates to a trade union—

(a) the individual's identity is disclosed to the union unless the Certification Officer thinks the circumstances are such that it should not be so disclosed;
(b) the individual's identity is disclosed to such other persons (if any) as the Certification Officer thinks fit.'

23. After section 256 there shall be inserted—

'256A Vexatious litigants

(1) The Certification Officer may refuse to entertain any application or complaint made to him under a provision of Chapters III to VIIA of Part I by a vexatious litigant.

(2) The Certification Officer must give reasons for such a refusal.

(3) Subsection (1) does not apply to a complaint under section 37E(1)(b) or to an application under section 41.

(4) For the purposes of subsection (1) a vexatious litigant is a person who is the subject of—

(a) an order which is made under section 33(1) of the Employment Tribunals Act 1996 and which remains in force,
(b) a civil proceedings order or an all proceedings order which is made under section 42(1) of the Supreme Court Act 1981 and which remains in force,
(c) an order which is made under section 1 of the Vexatious Actions (Scotland) Act 1898, or
(d) an order which is made under section 32 of the Judicature (Northern Ireland) Act 1978.

256B Vexatious litigants: applications disregarded

(1) For the purposes of a relevant enactment an application to the Certification Officer shall be disregarded if—

(a) it was made under a provision mentioned in the relevant enactment, and

(b) it was refused by the Certification Officer under section 256A(1).

(2) The relevant enactments are sections 26(8), 31(7), 45C(5B), 56(8), 72A(10), 81(8) and 108A(13).'

Annual report by Certification Officer

24. In section 258(1) (Certification Officer: annual report) for 'calendar year' there shall be substituted 'financial year'.

Section 31 **SCHEDULE 7**

EMPLOYMENT AGENCIES

Introduction

1. The Employment Agencies Act 1973 shall be amended as provided in this Schedule.

General regulations

2.—(1) Section 5 (power to make general regulations) shall be amended a follows.

(2) In subsection (1) there shall be substituted for paragraphs (f) and (g) and the proviso following paragraph (g)—

'(ea) restricting the services which may be provided by persons carrying on such agencies and businesses;

(eb) regulating the way in which and the terms on which services may be provided by persons carrying on such agencies and businesses;

(ec) restricting or regulating the charging of fees by persons carrying on such agencies and businesses.'

(3) After subsection (1) there shall be inserted—

'(1A) A reference in subsection (1) (ea) to (ec) of this section to services includes a reference to services in respect of—

(a) persons seeking employment outside the United Kingdom;

(b) persons normally resident outside the United Kingdom seeking employment in the United Kingdom.'

Charges

3. For section 6(1) (restriction on demand or receipt of fee for finding or seeking to find employment) there shall be substituted—

'(1) Except in such cases or classes of case as the Secretary of State may prescribe—

(a) a person carrying on an employment agency shall not request or directly or indirectly receive any fee from any person for providing services (whether by the provision of information or otherwise) for the purpose of finding him employment or seeking to find him employment;

(b) a person carrying on an employment business shall not request or directly or indirectly receive any fee from an employee for providing services (whether by the provision of information or otherwise) for the purpose of finding or seeking to find another person, with a view to the employee acting for and under the control of that other person;

(c) a person carrying on an employment business shall not request or directly or indirectly receive any fee from a second person for providing services (whether by the provision of information or otherwise) for the purpose of finding or seeking to find a third person, with a view to the second person becoming employed by the first person and acting for and under the control of the third person.'

Inspection

4.—(1) Section 9 (inspection) shall be amended as follows.

(2) In subsection (1) (power to inspect)—

(a) for paragraph (a) there shall be substituted—

'(a) enter any relevant business premises;', and

(b) after paragraph (c) there shall be inserted—

'; and

(d) take copies of records and other documents inspected under paragraph (b).'.

(3) After subsection (1) there shall be inserted—

'(1A) If an officer seeks to inspect or acquire, in accordance with subsection (1)(b) or (c), a record or other document or information which is not kept at the premises being inspected, he may require any person on the premises—

(a) to inform him where and by whom the record, other document or information is kept, and

(b) to make arrangements, if it is reasonably practicable for the person to do so, for the record, other document or information to be inspected by or furnished to the officer at the premises at a time specified by the officer.

(1B) In subsection (1) "relevant business premises" means premises—

(a) which are used, have been used or are to be used for or in connection with the carrying on of an employment agency or employment business,

(b) which the officer has reasonable cause to believe are used or have been used for or in connection with the carrying on of an employment agency or employment business, or

(c) which the officer has reasonable cause to believe are used for the carrying on of a business by a person who also carries on or has carried on an employment agency or employment business, if the officer also has reasonable cause to believe that records or other documents which relate to the employment agency or employment business are kept there.

(1C) For the purposes of subsection (1)—

(a) "document" includes information recorded in any form, and

(b) information is kept at premises if it is accessible from them.'

(4) For subsection (2) (self-incrimination) there shall be substituted—

'(2) Nothing in this section shall require a person to produce, provide access to or make arrangements for the production of anything which he could not be compelled to produce in civil proceedings before the High Court or (in Scotland) the Court of Session.

(2A) Subject to subsection (2B), a statement made by a person in compliance with a requirement under this section may be used in evidence against him in criminal proceedings.

(2B) Except in proceedings for an offence under section 5 of the Perjury Act 1911 (false statements made otherwise than on oath), no evidence relating to the statement may be adduced, and no question relating to it may be asked, by or on behalf of the prosecution unless—

    (a) evidence relating to it is adduced, or
    (b) a question relating to it is asked,

by or on behalf of the person who made the statement.'

(5) In subsection (3) (offence)—

    (a) for 'or (b)' there shall be substituted ', (b) or (d)', and
    (b) after the words 'paragraph (c) of that subsection' there shall be inserted 'or under subsection (1A)'.

(6) In subsection (4)(a) (restriction on disclosure of information) in sub-paragraph (iv) (exception for criminal proceedings pursuant to or arising out of the Act) the words 'pursuant to or arising out of this Act' shall be omitted.

Offences

5. After section 11 there shall be inserted—

'11A Offences: extension of time limit

(1) For the purposes of subsection (2) of this section a relevant offence is an offence under section 3B, 5(2), 6(2), 9(4)(b) or 10(2) of this Act for which proceedings are instituted by the Secretary of State.

(2) Notwithstanding section 127(1) of the Magistrates' Courts Act 1980 (information to be laid within 6 months of offence) an information relating to a relevant offence which is triable by a magistrates' court in England and Wales may be so tried if it is laid at any time—

    (a) within 3 years after the date of the commission of the offence, and
    (b) within 6 months after the date on which evidence sufficient in the opinion of the Secretary of State to justify the proceedings came to his knowledge.

(3) Notwithstanding section 136 of the Criminal Procedure (Scotland) Act 1995 (time limit for prosecuting certain statutory offences) in Scotland proceedings in respect of an offence under section 3B, 5(2), 6(2), 9(4)(b) or 10(2) of this Act may be commenced at any time—

    (a) within 3 years after the date of the commission of the offence, and
    (b) within 6 months after the date on which evidence sufficient in the opinion of the Lord Advocate to justify the proceedings came to his knowledge.

(4) For the purposes of this section a certificate of the Secretary of State or Lord Advocate (as the case may be) as to the date on which evidence came to his knowledge is conclusive evidence.

11B   Offences: cost of investigation

The court in which a person is convicted of an offence under this Act may order him to pay to the Secretary of State a sum which appears to the court not to exceed he costs of the investigation which resulted in the conviction.'

Regulations and orders

6. For section 12(5) (regulations and orders: procedure) there shall be substituted—

'(5) Regulations under section 5(1) or 6(1) of this Act shall not be made unless a draft has been laid before, and approved by resolution of, each House of Parliament.

(6) Regulations under section 13(7)(i) of this Act or an order under section 14(3) shall be subject to annulment in pursuance of a resolution of either House of Parliament.'

Interpretation

7. In section 13(2) (definition of employment agency) for 'workers' (in each place) there shall be substituted 'persons'.

Exemptions

8. For section 13(7)(1) there shall be substituted—

'(i)   any prescribed business or service, or prescribed class of business or service or business or service carried on or provided by prescribed persons or classes of person.'

Section 41   **SCHEDULE 8**

NATIONAL SECURITY

1. The following shall be substituted for section 193 of the Employment Rights Act 1996 (national security)—

'193   National security

Part IVA and section 47B of this Act do not apply in relation to employment for the purposes of—

    (a)   the Security Service,
    (b)   the Secret Intelligence Service, or
    (c)   the Government Communications Headquarters.'

2. Section 4(7) of the Employment Tribunals Act 1996 (composition of tribunal: national security) shall cease to have effect.

3. The following shall be substituted for section 10 of that Act (national security, etc)—

'10   National security

(1) If on a complaint under—

    (a)   section 146 of the Trade Union and Labour Relations (Consolidation) Act 1992 (detriment: trade union membership), or

    (b)   section 111 of the Employment Rights Act 1996 (unfair dismissal),

it is shown that the action complained of was taken for the purpose of safeguarding national security, the employment tribunal shall dismiss the complaint.

(2) Employment tribunal procedure regulations may make provision about the composition of the tribunal (including provision disapplying or modifying section 4) for the purposes of proceedings in relation to which—

    (a)   a direction is given under subsection (3), or

    (b)   an order is made under subsection (4).

(3) A direction may be given under this subsection by a Minister of the Crown if—

    (a)   it relates to particular Crown employment proceedings, and

    (b)   the Minister considers it expedient in the interests of national security.

(4) An order may be made under this subsection by the President or a Regional Chairman in relation to particular proceedings if he considers it expedient in the interests of national security.

(5) Employment tribunal procedure regulations may make provision enabling a Minister of the Crown, if he considers it expedient in the interests of national security—

    (a)   to direct a tribunal to sit in private for all or part of particular Crown employment proceedings;

    (b)   to direct a tribunal to exclude the applicant from all or part of particular Crown employment proceedings;

    (c)   to direct a tribunal to exclude the applicant's representatives from all or part of particular Crown employment proceedings;

    (d)   to direct a tribunal to take steps to conceal the identity of a particular witness in particular Crown employment proceedings;

    (e)   to direct a tribunal to take steps to keep secret all or part of the reasons for its decision in particular Crown employment proceedings.

(6) Employment tribunal procedure regulations may enable a tribunal, if it considers it expedient in the interests of national security, to do anything of a kind which a tribunal can be required to do by direction under subsection (5)(a) to (e).

(7) In relation to cases where a person has been excluded by virtue of subsection (5)(b) or (c) or (6), employment tribunal procedure regulations may make provision—

    (a)   for the appointment by the Attorney General, or by the Advocate General for Scotland, of a person to represent the interests of the applicant;

    (b) about the publication and registration of reasons for the tribunal's decision;

    (c) permitting an excluded person to make a statement to the tribunal before the commencement of the proceedings, or the part of the proceedings, from which he is excluded.

(8) Proceedings are Crown employment proceedings for the purposes of this section if the employment to which the complaint relates—

    (a) is Crown employment, or

    (b) is connected with the performance of functions on behalf of the Crown.

(9) The reference in subsection (4) to the President or a Regional Chairman is to a person appointed in accordance with regulations under section 1(1) as—

    (a) a Regional Chairman,

    (b) President of the Employment Tribunals (England and Wales), or

    (c) President of the Employment Tribunals (Scotland).

10A Confidential information

(1) Employment tribunal procedure regulations may enable an employment tribunal to sit in private for the purpose of hearing evidence from any person which in the opinion of the tribunal is likely to consist of—

    (a) information which he could not disclose without contravening a prohibition imposed by or by virtue of any enactment,

    (b) information which has been communicated to him in confidence or which he has otherwise obtained in consequence of the confidence reposed in him by another person, or

    (c) information the disclosure of which would, for reasons other than its effect on negotiations with respect to any of the matters mentioned in section 178(2) of the Trade Union and Labour Relations (Consolidation) Act 1992, cause substantial injury to any undertaking of his or in which he works.

(2) The reference in subsection (1)(c) to any undertaking of a person or in which he works shall be construed—

    (a) in relation to a person in Crown employment, as a reference to the national interest,

    (b) in relation to a person who is a relevant member of the House of Lords staff, as a reference to the national interest or (if the case so requires) the interests of the House of Lords, and

    (c) in relation to a person who is a relevant member of the House of Commons staff, as a reference to the national interest or (if the case so requires) the interests of the House of Commons.

10B Restriction of publicity in cases involving national security

(1) This section applies where a tribunal has been directed under section 10(5) or has determined under section 10(6)—

    (a) to take steps to conceal the identity of a particular witness, or

    (b) to take steps to keep secret all or part of the reasons for its decision.

(2) It is an offence to publish—

    (a) anything likely to lead to the identification of the witness, or

    (b) the reasons for the tribunal's decision or the part of its reasons which it is directed or has determined to keep secret.

(3) A person guilty of an offence under this section is liable on summary conviction to a fine not exceeding level 5 on the standard scale.

(4) Where a person is charged with an offence under this section it is a defence to prove that at the time of the alleged offence he was not aware, and neither suspected nor had reason to suspect, that the publication in question was of, or included, the matter in question.

(5) Where an offence under this section committed by a body corporate is proved to have been committed with the consent or connivance of, or to be attributable to any neglect on the part of—

    (a) a director, manager, secretary or other similar officer of the body corporate, or

    (b) a person purporting to act in any such capacity,

he as well as the body corporate is guilty of the offence and liable to be proceeded against and punished accordingly.

(6) A reference in this section to publication includes a reference to inclusion in a programme which is included in a programme service, within the meaning of the Broadcasting Act 1990.'

4. Section 28(5) of the Employment Tribunals Act 1996 (composition of Appeal Tribunal: national security) shall cease to have effect.

5.—(1) Section 30 of that Act (Appeal Tribunal Procedure rules) shall be amended as follows.

(2) In subsection (2)(d) for 'section 10' substitute 'section 10A'.

(3) After subsection (2) insert—

'(2A) Appeal Tribunal procedure rules may make provision of a kind which may be made by employment tribunal procedure regulations under section 10(2), (5), (6) or (7).

(2B) For the purposes of subsection (2A)—

    (a) the reference in section 10(2) to section 4 shall be treated as a reference to section 28, and

    (b) the reference in section 10(4) to the President or a Regional Chairman shall be treated as a reference to a judge of the Appeal Tribunal.

(2C) Section 10B shall have effect in relation to a direction to or determination of the Appeal Tribunal as it has effect in relation to a direction to or determination of an employment tribunal.'

6. After section 69(2) of the Race Relations Act 1976 (evidence: Minister's certificate as to national security, etc) there shall be inserted—

'(2A) Subsection (2)(b) shall not have effect for the purposes of proceedings on a complaint under section 54.'

7. Paragraph 4(1)(b) of Schedule 3 to the Disability Discrimination Act 1995, (evidence: Minister's certificate as to national security, etc.) shall cease to have effect.

SCHEDULE 9

REPEALS

1. BALLOTS AND NOTICES

Chapter	Short title	Extent of repeal
1992 c 52	Trade Union and Labour Relations (Consolidation) Act 1992.	In section 226(2) the word 'and' at the end of paragraph (b). Section 227(2). In section 234A(7)(a) the words 'otherwise than to enable the union to comply with a court order or an undertaking given to a court.'.

2. LEAVE FOR FAMILY REASONS ETC

Chapter	Short title	Extent of repeal
1996 c 17	Employment Tribunals Act 1996.	In section 13(2)— the word 'or' after paragraph (a), paragraph (b), and the words ', or which she held before her absence,'.
1996 c 18	Employment Rights Act 1996.	In section 37, subsection (4), the word 'and' after subsection (5)(a), and subsection (5)(b). In section 43, subsection (4), the word 'and' after subsection (5)(a), and subsection (5)(b). Section 96. Section 97(6). Section 98(5). Section 105(2). Section 108(3)(a). Section 109(2)(a). Section 114(5). Section 115(4). In section 118(1)(b), the word ', 127'. Section 119(6). Section 127. Section 137. Section 145(7). Section 146(3).

Chapter	Short title	Extent of repeal
1996 c 18—*cont*	Employment Rights Act 1996—*cont*	Section 156(2). Section 157(6). Section 162(7). In section 199, the words 'subject to subsection (3)' in subsection (2), and subsection (3). In section 200(1), the words 'and section 137'. Section 209(6). In section 212— subsection (2), in subsection (3), the word 'or' after paragraph (c), and paragraph (d), in subsection (4) the words 'or (subject to subsection (2)) subsection (3)(d)'. Section 226(3)(a) and (5)(a). In section 235(1), the definitions of 'maternity leave period' and 'notified day of return'.
SI 1994/ 2479	Maternity (Compulsory Leave) Regulations 1994.	The whole instrument.

3. AGREEMENT TO EXCLUDE DISMISSAL RIGHTS

Chapter	Short title	Extent of repeal
1992 c 52	Trade Union and Labour Relations (Consolidation) Act 1992.	In Schedule A1, paragraph 163.
1996 c 18	Employment Rights Act 1996.	In section 44(4) the words from the beginning to 'the dismissal,'. In section 45A(4) the words from ', unless' to the end. In section 46(2) the words from the beginning to 'the dismissal,'. In section 47(2) the words from the beginning to 'the dismissal,'. In section 47A(2) the words from the beginning to 'the dismissal,'. In section 47B(2) the words from the beginning to 'the dismissal,'. Section 197(1) and (2). In section 197(4) the words '(1) or'.

Chapter	Short title	Extent of repeal
1996 c 18—*cont*	Employment Rights Act 1996— *cont*	In section 203(2)(d) the words '(1) or'. In section 209(2)(g) the words 'and 197(1)'.
1999 c 26	Employment Relations Act 1999.	Section 18(6).

4. POWER TO CONFER RIGHTS ON INDIVIDUALS

Chapter	Short title	Extent of repeal
1999 c 18	Employment Rights Act 1996.	Section 209(7).

5. ACAS: GENERAL DUTY

Chapter	Short title	Extent of repeal
1992 c 52	Trade Union and Labour Relations (Consolidation) Act 1992.	In section 209 the words from ', in particular' to the end.
1993 c 19	Trade Union Reform and Employment Rights Act 1993.	Section 43(1).

6. COMMISSIONERS

Chapter	Short title	Extent of repeal
1967 c 13	Parliamentary Commissioner Act 1967.	In Schedule 2, the entries relating to— the Office of the Commissioner for Protection Against Unlawful Industrial Action, and the Office of the Commissioner for the Rights of Trade Union Members.
1975 c 24	House of Commons Disqualification Act 1975.	In Part III of Schedule 1, the entries relating to— the Commissioner for Protection Against Unlawful Industrial Action, and the Commissioner for the Rights of Trade Union Members.
1975 c 25	Northern Ireland Assembly Disqualification Act 1975.	In Part III of Schedule 1, the entries relating to— the Commissioner for Protection Against Unlawful Industrial Action, and

Chapter	Short title	Extent of repeal
1975 c 25— *cont*	Northern Ireland Assembly Disqualification Act 1975—*cont*	the Commissioner for the Rights of Trade Union Members.
1992 c 52	Trade Union and Labour Relations (Consolidation) Act 1992.	In section 65(3) the words 'the Commissioner for the Rights of Trade Union Members or'. In Part I, Chapter VIII. Sections 235B and 235C. Section 266 (and the heading immediately preceding it) and sections 267 to 271. In Schedule 2, paragraphs 1 and 4(4).
1993 c 19	Trade Union Reform and Employment Rights Act 1993.	In Schedule 7, paragraph 20. In Schedule 8, paragraphs 2, 6, 7, 58 to 60 and 79 to 84.

7. THE CERTIFICATION OFFICER

Chapter	Short title	Extent of repeal
1992 c 52	Trade Union and Labour Relations (Consolidation) Act 1992.	In section 24(6), the second sentence. In section 24A(6), the second sentence. In section 25(2)(b) the words 'where he considers it appropriate,'. Section 26(2). In section 45C(2)(a) the words ', where he considers it appropriate,' and section 45C(3) and (4). In section 54(1), the second sentence. In section 55(2)(b) the words 'where he considers it appropriate,'. Section 56(2). In section 79(1), the second sentence. In section 80(2)(b) the words 'where he considers it appropriate,'. Section 81(2).

8. EMPLOYMENT AGENCIES

Chapter	Short title	Extent of repeal
1973 c 35	Employment Agencies Act 1973.	In section 9(4)(a)(iv) the words 'pursuant to or arising out of this Act'.

9. EMPLOYMENT RIGHTS: EMPLOYMENT OUTSIDE GREAT BRITAIN

Chapter	Short title	Extent of repeal
1996 c 18	Employment Rights Act 1996.	Section 196. In section 199(6), the words 'Section 196(6) does not apply to an employee, and'. In section 201(3)(g), the word '196,'. Section 204(2). In section 209(2)(g), the words '196(1) and'. In section 209(5), the words ', 196(2), (3) and (5)'.

10. SECTIONS 33 TO 36

Chapter	Short title	Extent of repeal
1996 c 52	Trade Union and Labour Relations (Consolidation) Act 1992.	Section 157. Section 158. Section 159. Section 176(7) and (8).
1996 c 18	Employment Rights Act 1996.	In section 117, subsection (4)(b) and the word 'or' before it, and subsections (5) and (6). Section 118(2) and (3). Section 120(2). Section 124(2). Section 125. Section 186(2). Section 208. Section 227(2) to (4). Section 236(2)(c).

Chapter	Short title	Extent of repeal
1996 c 18—*cont*	Employment Rights Act 1996—*cont*	In section 236(3) the words '120 (2), 124(2)'. In Schedule 1, paragraph 56(10) and (11).
1998 c 8	Employment Rights (Dispute Resolution) Act 1998.	Section 14(1).

11. COMPENSATORY AWARD: REMOVAL OF LIMIT IN CERTAIN CASES

Chapter	Short title	Extent of repeal
1996 c 18	Employment Rights Act 1996.	In section 112(4), the words 'or in accordance with regulations under section 127B'. In section 117(2) and (3), the words 'and to regulations under section 127B'. In section 118(1), the words 'Subject to regulations under section 127B,'. Section 127B.
1998 c 23	Public Interest Disclosure Act 1998.	Section 8. Section 18(4)(b).

12. NATIONAL SECURITY

Chapter	Short title	Extent of repeal
1995 c 50	Disability Discrimination Act 1995.	Paragraph 4(1)(b) of Schedule 3, and the word 'or' immediately before it.
1996 c 17	Employment Tribunals Act 1996.	Section 4(7). Section 28(5).
1998 c 23	Public Interest Disclosure Act 1998.	Section 11.

INDEX

References are to paragraph numbers.

ACAS   5.2
  Central Arbitration Committee
    5.1.2
  codes of practice   4.1.1, 4.1.3, 5.2.1
  collective bargaining   5.2.2
  deregulation of trade unions   2.5.6
  disciplinary hearings
    right to be accompanied   4.1.1,
      4.1.3
  general duty   5.2.2
  membership   5.2.1
  role   5.2
Accompanied, right to be
  ACAS Code of Practice   4.1.1, 4.1.3
  choice of companion   4.1.1
  compensation   4.1.5, 4.1.6
  detriment   4.1.6
  disciplinary hearings   1.1.7, 4.1,
    6.2.1, 6.4.1
  employment agencies   6.2.1
  employment tribunals   4.1.5–4.1.6
  grievance hearings   1.1.7, 4.1,
    6.2.1, 6.4.1
  interim relief   4.1.7
  national security   4.1.8, 6.4.1
  remuneration   4.1.2
  time off   4.1.2
  unfair dismissal   4.1.1, 4.1.6–4.1.7
  warnings   4.1.1
Advisory, Conciliation and Arbitration
    Service, *see* ACAS
Agencies, *see* Employment agencies
Associated companies
  recognition of trade unions   2.2.2,
    2.3.5
Awards   6.3

Ballots
  accidental failures, disregarding
    2.12.10
  bargaining units   2.2.17, 2.4.9
  breaches, disregarding minor
    2.12.10

call out bans   2.12.8
Central Arbitration Committee
    2.2.16–2.2.17
Certification Officers   5.4.11–5.4.12
conduct of   2.12.9
costs   2.2.17
deregulation of trade unions
    2.5.6–2.5.8, 2.6.2, 2.7.3
detriment   2.9.4
effectiveness periods   2.12.11
guidance   2.9.4
industrial action   1.1.7, 2.12
  inducing members to take
    2.12.6
  suspension of   2.12.12
merchant seamen   2.12.9
notices   2.12
  writing, in   2.12.4
overtime   2.12.8
political   5.4.10–5.4.11
postal   2.2.17
results, informing employers of
    2.12.2
sample voting papers   2.12.5
secret   2.2.16–2.2.17
separate workplace   2.12.7
Bargaining units
  agreements on   2.2.4
  appropriate   2.2.12, 2.4.2–2.4.7,
    2.4.10
  ballots   2.2.17, 2.4.9
  Central Arbitration Committee
    2.2.6, 2.2.12–2.2.16, 2.4.2–2.4.10
  changes to   2.4.1–2.4.10
  definition   2.2.1
  deregulation of trade unions
    2.5.6–2.5.8, 2.6.2, 2.7.2
  employer believes unit has ceased to
    exist   2.4.5
  negotiations   2.2.4
  new units, deciding on   2.4.8–2.4.9
  notice   2.4.5–2.4.6, 2.4.9

Bargaining units – *cont*
  number of   2.4.4
  outside   2.4.3
  recognition of trade unions   2.2.1,
    2.2.4, 2.2.6, 2.2.9–2.2.17, 2.4.1–
    2.4.10, 2.8.1
  residual workers   2.4.10
  training   2.13.2–2.13.3
Blacklisting   1.1.7, 2.11.1–2.11.2

Call out bans   2.12.8
Central Arbitration Committee   5.1
  ACAS   5.1.2
  ballots   2.2.16–2.2.17
  bargaining units   2.2.6, 2.2.12–
    2.2.16, 2.4.2–2.4.10
  collective bargaining   2.2.1, 2.2.18–
    2.2.19, 5.1.1
  derecognition of trade unions
    2.5–2.7.4, 5.1.1, 5.1.3
  membership   5.1.2
  proceedings   5.1.3
  recognition of trade unions   2.2.1–
    2.2.2, 2.2.6–2.2.7, 2.2.9–2.3.5,
    5.1.1, 5.1.3
  role   5.1
Certification Officer   5.4
  accounting records   5.4.6
  amalgamations   5.4.13
  ballots   5.4.10–5.4.11
  breach of union rules   5.5.2–5.5.5
  certificates of independence   5.4.1
  Commissioner for the Rights of Trade
    Union Members   5.3.2
  dispute resolution   5.4.2–5.4.6
  elections   5.4.8
  employers' associations   5.5.4
  enforcement orders   5.4.4
  functions   5.4.1
  funds   5.4.9
  offenders   5.4.7
  political funds   5.4.12, 5.5.4
  political objects, application of funds
    for   5.4.9
  powers   5.4.2
  procedure   5.5.5
  register of members   5.4.3–5.4.4
  role   5.4
  transfer of engagements   5.4.13
Codes of practice
  ACAS   4.1.1, 4.1.3, 5.2.1

disciplinary hearings
  right to be accompanied   4.1.1,
    4.1.3
  part-time workers   4.5.3
Collective bargaining, *see also* Bargaining
    units
  ACAS   5.2.2
  Central Arbitration Committee
    2.2.1, 2.2.18–2.2.19, 5.1.1
  definition   2.7.1
  deregulation of trade unions   2.7.1
  negotiations   2.3.5
  recognition of trade unions   2.1,
    2.2.18–2.2.19, 2.3.2, 2.3.5, 2.8.1
  training   2.13.2
Collective rights, *see also* Collective
    bargaining, Trade unions
  agreements   4.3
  ballots   1.1.7
  blacklisting   1.1.7
  detriment   1.2.4, 4.3.1
  disciplinary hearings   1.1.7
  discrimination   1.1.7
  Employment Relations Bill   1.2.5–
    1.2.6
  trade union recognition   1.1.7
  training   1.1.7
  unfair dismissal   4.3.1
  voluntary agreements   1.1.7
Commissioner for Protection against
    Unlawful Industrial Action   1.1.7
  abolition   1.1.7, 5.3
  Fairness at Work White Paper   1.1.7
Commissioner for the Rights of Trade
    Union Members
  abolition   1.1.7, 5.3
  Certification Officers   5.3.2
  Fairness at Work White Paper   1.1.7
Compensation   6.3
  calculation   4.1.5–4.1.6, 6.3.2
  compromise   6.3.3
  conduct   4.1.6
  detriment   2.9.2
  discrimination   6.3.1
  employment tribunals   2.9.2,
    2.13.3, 3.2.5, 3.3.5, 4.1.5–4.1.6
  Fairness at Work White Paper   1.1.6
  guarantee payments   6.3.4
  index-linked   1.1.6, 1.2.3, 6.3.2–
    6.3.3
  limits on   1.1.6, 6.3.3

Compensation – *cont*
  parental leave   3.2.5
  purpose   6.3.3
  re-engagement   6.3.1
  reinstatement   6.3.1
  sex discrimination   1.1.6
  special and additional awards   6.3.1
  time off   3.3.5
  trade unions   6.3.1
  training   2.13.3
  unfair dismissal   1.1.6, 1.2.3, 6.3.1
Compromise   6.3.3
Continuity period
  Fairness at Work White Paper   1.1.5
  parental leave   3.2.2
  unfair dismissal   1.1.5
Contracts of employment, *see also* Terms
    and conditions
  breach   2.9.1, 4.2.1
  detriment   2.9.1
  industrial action   4.2.1
  outside UK   6.5.1
  persons not employed under
    detriment   2.9.2
    Fairness at Work White Paper
      1.1.4
    individual rights   1.2.3, 4.7.2
Costs
  ballots   2.2.17
Crew   2.12.9
Criminal offences
  blacklisting   2.11.2
  employment agencies   6.2.5–6.2.6
  maternity leave   3.1.4
  part-time workers   4.5.2
  trade unions   2.11.2

Dependants
  definition   3.3.3
  detriment   3.3.6
  dismissal   3.3.7
  time off for   3.3
Derecognition of trade unions   2.5.1–
    2.7.4
  ACAS   2.5.6
  applications
    admissibility   2.5.3, 2.5.6, 2.6.2,
      2.7.2–2.7.3
    prescribed forms   2.5.7, 2.7.2
    relevant   2.5.7

  automatic recognition   2.6
  ballots   2.5.6–2.5.8, 2.6.2, 2.7.3
  bargaining units   2.5.6, 2.5.7, 2.6.2,
    2.7.2
  Central Arbitration Committee
    2.5.1–2.7.4, 5.1.1, 5.1.3
  collective bargaining   2.7.1
  detriment   4.3.1
  employees
    number of   2.5.2
    request to end arrangements
      2.7.2–2.7.3
  employer's request to end
    arrangements   2.5.4–2.5.7,
      2.6.2
  negotiations   2.5.5, 2.5.6, 2.5.7,
    2.6.2
  non independent unions   2.7
  notice   2.5.2–2.5.3, 2.5.6, 2.6.2
  statutory   2.2, 2.5.1, 2.5.4, 2.7.1
  unfair dismissal   4.3.1
  voluntary recognition   2.3.1–2.3.5
Detriment
  ballots   2.9.4
  collective rights   4.3.1
  compensation   2.9.2
  contracts of employment   2.9.1
    persons not employed under
      2.9.2
  discrimination   2.10.2
  employment agencies   6.2.1
  employment tribunals   2.9.2, 2.10.3
  fixed-term contracts   4.4.2
  maternity leave   3.1.1
  national security   6.4.1
  time off   3.3.6
  trade unions   2.9, 2.10
    recognition and derecognition
      4.3.1
  unfair dismissal   2.9.1–2.9.4
Disciplinary hearings
  definition   4.1.3
  Fairness at Work White Paper   1.1.7
  right to be accompanied   1.1.7, 4.1,
    6.2.1, 6.4.1
Discrimination, *see also* Sex
    discrimination
  blacklisting   2.11.1–2.11.2
  compensation   6.3.1
  detriment   2.10.1
  part-time workers   4.5.1, 4.5.3

Discrimination – *cont*
 trade unions 1.1.7, 2.10.1, 2.11.1–
 2.11.2, 4.3.1
Dismissal, *see* Unfair dismissal

Employees
 contracts of employment, not
 employed under
 detriment 2.9.2
 individual rights 1.2.3, 4.7.2
 meaning 1.1.4
 representatives
 unfair dismissal 2.14.1
 school staff 6.8.1
Employers' associations 5.5.4
Employment agencies 6.2
 agency workers 6.2.2
 definition 4.1.4
 status 6.2.1
 unfair dismissal 6.2.1
 conduct of agencies 6.2.1
 contracts 6.2.2
 definition 6.2.2
 fees 6.2.2–6.2.3
 Fairness at Work White Paper 6.2.1
 inspection 6.2.4
 self-incrimination 6.2.5
 offences 6.2.5–6.2.6
 regulation 6.2.1
 procedure 6.2.7
Employment protection 2.9
 detriment 4.3.1
 rights 1.2.6, 4.7
 unfair dismissal 2.9.3, 4.3.1
Employment Relations Bill 1999
 1.2.1–1.2.6
 amendments 1.2.1
 collective rights 1.2.4, 1.2.6
 compensation 1.2.3
 employment agencies 1.2.6
 family friendly policies 1.2.5
 fixed-term contracts 1.2.3
 individual rights 1.2.3
 minimum wage 1.2.6
 national security 1.2.6
 part-time workers 1.2.6
 time off 3.3.4
 trade unions 1.2.4, 1.2.6
 unfair dismissal 1.2.3

Employment tribunals
 accompanied, right to be 4.1.5–
 4.1.6
 compensation 2.9.2, 2.13.3, 3.2.5,
 3.3.5, 4.1.5–4.1.6
 detriment 2.9.2, 2.10.3
 national security 6.4.1–6.4.2
 parental leave 3.2.5
 part-time workers 4.5.2
 time-limits 2.9.2, 2.10.3, 3.2.5,
 3.3.5, 4.1.5
 time off 3.3.4–3.3.5
 training 2.13.3
European Union
 family friendly policies 1.1.8
 maternity leave 3.1.2, 3.1.4
 parental leave 1.1.8, 3.2.1, 3.2.4
 part-time workers 1.2.6, 4.5.1–4.5.2
 posted workers 6.5.1
 time off 3.3.1, 3.3.6
 transfer of undertakings 6.6.1
 working time 1.1.8

Fairness at Work White Paper 1.1–
 1.1.8
 collective rights 1.1.7
 Commissioner for Protection against
 Unlawful Industrial Action
 1.1.7
 Commissioner for the Rights of Trade
 Union Members 1.1.7
 compensation 1.1.6
 continuity period 1.1.5
 contracts of employment, employees
 not employed under 1.1.4
 disciplinary procedure 1.1.7
 'employees' 1.1.4
 family friendly policies 1.1.8
 grievance procedure 1.1.7
 individual rights 1.1.6
 industrial action 1.1.7
 Partnerships at Work 6.1
 trade unions 1.1.7
 unfair dismissal 1.1.5, 1.1.6
Family friendly policies
 Employment Relations Bill 1.2.5
 European Union 1.1.8
 Fairness at Work White Paper 1.1.8
 maternity leave 1.1.8
 parental leave 1.1.8

Family friendly policies – *cont*
 small businesses   1.2.5
 time off   1.2.5, 3.3
 working time   1.1.8
Fixed-term contracts
 detriment   4.4.2
 qualifying period   6.8.1
 school staff   6.8.1
 unfair dismissal   1.2.3, 4.4, 6.8.1
 waiver provisions   1.2.3, 4.4

Grievance hearings
 definition   4.1.3
 Fairness at Work White Paper   1.1.7
 right to be accompanied   1.1.7, 4.1,
  6.2.1, 6.4.1
Guarantee payments   6.3.4

Health and safety
 maternity leave   3.1.4
 representatives   2.14.1
 unfair dismissal   2.14.1
Hours of work, *see* Working time

Individual rights
 contracts of employment, persons not
  employed under   1.2.3, 4.7.2
 definition   4.1.4
 detriment   4.1.6, 4.3
 disciplinary hearings
  right to be accompanied   4.1
 dismissal   4.1.6–4.1.7, 4.3
 employment protection rights   4.7
 Employment Relations Bill   1.2.3
 Fairness at Work White Paper   1.1.6
 fixed-term contracts   4.4
 national minimum wage   4.6
 national security   4.1.8
 part-time workers   4.5
  codes of practice   4.5.3
 religious and other communities
  4.6.1
 striking workers
  unfair dismissal   4.2
 unfair dismissal   1.2.3
Industrial action
 ballots   1.1.7
 call out bans   2.12.8

Commissioner for Protection against
  Unlawful Industrial Action
  1.1.7, 5.3
 contracts of employment   4.2.1
 Fairness at Work White Paper   1.1.7
 inducing members to take   2.12.6,
  2.12.12
 notices   2.12
 overtime   2.12.8
 redundancy   4.2.2
 re-engagement   4.2.1
 suspension of   2.12.12
 unfair dismissal   1.1.7, 4.2
 unofficial action   4.2.1
Interim relief
 recognition   2.14
 right to be accompanied   4.1.7
 unfair dismissal   2.14

Leave, *see* Maternity leave, Parental leave

Maternity leave   3.1–3.3.7
 compulsory   3.1.4
 criminal offences   3.1.4
 detriment   3.1.1
 duration of   3.1.3
 European Union   3.1.2, 3.1.4
 family friendly policies   1.1.8
 health and safety   3.1.4
 notification   3.1.7
 ordinary   3.1.2–3.1.3
 redundancy   3.1.6
 return, right to   3.1.2, 3.1.7
 statutory   3.1.3
 unfair dismissal   3.1.1, 3.1.4, 3.3.7
Maternity pay
 maternity leave   3.1.3
 statutory   3.1.3
Merchant seamen   2.12.9
Minimum wage
 Employment Relations Bill 1999
  1.2.6
 exemption from   4.6.1
 information   6.7.1
 national insurance contributions
  6.7.1
 taxation   6.7.1
 voluntary workers   1.2.6
Miscellaneous provisions
 compensation

Miscellaneous provisions – *cont*
  awards   6.3
    guarantee payments   6.3.4
    unfair dismissal   6.3.1
  dismissal of school staff   6.8
  employment agencies   6.2
    charges   6.2.3
    definition   6.2.2
    inspection   6.2.4
    offences   6.2.6
    regulations   6.2.1
    self-incrimination   6.2.5
  employment outside UK   6.5
  minimum wage   6.7
  national security   6.4
  partnerships at work   6.1
  transfer of undertakings   6.6

National insurance contributions
  6.7.1
National minimum wage, *see* Minimum
  wage
National security   6.4
  detriment   6.4.1
  Employment Relations Bill 1999
    1.2.6
  employment tribunals   6.4.1–6.4.2
  right to be accompanied   4.1.8,
    6.4.1
  trade unions   6.4.1
  unfair dismissal   6.4.1

Overtime bans   2.12.8

Parental leave, *see also* Maternity
  leave   3.1.1
  adoptive parents   3.2.2
  compensation   3.2.5
  employment tribunals   3.2.5
  entitlement   3.2.2
  European Union   1.1.8, 3.2.1, 3.2.4
  family friendly policies   1.1.8
  part-time employment   3.2.3
  postponement   3.2.5
  qualifying period   3.2.2
  redundancy   3.2.3
  return, right to   3.2.3
  rights during and after   3.2.3
  terms and conditions   3.2.3

  transfer of   3.2.2, 3.2.3
  unfair dismissal   3.2.3, 3.3.7
Part-time workers
  codes of practice   4.5.3
  criminal offences   4.5.2
  discrimination   4.5.1, 4.5.3
  Employment Relations Bill 1999
    1.2.6
  employment tribunals   4.5.2
  European Union   1.2.6, 4.5.1–4.5.2
  Framework Agreement   4.5.1
  parental leave   3.2.3
Partnerships at Work   6.1
Pay, *see* Minimum wage,
  Remuneration   1.2.6
Political funds   5.4.12
Posted workers   6.5.1

Qualifying period
  Employment Relations Bill 1999
    1.2.3
  Fairness at Work White Paper   1.1.6
  fixed-term contracts   6.8.1
  parental leave   3.2.2
  unfair dismissal   1.1.6, 1.2.3, 6.8.1

Recognition of trade unions, *see also*
  Derecognition of trade unions
    1.1.7, 1.2.4, 2.1
  agreements   2.2.4, 2.3.2
    termination   2.3.4
    types of   2.3.3
  applications
    admissibility   2.2.9–2.2.10
    competing   2.2.15–2.2.16
    form of   2.2.6
    notice to cease consideration of
      2.2.11
    rejection of   2.2.2
    validity   2.2.7–2.2.8
    withdrawal of   2.2.11
  associated employers   2.2.2, 2.3.5
  automatic   2.6
  ballots   2.2.16–2.2.17
  bargaining units   2.2.1, 2.2.4, 2.2.6,
    2.2.9–2.2.17, 2.4.1–2.4.10,
    2.8.1
  Central Arbitration Committee
    2.2.1–2.2.2, 2.2.6–2.2.7, 2.2.9–
    2.3.5, 5.1.1, 5.1.3

Recognition of trade unions – *cont*
collective bargaining   2.2.18–
2.2.19, 2.3.2, 2.3.5, 2.8.1
competing applications   2.2.15
consequences of   2.2.18
detriment   4.3.1
interim relief   2.14
methods of   2.3.5
negotiations   2.2.4, 2.2.6, 2.3.5
notice to cease consideration of
application   2.2.11
number of workers   2.2.2–2.2.3
requests   2.2.2
rejection of   2.2.5, 2.3.5
small businesses   2.2.3
statutory   2.2
unfair dismissal   2.14, 4.3.1
voluntary   2.3.1–2.3.5
withdrawal of application   2.2.11
Redundancy
industrial action   4.2.2
parental leave   3.2.3
waiver of rights   4.4.1
Re-engagement   4.2.1, 6.3.1
Reinstatement   6.3.1
Remuneration, *see also* Minimum wage
accompanied, right to be   4.1.2
time off   3.3.3, 4.1.2
Residual workers
bargaining units   2.4.10

School staff   6.8.1
Seamen   2.12.9
Secret ballots   2.2.17
Self-employment
employment agencies   6.2.1
Self-incrimination   6.2.5
Settlement   6.3.3
Sex discrimination
compensation   1.1.6
Small businesses
family friendly policies   1.2.5
recognition of trade unions   2.2.3
time off   1.2.5
trade unions   2.2.3

Taxation   6.7.1
Terms and conditions of employment
parental leave   3.2.3

Time off
accompanied, right to be   4.1.2
compensation   3.3.5
dependants   3.3
definition   3.3.3
detriment   3.3.6
Employment Relations Bill 1999
3.3.4
employment tribunals   3.3.4–3.3.5
European Union   3.3.1, 3.3.6
family friendly policies   1.2.5, 3.3
notice   3.3.4
reasonableness   3.3.1, 3.3.3–3.3.4
remuneration   3.3.3, 4.1.2
small businesses   1.2.5
unfair dismissal   3.3.7
Time-limits
employment tribunals   2.9.2,
2.10.3, 3.2.5, 3.3.5, 4.1.5
extension of   4.1.5
Trade unions, *see also* Collective rights,
Recognition of trade unions
2.1–2.14
accounts   5.4.6
amalgamations   5.4.13
bargaining units   1.2.6, 2.2.1
blacklisting   1.1.7, 1.2.4, 2.11.1–
2.11.2
breach of rules   5.5
Certification Officers   5.4, 5.5.2–
5.5.5
Commissioner for the Rights of Trade
Union Members   1.1.7, 5.3
compensation   6.3.1
criminal offences   2.11.2
detriment   2.9.1–2.9.4, 2.10
discrimination   1.1.7, 2.10.1,
2.11.1–2.11.2, 4.3.1
elections   5.4.8
employers' associations   5.5.4
Fairness at Work White Paper   1.1.7
independence
certificates of   5.4.1
loss of   2.8
national security   6.4.1
political funds   5.4.9, 5.4.12, 5.5.4
residual workers   2.4.10
rules, breach of   5.5
secret ballots   2.2.17
small businesses   2.2.3
statutory recognition   2.2

Trade unions – *cont*
  training   1.1.7, 1.2.6, 2.13
  transfer of engagements   5.4.13
  unfair dismissal   2.9.1–2.9.4
  voluntary recognition   2.1.1, 2.3
Training
  bargaining units   2.13.2–2.13.3
  collective bargaining   2.13.2
  compensation   2.13.3
  employment tribunals   2.13.3
  trade unions   1.1.7, 1.2.6, 2.13
Transfer of undertakings   6.6.1

Unfair dismissal
  collective rights   4.3.1
  compensation   1.1.6, 1.2.3, 6.3.1
  continuity period   1.1.5
  detriment   2.9.1–2.9.4, 2.10
  disciplinary hearing
    right to be accompanied   4.1.7
  employee representatives   2.14.1
  employment agencies   6.2.1
  Fairness at Work White Paper   1.1.5,
    1.1.6
  fixed-term contracts   4.4, 6.8.1
  health and safety representatives
    2.14
  individual rights   1.2.3
  industrial action   1.1.7, 4.2
  interim relief   2.14

  maternity leave   3.1.1, 3.1.6, 3.3.7
  national security   6.4.1
  parental leave   3.2.3, 3.3.7
  pregnancy   3.3.7
  qualifying period   1.1.6, 1.2.3, 6.8.1
  re-engagement   4.2.1, 6.3.1
  reinstatement   6.3.1
  school staff   6.8.1
  time off   3.3.7
  trade unions
    derecognition   4.3.1
    recognition   2.14, 4.3.1
  waiver provisions   4.4

Voluntary workers
  minimum wage   1.2.6

Wages, *see* Minimum wage,
    Remuneration
Waiver provisions   1.2.3, 4.4
White Paper, *see Fairness at Work* White
    Paper
Working time
  European Union   1.1.8
  family friendly policies   1.1.8

Zero hours contracts   1.1.5